I0114648

JOURNEY TO MUSICAL THEATRE

College Admissions & Profiles

Rachel A. Winston, Ph.D.

ISBN 978-1946432612 (hardback); 978-1946432605 (paperback); 978-1946432629 (e-book)

LCCN: 2022904442

Lizard Publishing, 7700 Irvine Center Drive, Suite 800, Irvine, CA 92618 *www.lizard-publishing.com*

Lizard Publishing creates, designs, produces, and distributes books and resources to provide academic, admissions, and career information. Our mental process is fueled by three tenets:

- Ignite the hunger to learn and the passion to make a difference
- Illuminate the expanse of knowledge by sharing cutting edge thinking
- Innovate to create a world that makes the transition from dreams to reality

We work with academic leaders who transform the educational landscape to publish relevant content and advise students of their educational and professional options, with the aim of developing 21st-century learners and leaders. We also work with students to publish their books and present widely diverse ideas to the college/graduate school-bound community. With headquarters in Irvine, California, Lizard Publishing works virtually with authors to edit, publish, and distribute both hard copy and paperback books.

This book was published in the U.S.A. Lizard Publishing is a premium quality provider of educational reference, career guidance, and motivational publications/merchandise for global learners, educators, and stakeholders in education.

Book design by Michelle Tahan *www.michelletahan.com*

Book formatting by Obinna Chinemerem Ozuo

Book website: *www.collegetheatreprograms.com*

LIZARD PUBLISHING

This book is dedicated to the hundreds of talented directors, actors, musicians, choreographers, and backstage personnel with whom I performed in musicals at Montgomery Blair High School (Silver Spring, MD) and Syracuse University. Their creativity, genius, and dedication left an indelible impression. Best wishes to everyone who chooses musical theatre and delights new audiences in each and every performance.

From *Guys and Dolls'* "More I Cannot Wish You" written by Frank Loesser,

"Music I can wish ya

Merry music while you're young

And wisdom when your hair has turned to gray."

This book is also dedicated to the performers, stagehands, and docents I have known throughout the years at the Orange County Performing Arts Center and Segerstrom Hall, who epitomize dedication and professionalism.

ACKNOWLEDGMENTS

There is never enough room to acknowledge every person. Numerous people contributed to my perspective about musical theatre. Students, performers, faculty, directors, counselors, admission directors, and researchers assisted in enhancing my knowledge base or taught me indelible lessons. Over a lifetime of experiences working with students and actors, I am wiser and more worldly.

I gratefully acknowledge Michelle Tahan, Jasmine Jhunjhnuwala, E. Liz Kim, and Jacqueline Xu, as well as my family, friends, colleagues, and professors. It is with profound gratitude that I also acknowledge those performers I have known in the musical theatre world.

As a faculty member in the UCLA College Counseling Certificate Program, I met many dedicated counselors who spend their life serving and supporting students. Meaningful contributions to the book have been made indirectly by admissions representatives, college counselors, and faculty members who took a special interest in this book's success.

I would also like to thank the thousands of students I have taught, counseled, or supported in my nearly four decades of service.

> *"If I see so far, it is because I stand on the shoulders of giants."*
> *– Isaac Newton*

Isaac Newton once said, "If I see so far, it is because I stand on the shoulders of giants."

A few of those giants whose broad shoulders lifted me higher and helped teach invaluable lessons include: Davis Ferrero, Danny Casey, Morgan Higgins, Corina Lee, Emma Mermilliod, Nathan Mermilliod, Sophia Tazerouni, Mark Wolf, Zayd Kuba, Marissa Kotch, Rachel Richardson, Grant Smith, and Jackson Ellison.

Finally, there would be no book on musical theatre schools and no career college admissions counseling without the support of Robert Helmer, whose tireless efforts support me every single day.

ABOUT THE AUTHOR

Dr. Rachel A. Winston is a tireless student advocate. She has served the educational community as a university professor, college advisor, statistician, researcher, author, cryptanalyst, motivational speaker, publishing executive, and lifelong student. As one of the leading experts in college counseling and an award-winning faculty member, Dr. Winston has spent her lifetime learning, teaching, mentoring, and coaching students. Her counseling practice centers around college admissions, college essays, portfolios, and intellectual conversations about life and career pursuits.

She started college at thirteen and graduated from college programs in such widely ranging disciplines as chemistry, mathematics, computers, liberal arts, international relations, negotiation, conflict resolution, peacebuilding, business administration, higher education leadership, interpreting, college counseling, and publishing. Throughout her education, she attended and graduated from Harvard, University of Chicago, GWU, UCLA, Syracuse, CSUF, CSUDH, Pepperdine, Claremont Graduate University, and Gallaudet University.

Her position working in Washington, D.C. on Capitol Hill and with the White House in the 1980s took her to approximately a hundred universities training campaign managers at colleges from Colorado to California, thoroughly dotting the western states. Later, she led college tours with students and their families on road trips throughout the United States. She has taught or counseled thousands of students over her career and speaks at conferences and academic programs throughout the world.

As a professor and avid writer for numerous publications, she won the 2012 McFarland Literary Achievement Award, Bletchley Park Cryptanalyst Award, and numerous other awards, including Faculty Member of the Year, Leadership Tomorrow Leader of the Year, and college service and leadership awards. While studying Human Capital at Claremont Graduate University, she was a scholarship recipient at the Drucker School of Management. She was also elected to the statewide Board of Governors for the Faculty Association for California Community Colleges, where she served on the executive committee.

She also served as a faculty member for the UCLA College Counselor Certificate Program, the Director of Mathematics at Brandman University, and Embry Riddle Aeronautical University, Chapman University, Cal State Fullerton, and a handful of California Community Colleges, including Cerro Coso College where she represented the entire faculty as the Academic Senate President and retired in 2016. Over her career, she taught mathematics online, on television, live interactive satellite, telecourses, and in large and small lecture halls.

AUTHORS' NOTE

You are reading this book because you are considering admission to colleges where you open the doors to the world of musical theatre. Whatever route you took to get to this point, you are in the right place. Right now, you need to gather information to make informed decisions.

While many people offer advice, suggestions differ. Friends will tell you the 'right' way or the way their neighbor was accepted. Graciously accept this anecdotal information, pursuing theatre with your heart and mind as you commit to learning more.

Dig deeper to consider current, expert information from counselors who have worked with hundreds of students. Changes in programs, curricula, requirements, and links happen each year.

Doublecheck each program's specifics yourself. Each school's profile information is current as of March 2022. However, since researching this book, changes may have taken place. There are other books about musical theatre programs written by talented and experienced counselors. I admire and cheer on their efforts.

"We are what we think. All that we are arises with our thoughts. With our thoughts, we make the world."
— Buddha

This resources about colleges, admissions, profiles, and lists is different in that it also provides unique tidbits. I hope you find the information valuable. Your job is to begin early by assembling lists of possible schools to consider. Create a road map and set yourself on a clear path.

If you see an error in this book or even a suggestion for a future edition, please write to Dr. Rachel A. Winston at collegeguide@yahoo.com. We will fix the entry with the next printed version. All of that said, this book was written with you in mind.

There is a wealth of information on the Internet with free downloads, FAQs, testimonials, and offers to help you with your applications. Some of these advisors are knowledgeable and can help you. Unfortunately, students and parents hunt around the web, searching for a tremendous number of hours to seek the information they need. This book aims to resolve this problem with college admissions data and profiles to make your search easier.

For now, though, I assume you want to attend college to study theatre and are exploring this book to find a program that will get you on your way toward your goal. You are undoubtedly a talented candidate who is willing to work very hard. Whether your goals include regional shows, Broadway, or international stages, keep believing that anything is possible. There is a perfect character fit for you.

As you investigate colleges, you might find that some programs are listed in the School of Theatre, School of Drama, School of Acting, or School of Music. Either way, this book will help you reach your goal. Investigating these programs, applying, prescreening, auditioning, and writing personal statements for each college will require research to determine which is right for you and the specific reasons you are good fit.

While you might believe that musical theatre programs are relatively similar, each college's nuances make them very different. These small differences may seem confusing. My goal with this book is to demystify the information and process.

CONTENTS

CHAPTER 1

FOR THE LOVE OF THEATRE: CREATING MAGICAL MOMENTS FOR PATRONS OF THE DRAMATIC ARTS

"...Everyone deserves a chance to fly!"

– Stephen Schwartz, Wicked: ***The Complete Book and Lyrics of the Broadway Musical***

A theatre, hushed just before the curtains open, is magical. Patrons who sense that magnificent enchantment discover a transformative, goosebump-eliciting experience, reminding them that anything is possible. Even a river can be turned into chocolate as Willy Wonka and Charlie Bucket discovered in their search for inner peace and happiness in *Charlie and the Chocolate Factory.* Similarly, Dorothy took a yellow-brick road, discovering new friends and braving a menacing forest filled with winged monkeys to discover that her family loved her dearly in *The Wizard of Oz.* Willy, Charlie, Dorothy, and every other character in drama, musical theater, and films come alive through the vision of directors, the talent of actors, singers, and dancers, and the inventive imaginations of costume, lighting, and set designers.

Stories transform from imagination to written text and from scripts to dramatic re-enactment. Those who eat the cake in *Alice in Wonderland* grow to new heights drinking in the magnificence of the theatre. Simply standing on a pitch-black stage with rows upon rows of empty chairs is a remarkable experience. The stage is a metaphor for life as everyone lives on a stage, performing in their own play. It's humbling.

Shakespeare provided his own commentary.

> "All the world's a stage,
> and all the men and women merely players:
> they have their exits and their entrances;
> and one man in his time plays many parts ..."
>
> —*As You Like It,* Act II, Scene 7, 139–142

Behind the curtain, a different kind of magic happens. Costumes and sets create mood and ambiance, sensationalising grand moments like the balcony scene in *Romeo and Juliet* depicting societal barriers that can thwart love. The riverboat, *Cotton Blossom*, in Jerome Kern and Oscar Hammerstein's musical comedy *Show Boat*, provides a floating palace addressing the social issues of racism and inequality. As the show begins and the curtain rises, excitement builds, as the actors begin their onstage performance in the glow of the lights, donning dramatic costumes, and backed by a captivating set.

Iconic set pieces like the Paris Opera House chandelier in *Phantom of the Opera*, dramatic moments like the helicopter scene in *Miss Saigon*, and a carnivorous, human-eating plant in *Little Shop of Horrors* bring theatre to spectacular glory. Audience members become enraptured by exuberant, emotion-filled acting and the dynamic sight and sound display.

Meanwhile, costume designers enchant audiences. Elsa's outfit magically transforms into her icy blue gown in *Frozen*, Eliza Doolittle stuns donning her ascot dress in *My Fair Lady*, the King of Siam's iconic outfit wows at the British envoy reception in *The King and I*, Aurora mesmerizes in her *Kiss of the Spider Woman* dress, and Dorothy dazzles the Munchkins with her spectacular ruby red slippers. Identifiable masks like the iconic masterpiece designed by Maria Björnson and worn by the Phantom in *Phantom of the Opera* or the outfits designed by Paul Tazewell and showcased by the *Hamilton* cast stand out in our memories.

As you pursue your goal in musical theatre, you will explore all aspects of the stage, learning fine details of how sets are constructed, costumes are assembled, accessories added, and props are envisioned to add flair that realistically portrays your character. While you intensely study acting, singing, and dancing, have fun using your creative talents, and live each moment fully, developing invaluable skills that are transferable to other jobs you might choose. As you transition, remember that life is a journey, not a destination. Theatre is a thrill ride of grand proportions.

Learning basic sewing skills could come in handy if you need to fix a costume quickly. Knowing a bit about carpentry could help you repair a loose board on a set if you are practicing after hours or build creative spaces in a home or office. With the transferrable skills you learn studying technical theatre, even Halloween sets and costumes can be remarkably fun to produce.

Many actors working in theatre, musical theatre, and film have a Bachelor of

Fine Arts (BFA) or Master of Fine Arts (MFA), though this degree is not necessary to perform, and half of the performers on Broadway have a college degree. Nevertheless, somewhere down the line, a college education is valuable and some of the best actors on stage continue to train, study with coaches, and develop new skills throughout their life.

You can earn your degree in theatre arts, musical theatre, dance, or music, though some students attend liberal arts colleges to pursue majors in dramatic writing, literature, or history. Either way, a bachelor's degree gets you started with general skills to fine-tune your craft while diversifying your skills. Before, during, and after your educational foundation, you just need experience.

The journey you are taking will have its ups and downs, but you will have stories to tell for the rest of your life. Enjoy this magical experience.

IMAGINE DOROTHY'S RUBY RED SLIPPERS OR MARY POPPIN'S BLACK UMBRELLA

Acting is not simply pretending to be someone else. In fact, the heart of any role is in the impassioned expression of human nature. Actors must embody a character and bring its essence to life in words, diction, and song. There is a certain *je ne sais quoi*, a mysteriousness that captures the lives of people during a certain moment in history.

To understand *Les Misérables*, actors must internalize the social issues of 19th-century France including the period's destitute poverty, the immoral justice system, and the excruciating hardships during the industrial revolution. Victor Hugo wrote *Les Misérables* in 1862, telling the profound story of life at that time. Audiences can feel the chanting march reverberate when the chorus sings,

When the beating of your heart

Echoes the beating of the drums

There is a life about to start

When tomorrow comes!

Meanwhile, the audience comes along for the ride from highs to lows and back. Actors and crew stage and creatively perform as a team. Stage design helps tell the story through lighting, sound, effects, costume, scenery, and props. All the while, actors must embrace the following seven Cs of theatrical shows.

1. Creative
2. Clear
3. Concise
4. Compact
5. Communication
6. Collaboration
7. Complete

Creativity is fundamental. Afterward, the story's visual imagery needs to be told clearly so that people can see the story and internalize the mood, meaning, purpose, time period, socioeconomic climate, and emotion. The elements of a story are folded into one or more sets of visual pieces – moving parts in a jigsaw puzzle that, alone, says little, but together illuminates the entire picture.

At the same time, the show is not long. The limited timeframe necessitates brevity and conciseness. While plays, musicals, films, and commercials can range in duration, each has a beginning, middle, and end. Films, plays, and musical theatre must complete the entire thought with all components fitting together.

The stage or scene is compact in space. All of the action needs to happen within the frame of the stage or a lens. Yet, these components are confined to spatial limitations within the given area. While theatrical stages range in size, film locations can be much larger. Nevertheless, there are still bounds on action scenes that can take place on set. Every image, costume, or set piece that is needed to tell the story must be within the borders.

Shows do not take place in a vacuum. They are visualized and constructed as a team. Not only must the actors, choreographers, costume designers, and those in technical theatre know the story and understand the context, but they must also communicate effectively with the director at the start. From the very beginning, there should be a clear line of communication.

Collaboration is essential. Actors must listen attentively and propose ideas, though the performance must be conceptualized with the director's leadership. Consultation with other cast and crew members is also necessary. By discussing opportunities for improvement, pitfalls in design elements, and financial and spatial limitations, the team can efficiently and effectively produce the synergy to craft the best representation of the story.

In the end, the story must be complete. Whatever needed to be communicated must have its rise and fall. The costumes and sets must reflect the perspective, conflict, climax, resolution, and overall theme.

Theatres are alive, buzzing with activity. Although the pandemic presented challenges to in-person plays and musicals, films continued to be created and theatres returned to enthusiastic audiences. Omicron's December 2021 last-minute heartbreaking shutdown disappointed thousands, though the song "No Day But Today", in the musical *Rent* reminds us,

There's only us,
There's only this,
forget regret,
or life is yours to miss.
No other road,
no other way,
No day but today.

Historically, theatres have always bounced back, even in the most catastrophic times. Shows and styles may change; budgets may tighten; designs may reflect the momentary mood.

While few alive today will ever forget the impact the pandemic had on life, liberty, and disparity, people will remember that "somewhere over the rainbow, bluebirds fly." We, too, will fly again, as will theatre. Unfortunately, the saddest moments will not completely disappear.

Theatres took a huge hit, stopping production teams. Theatre will come back stronger as will those who bring energy and life to the stage. People hunger to be inspired with messages that transcend the anguish of disease and war. We can still hear Liza Minnelli's voice ring.

What good is sitting alone in your room?

Come hear the music play.

Life is a Cabaret, old chum,

Come to the Cabaret.

Actors must act. Singers must sing. Dancers must dance. Costumes will again be created and stitchers will resume their roles. Feverish tech crews will construct sets, create props, paint miniature villages, and move tons of material.

We will all move on.

The song "Seize the Day" from the musical *Newsies* tells us,

Now is the time to seize the day

They're gonna see there's hell to pay

Nothing can break us

No one can make us quit before we're done

One for all and all for one!

Ultimately, musical theatre will return worldwide, and life will continue despite adversity, challenges, and global strife as we keep striving for our dreams.

CHAPTER 2

EXPECTATIONS AND TRAINING: ACTING, SINGING, AND DANCE

"Art doesn't give rise to anything in us that isn't already there. It simply stirs our curious consciousness and sparks a fire that illuminates who we have always wanted to be."

– **Kamand Kojouri**

THE UNPREDICTABLE YELLOW BRICK ROAD

The road to theatre performance is neither straight nor predictable. Think of it like Dorothy's yellow brick road. You are off to see the Wizard, skipping merrily to some upbeat music, when you stumble upon a field where a scarecrow hangs from a pole. You know that somewhere over the rainbow, big city lights and a grand theatre were just ahead. Theatres beckon you to enter, but you are now in a cornfield in Munchkin Country helping a lonely straw-stuffed gentleman off of the pole. You continue along your path as you find a tin man and a lion. Your road takes twists and turns as you fall asleep in a field of poppies, missing a grand opportunity, or are carried away in the beaks of birds to some never, neverland.

Given that acting contracts are short-term, a performer's value only lasts while actors are healthy and free of injury. Life's successes rest perilously on ability and showmanship. During college, freelance work typically begins in a small company where actors gain professional experiences. Later, individuals may create shows or audition among many other talented actors. One day, a part fits like a glove and you are simply a perfect match for the character. Other times, it is serendipity, like how Yul Brynner landed the role of the King of Siam in *The King and I.*

Personal character is essential in the acting world since actors spend so much time together, personally and professionally, while sharing emotional experiences on and off the stage. Relationship building and collaboration are essential as actors strive for value-centered living, while endlessly searching for the essence of their moral fabric and developing lifelong relationships. Toxic personalities, prima donnas, and drama queens often blend like oil and water. Marilyn Monroe once said, "I restore myself when I'm alone. A career is born in public – talent in privacy." Patti Smith said, "We go through life. We shed our skins. We become ourselves." We are unstoppable in life when we discover ourselves, our passions, and our destiny.

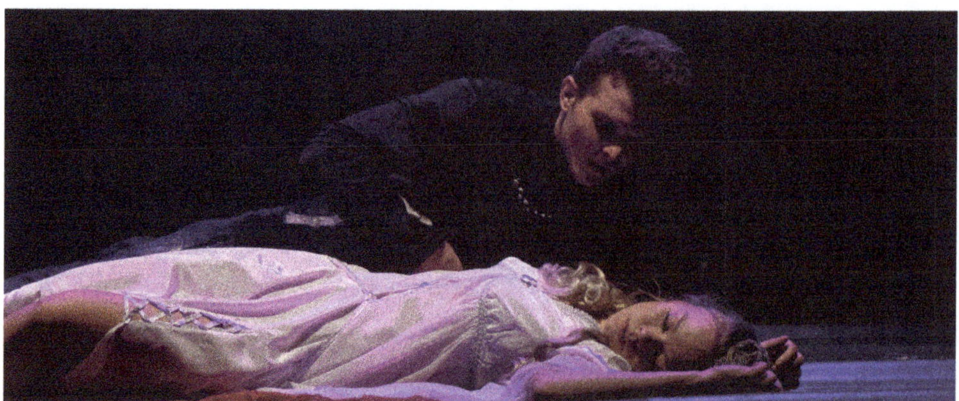

Thus, actors must be able to:

1. Take direction from the director and stage manager
2. Work well with the choreographer, blending seamlessly with other dancers
3. Be punctual and reliable, attending scheduled rehearsals
4. Work as a team on and off the stage
5. Show up at all costume fittings and props rehearsals
6. Understand how their character fits into the play's story
7. Memorize lines, songs, dances, and timings
8. Learn their role independently and collectively
9. Improvise, perform, ad-lib
10. Project their character's persona confidently and convincingly
11. Assist where necessary, supporting cast and crew members
12. Laugh

MUSICAL THEATRE'S MULTI-DISCIPLINARY TRAINING

You are embarking on a thrilling, demanding, and disciplined pursuit. You will work with extremely skilled performers who started when they entered elementary school. Some have performed professionally on stages worldwide and will blow you away with their abilities. However, rarely are musical theatre students equally skilled in singing, dancing, and acting.

Some thespians are amazingly talented. Do not let their abilities bring you down or make you feel as if you are not good enough. You may significantly improve during college with the right training. Besides, your enthusiasm for musical theatre will show through in your auditions. Furthermore, many directors and college talent scouts are more interested in your potential, commitment, and attitude.

NEW STYLES AND CHANGING DYNAMICS

Musical theatre's introduction of rap and hip-hop into the wildly successful show *Hamilton,* that premiered in 2015, added a contemporary flair to the stage while adapting the dynamic musical theatre curricula. Other musicals like Cindy Lauper's pop-punk sound in *Kinky Boots*, which premiered in 2012, set the stage for this slow transformation. Even before *Kinky Boots* came the 1998 premiere of *Hedwig and the Angry Inch* with its rock music and lyrics by Stephen Trask.

Here are 100 Broadway musicals theatre lovers should see in their lifetime.[1]

1. *The Sound of Music*
2. *The Wizard of Oz*
3. *Oklahoma*
4. *Guys and Dolls*
5. *The Phantom of the Opera*
6. Gypsy
7. *Les Misérables*
8. *How To Succeed in Business Without Really Trying*
9. *Annie*
10. *Wicked*
11. *West Side Story*
12. *Chicago*
13. *The Music Man*
14. *Grease*
15. *A Chorus Line*
16. *Sweeney Todd*
17. *Fiddler on the Roof*
18. *Annie Get Your Gun*
19. *Singing in the Rain*
20. *Carousel*
21. *My Fair Lady*
22. *42nd Street*
23. *Hello, Dolly!*
24. *South Pacific*
25. *Into the Woods*
26. *Damn Yankees*
27. *Man of La Mancha*
28. *Hair*
29. *Ragtime*
30. *The King and I*
31. *The Fantasticks*
32. *Rent*
33. *Miss Saigon*
34. *A Funny Thing Happened on the Way to the Forum*
35. *Joseph and the Amazing Technicolor Dreamcoat*
36. *Aida*
37. *Sunday in the Park with George*
38. *The Wiz*
39. *The Best Little Whorehouse in Texas*
40. *Bye Bye Birdie*
41. *The Book of Mormon*
42. *Evita*
43. *La Cage Aux Follies*
44. *The Producers*
45. *Jersey Boys*
46. *Oliver!*
47. *The Lion King*
48. *Memphis*
49. *Billy Elliot*

---

1 Johnny Hebda, "Johnny Hebda: Best Broadway Musicals of All Time," *Blogspot*, July 9, 2012, http://johnnyhebda.blogspot.com/2012/07/johnny-hebda-best-broadway-musicals-of.html

50. *Avenue Q*
51. *Thoroughly Modern Millie*
52. *Company*
53. *Little Shop of Horrors*
54. *Parade*
55. *Hairspray*
56. *Jekyll and Hyde*
57. *Spamalot*
58. *Anything Goes*
59. *Follies*
60. *The Light in the Piazza*
61. *Mamma Mia*
62. *The Secret Garden*
63. *Seven Brides for Seven Brothers*
64. *Spring Awakening*
65. *Big River*
66. *Pippin*
67. *The 25th Annual Putnam County Spelling Bee*
68. *Porgy and Bess*
69. *The Scarlet Pimpernel*
70. *The Pajama Game*
71. *The Drowsy Chaperone*
72. *Pirates of Penzance*
73. *She Loves Me*
74. *1776*
75. *Sweet Charity*
76. *Dreamgirls*
77. *Sunset Boulevard*
78. *Blood Brothers*
79. *A Little Night Music*
80. *Jesus Christ Superstar*
81. *Footloose*
82. *Dirty, Rotten Scoundrels*
83. *Next to Normal*
84. *Crazy for You*
85. *Beauty & The Beast*
86. *Newsies*
87. *Camelot*
88. *Mary Poppins*
89. *Seussical the Musical*
90. *Once on this Island*
91. *You're a Good Man Charlie Brown*
92. *Brigadoon*
93. *The Last Five Years*
94. *Show Boat*
95. *Side Show*
96. *Assassins*
97. *Passion*
98. *Peter Pan*
99. *In the Heights*
100. *Urinetown*

NO SURPRISES – PLAN AND PREPARE AHEAD OF TIME

Musical theatre students must have the ability to sing, dance, and act. Intense college training in these areas enhances these skills. However, most students enter with these abilities and must demonstrate their skills in pre-screening videos and audiotapes. As soon as you can, obtain video and audio of your performances, showcases, acting, and training.

Many students do not consider taping their music lessons with their vocal coach or videoing their dance instruction or rehearsal choreography. However, even practice sessions can give admissions officers and theatre faculty an idea of your talents and skills. Photographs, like a headshot or a screen capture of you on stage, may come in handy when you are applying to college, creating a resume, or producing a one-sheet. There are times when you feel bright, light, and effortless in your body and mind. Those unpredictable times may offer you the best photo-ops.

For your dance pre-screen taping, find a time when your studio room is quiet and empty, possibly before anyone arrives or after everyone has left. You can get a friend or family member to capture the recording or bring a camera and a tripod. You are likely to need an accompanist, whether an audiotape, piano, or other instrumental for your pre-screen taping. A recording studio is best for your songs and monologues. However, if this is not possible, locate a music room, acoustically sound hall, or some other place where you can create an environment with the best sound.

PRE-SCREENING AND AUDITION PREPARATION

Whether you are preparing monologues, song selections, or choreography, work with your theatre, dance, or choir teacher or a private coach. Someone who is a trained listener can hear whatever you miss. Remember, your goal is to put your best foot forward. Iron out the kinks in your performance before you press submit.

PROFESSIONAL THEATRE OR COLLEGE OR BOTH

Note: Some colleges do not allow or strongly discourage their students to perform professionally while they are enrolled in their college program.

Nevertheless, uber-talented musical theatre students often hunger for the big stage to gain professional experiences while studying at school. Particularly in theatre hubs like New York, Los Angeles, Atlanta, Chicago, Cleveland, Dallas, Philadelphia, and Washington, D.C., students do not want to wait for their big break. However, colleges often want students to focus on academics. This tricky space between college and professional theatre results in students mulling over their future while they are living in the present.

When casting sheets open, students believe that it could not hurt to try. Besides, in their mind, they can rehearse and practice between classes and perform in weekend and evening shows outside of class time. However, being in a professional cast often necessitates missing a class or turning down a role at the university. Additionally, with dual commitments, often something has to give. Homework is the loser and academic performance drops. Resolution of the conflict often leans to the professional stage rather than the college.

A college could decide professional theatre concurrently with college is not acceptable. Universities could pull a scholarship that was predicated on performing in college shows. However, the rules that guide a student's ability to perform outside of school are listed in the college catalog. Students must do their due diligence and decide.

Many theatre directors or division deans believe that students should choose. Do you want to perform professionally now or focus on your college education - one or the other? They might tell students that if they miss a class, rehearsal, or show due to an outside professional commitment they may not remain in the program. While theatre directors or division deans are reticent about student participation in professional theatre during the school year, they often encourage students to perform each summer and during winter break.

CHAPTER 3

ACADEMIC SKILLS: FOUNDATIONAL KNOWLEDGE FOR MUSICAL THEATRE

"Without writers, stories would not be written. Without actors, stories could not be brought to life."

– **Angie-Marie Delsante**

Students applying to college programs in musical theatre are expected to be dynamic, multidisciplinary, and extraordinarily talented. However, since majoring in musical theatre is more than just studies in singing, dancing, and acting, students must possess intellectual curiosity for literature, dramatic writing, history, sociology, psychology, economics, communication, and foreign language.

The liberal arts offer a valuable core of knowledge, preparing students for life. This importance is no different for musical theatre students. Liberal arts classes offer students a range of academic studies from which they can view the world. This interdisciplinary foundation is the core essence of knowledge to build a future and a life that extends beyond auditioning, casting, and acting.

Connecting the past to the present delivers a sense of captivating tension, underlying frustrations, and societal conflict to audiences. Pulitzer Prize winner, Lin-Manuel Miranda, who wrote the book, music, and lyrics for the musical *Hamilton*, studied at Wesleyan University in Connecticut. Wesleyan University's President, Michael Roth, explained that *Hamilton* makes "the past come alive in ways that expand possibilities in the present." This is a key skill for everyone involved in theatre.

Simply learning how to conduct research, write clearly, and use technology is valuable. However, the academic skills in developing scholarly papers not only aids in personal self-expression but in delving into big picture concepts and fine-tuned grammar. When an individual writes an e-mail, letter, or paper, others know whether the person has strong English skills. Knowing proper English is not a necessity in theatrical performance if you know your lines, but a person's written communication speaks loudly.

Students learn to collect, organize, and synthesize information in imaginative ways that inspire new points of creativity and opportunity. While diving into problem-solving and critical thinking students can test their ideas, tossing them around with classmates and professors, improving skills in collaboration, interpretation, and originality. Thinking outside of the box in small group discussions can refine character portrayals, remove philosophical biases, and clarify what lies under the surface of the story.

Academic skills also allow students to have a more global and historical worldview. Students who study world history can delve into the past to understand prejudices and challenge today's intellectual thinking. Taking liberal arts classes can teach skills that can help eliminate bias and bigotry. Thespians profoundly shape our world, bringing people together and offering new ways of thinking.

Although students applying to BA or BS programs will take approximately one-third to one-half of their credits in the liberal arts, even BFA students will typically take one-quarter of their classes in required humanities and social science courses to better understand time periods, social conditions, and environmental contexts that set the stage for each show.

Thus, pursuing musical theatre is not just the ability to perform, although auditions will focus on performance quality and skill development. Some schools may require tangential skills like the ability to play the piano or know music theory. Imagination is also essential. Students must be able to dream and envision bold and provocative new worlds. Without hesitation, they must step into new complex settings fresh and renewed.

Initiative is also essential. Listening, attentiveness, and taking direction are all important. However, going one step further demonstrates the commitment to practice, rehearse, and get things right. You can wait until a fitter checks sizes and seams or you can check that costumes fit, ensuring there are no tears or missing accessories. Remember, you are the one going on-stage and a hole or trailing tulle fabric could mean you might trip or have some other kind of accident.

While some students believe that their one moment in time will evaporate if they do not perform professionally as a teenager, training the mind is equally important as training the body. Disciplined preparation in artistic talent is sometimes not sufficient. The ability to read, write, analyze, and interpret characters, sociocultural lifestyles, and political atmospheres of the time is immensely helpful.

Ambition is sometimes seen as derogatory, particularly when egos get involved and students are not kind to others in the competitive environment. However, ambition is essential. You must be willing to go the extra mile since other standouts will. Only the best, brightest, and most focused students will get past the first call. Directors look for those who will collaborate as team players and support the artistry of fellow students while also seeking those people who are "in it to win it."

Academic skills will take you far. While many musical theatre success stories include award-winning actors who never went to college, there is a certain sense of respect in the industry for the smart, disciplined, prepared, and flexible. Scholarship can help you succeed if you decide not to continue with theatre, or you are unable to because of some unforeseen reason. Albert Einstein once said, "The value of an education in a liberal arts college is the training of the mind to think something that cannot be learned from textbooks."

Studying and performing in musical theatre demands resilience and flexibility. Even with all good intentions, unexpected events happen with sets, costumes, or lights. Regardless, actors go on stage to perform. Not all shows are flawless; sometimes there are imperfections. Grace and mercy must be extended if unfortunate events unfold, or important details are left out. When the milk spills, it cannot be returned to its carton.

Interpersonal communication, thus, is an equally important academic and social skill. Everyone in theatre must be patient and deliver written and verbal messages thoughtfully. Broken relationships due to irrational or inappropriate outbursts are hard to repair. Individuals must communicate effectively and ensure that the intended receiver gets the delivery of information. George Bernard Shaw once said, "The single biggest problem in communication is the illusion that it has taken place."

Likewise, singers must emote songs and lyrics with the feeling, sensitivity, and comprehension of the conceptions to be conveyed and the underlying meaning of the words. Vocalists must be able to project. In workshops and classes, musical theatre students develop tone quality, sight-reading, piano skills, and lyrical abilities. Students build upon any deficient skills or learn new talents they may not know like tap or ballet.

However, the most important aspects of academic and artistic training are conceived with passion. When a student is driven to work hard and learn new skills, they can overcome most areas in which they are not quite as skilled. Directors in theatre, television, and film worldwide look for the most expressive, committed, talented, and passionate artists. If you have interests beyond the arts that make you interesting, knowledgeable, and wise, you can make a tremendous impact with audiences as well as with fellow cast members.

Review websites and research programs. Look through official publications, but also review the internet, YouTube, and past shows. Contact someone in the theatre department to learn more about specific details in programs you want to pursue. This is your future. Jump in and learn about the environment to find the best fit for your undergraduate college or conservatory education.

CHAPTER 4

THEATRE EXPERIENCES: INTERNSHIPS FOR HIGH SCHOOL, COLLEGE, AND BEYOND

"I love it when you go to see something, and you enter as an individual, and you leave as a group. Because you've all been bound together by the same experience."

– **Tom Hiddleston**

ACKNOWLEDGMENT OF THE PANDEMIC'S IMPACT ON THEATRE

To begin, the pandemic's impact on theatre cannot go unnoticed. Theatres around the world were impacted by COVID-19 and its numerous repercussions. Theatres were shuttered. Though many that could survive the financial impact reopened, casts, crew, and directors needed to find alternative opportunities, retrain, or use their skills in creative ways. Internships were difficult to find for students who counted on gaining experience. Many school plays and musicals were canceled. However, new opportunities opened. Schools resumed. Theatre programs from high school to graduate school began once again.

INTERNSHIP LOCATIONS

Some geographical locations lend themselves better to theatre opportunities. Larger cities where there are big stages or where the region's donors support theatre offer more chances to obtain internship experiences. However, colleges with theatre programs also provide their students with internal opportunities to gain experience.

For example, New York City offers the greatest diversity of theatre internship options. In addition, nearby areas in New Jersey, Connecticut, Long Island, and Westchester County also offer significant opportunities for internship experience and professional positions. Some colleges in the New York and New England areas have a close affiliation with major theatres. For example, the University of Connecticut is connected to the Hartford Stage where the Metropolitan Opera offers study abroad opportunities with University of the Arts London's Wimbledon College of the Arts in the United Kingdom.

London is a mecca for theatre. An internship or semester abroad at a school, particularly in London to train as an actor in West End theatres, would be a phenomenal opportunity. Though the theatre community suffered during the pandemic, London theatre will rebound with the robust support of patrons of the arts.

Other locations where there are significant opportunities for theatre include:

Atlanta
Austin
Boston
Chicago
Cleveland
Dallas/Ft. Worth
Hartford
Los Angeles/Orange County
Miami/Ft. Lauderdale
Minneapolis/St. Paul
Philadelphia
Phoenix
Portland
San Diego
San Francisco/Oakland/Berkeley
Washington, D.C./Maryland/Virginia

ArtsAmerica also explains, "But even some cities and towns that don't have an especially large or active year-round theatre scene are noteworthy for festivals and other events; one famous example is Louisville, Kentucky, where the Actors Theatre of Louisville hosts the annual Humana Festival of New American Plays."[1]

Look through TheatreWorksUSA for some of the many opportunities available: *https://twusa.org/about/work-with-us/*

AMERICANS FOR THE ARTS INTERNSHIP

If you are committed to arts education in the United States there are numerous opportunities to support students. One of those is with Americans for the Arts where you can make a difference. Undergraduates, recent graduates, and graduate students are invited to apply and become a part of the team. This internship can be for college credit or as an hourly-paid position. Apply online through their portal.

Americans for the Arts also has a program called Diversity in Arts Leadership Internship, which seeks applicants from underrepresented groups who are passionate about community arts and education leadership. Locations for these internships are in New York City, New Jersey, Nashville, Boston, Sarasota, and Raleigh-Wake County.

---

1 Arts America, "Theater," *Arts America,* n.d., http://artsamerica.org/genres/genres-theater/

Additional Opportunities for Underrepresented Groups Include:

CALIFORNIA

- **The Getty Center** offers summer internships to undergraduates of culturally diverse backgrounds who reside or attend college in Los Angeles County.
- **Stanford Institute for Diversity in the Arts** - ***Community Arts Fellowships*** engage artists, students, and the local community collaboratively to create performance and visual art that examine the complex intersections between race, diversity, and social action.
- **Film Independent -** ***Project Involve*** offers up-and-coming film professionals from under-represented communities the opportunity to hone skills, form creative partnerships, utilize free or low-cost production resources.

COLORADO

- **The Diversity in the Arts Internship Program (DITA)** is a cohort of diverse arts and culture interns that learn from and support art and culture nonprofits in the diverse Denver metro community.

ILLINOIS

- **Steppenwolf Theatre -** ***Multicultural Fellowship*** *is* for early-career persons of color interested in working in arts administration.

MARYLAND

- **Greater Baltimore Cultural Alliance - *Urban Arts Leadership Program*** supports historically underrepresented, particularly those of color, in the management of cultural and artistic organizations.
- **The Walters Art Museum** offers a research and fellowship program for training and diversifying the fields of art history and museum practice.

NEW YORK

- **The New York Foundation for the Arts** has a classified section with various opportunities and is especially good for finding internships with galleries in New York.
- **Studio in a School - *ARTS Intern Program*** provides opportunities for college undergrads to learn about museum professions through internships in museums and cultural institutions.
- **4A - *Multicultural Advertising Intern Program*** allows students to work at prestigious advertising agencies, interact w/ advertising professionals, and gain credentials in arts management, production, and planning.
- **Center for Communication - VICE Cencom Fellowship** ensures greater access to careers in journalism for the next generation of innovative storytellers.
- **Pentacle - *Cultivating Leadership in Dance*** provides a structured internship program working closely with dance artists/choreographers and non-profit organizations.
- **International Radio & Television Society (IRTS) - *Summer Fellowship Program*** brings together to train & educate the next generation of media & communication professionals.
- **ArtTable - *Diversity Internship Initiative*** provides opportunities and mentorship for GRADUATE students from underrepresented backgrounds to aid their transition from academic to professional careers.
- **The CUNY Cultural Corps** creates opportunities for CUNY students and CUNY recent graduates to work in NYC's cultural sector.
- **The PENCIL Internship Program** provides NYC area students with access to career readiness training, connections to professional mentors, and the opportunity to secure a paid summer internship.
- **American Ballet Theatre Internship Program** expands ethnic and cultural diversity in classical ballet. ABT is committed to facilitating inclusive programs through its Project Plié initiative.

NORTH CAROLINA

- **Creative Catalyst Fellowship** allows participants to gain experience and develop visionary leadership in paid fellowships in residence at our partner organizations.

PENNSYLVANIA

- **Philadelphia Museum of Art *Honickman Diversity Internship*** provides students from diverse backgrounds with exposure to the inner-workings of a major metropolitan museum.

VIRGINIA

- **Wolf Trap - *Diversity Initiative Internship Program*** provides opportunities for promising young professionals, especially those from cultural or ethnic backgrounds underrepresented in arts management.

WASHINGTON, DC

- **Smithsonian – *Minority Awards Program*** aims to increase participation of groups who are underrepresented in the museum field.
- **Archives of American Art - *Horowitz-Fraad Minority Internships*** provides professional experiences in archival science, information management, museum studies, art administration, art history, and cultural studies.
- **Arena Stage - *Allen Lee Hughes Internship Program*** provides the highest standard of training through immersion in the art and business of producing theatre.
- **The National Museum of African American History and Culture** offers internships and fellowships for college, recent graduates, and graduate students opportunities to work closely with professionals and scholars in the museum field.

MULTIPLE CITIES

- **T. Howard Foundation - *Diversity in Media & Entertainment Internships*** provides minority students who are interested in media & entertainment with internships, networking opportunities, professional development training, scholarships, mentors, and more.

CASTING OPPORTUNITIES WITH THEATERWORKSUSA

TheaterWorksUSA (TWUSA) constantly looks for performers, holding auditions year-round. TWUSA is eager to find actors prepared to tour North America for two to six months. Contracts under American Actors' Equity Association's TheaterWorksUSA are available for actors signed as Assistant Stage Managers. Submit basic information, resume, and headshot to: twusa.org/about/work-with-us/.

You must be 18 years old to audition, though there are both Equity and Non-Equity calls. Auditions and rehearsals are held in New York City. You will have the opportunity to become a member of Actor's Equity Association, although this is not a requirement. Duties include load-in, load-out, props, and costumes.

SUMMER INTERNSHIPS IN ARTISTIC SERVICES, AUDIENCE SERVICES, CASTING LITERARY, STAGE MANAGEMENT, AND THEATRE OPERATIONS

One hundred internships are highlighted at https://www.playbill.com/article/over-100-theatrical-internships-you-can-apply-for

A few include:

Lincoln Center – New York, NY - Performance Marketing

Manhattan Theatre Club – New York, NY - Artistic and Literary, Individual Giving, Company Management, Marketing Analytics, Marketing, Business, Casting, Production Management, and Stargate Theatre

Signature Theatre – New York, NY – Artistic, Literary, Development, Special Events, Company Management, Business Management, Company Management/General Management, and Marketing

MCC Theatre – New York, NY – Audience Services, Development, Education and Public Engagement, Operations, Marketing, and Executive Office

Atlantic Theatre – New York, NY - School Education, School Artistic, and School Administration

Roundabout Theatre Company – New York, NY – Artistic, Literary, Audience Services, Development, Education Intern, Facilities/House Management, Finance, Human Resources, Management, IT, and Marketing

Telsey & Company - New York, NY - Casting

Stewart/Whitley - New York, NY – Casting

Tara Rubin Casting - New York, NY – Casting

5th Avenue Theatre – Seattle, WA – Artistic, New Works, Development, Education/Engagement, Company Management, Marketing/Communications, Casting, and Production Intern

La Jolla Playhouse – La Jolla, CA – Artistic, Philanthropy, Special Events, Administrative Education, YP@LJP Summer Program, Company Management, Marketing, Public Relations, Production Intern, and Stage Management

Steppenwolf Theatre Company – La Jolla, CA - Education

Steppenwolf Theatre Company – Chicago, IL – Literary, Fundraising/Development, Theatre Management, Marketing, Public Relations, Artistic/Casting, Production Intern, Electrics, Properties, Scenic Art, and Sound

American Repertory Theater – Cambridge, MA – Access and Equity, Fundraising/Development, Education, Community Engagement, and Public Relations

SUMMER TRAINING & INTERNSHIPS – MIDDLE SCHOOL & HIGH SCHOOL

In theatre, students learn by doing. Thus, initial and necessary experiences often begin in school and community-based theatre programs. Some of the following internships are for acting, musical theatre, technical theatre, and backstage opportunities. However, there are numerous summer options for students to pursue their dream and hone their craft. The following are a few of the summer options.

- ArtsBridge Summer Drama Programs
- AMDA (American Musical and Dramatic Academy) High School Summer Conservatory (Los Angeles and New York)
- Boston Conservatory
- Broadway Artists Alliance Summer Intensives
- BroadwayEvolved NYC Summer Intensive
- Carnegie Mellon University, Pre-College Drama
- Emerson College

- Florida State University
- French Woods Festival of the Performing Arts
- Idyllwild Arts Teens & Kids Summer Program
- Interlochen Arts Camp
- Ithaca College Summer Theatre Intensive
- La Jolla Playhouse Conservatory
- Marymount Manhattan
- Muny/Webster Intensive – St. Louis, Missouri
- Neighborhood Playhouse, Six Week Summer Acting Intensive
- Northwestern University, National High School Institute (Cherubs)
- NYU, Tisch, Summer High School
- Oklahoma City University
- Paper Mill Playhouse, Summer Musical Theater Conservatory
- Penn State University
- The Performing Arts Project (TPAP) – Wake Forest University
- Perry-Mansfield Intensives
- Rutgers Summer Conservatory
- Southeastern Summer Theater Institute (SSTI)
- Stagedoor Manor
- Stella Adler Teen Summer Conservatory
- Syracuse University, Summer College
- Texas State University, NEXUS Musical Theatre Pre-College Intensive
- UCLA, Acting and Performance Summer Institute
- University of Cincinnati, College Conservatory of Music
- University of Michigan, MPulse Summer Performing Arts Institutes
- University of North Carolina School of the Arts
- University of Southern California High School Summer Conservatory
- Walnut Hill School for the Arts

FESTIVAL JOBS AND INTERNSHIPS

ALABAMA

Alabama Shakespeare Festival
Location: Montgomery, AL
Career Opportunities: Positions open as available across the spectrum of theatre positions.[2]

CALIFORNIA

Marin Shakespeare Festival
Location: San Rafael, CA (Dominican University)
Paid Positions:[3] Stage Manager, Assistant Stage Manager, Carpenters, Costume Designers, Costume Assistants, House Manager/Assistant House Manager, Lighting Designer, Master Carpenter, Master Electrician, Prop Designer, Scenic Painters, Set Designer, and Wardrobe Supervisor
Volunteer Positions:[4] Carpenters / Scenic Painters, Costume Helpers, Dressers, Technicians, Sound and Light Operators, and Ushers.

---

2 Alabama Shakespeare Festival, "Career Opportunities," *Alabama Shakespeare Festival*, n.d., https://asf.net/careers/

3 Marin Shakespeare Company, "Job Openings," *Marin Shakespeare Company*, n.d., https://www.marinshakespeare.org/jobs/

4 Idaho Shakespeare Festival, "Volunteer," *Idaho Shakespeare Festival*, n.d., https://idahoshakespeare.org/volunteer/

Location: Santa Cruz, CA (University of California, Santa Cruz)
Internships: The summer season opens for intern applications in late fall and closes in February. Applications will be reviewed in February.[5] For more information, contact intern@santacruzshakespeare.org

Will Geer Theatricum Botanicum
Location: Topanga, CA
Internships:[6] Acting, administration, technical design, education and production – we have an internship for every aspect of Theatricum's operation.

COLORADO

Colorado Shakespeare Festival
Location: Boulder, CO (University of Colorado, Boulder)
Positions/Internships: For positions as they open, see https://cupresents.org/about-cu-presents/job-opportunities/

Casting for the following summer season is announced in October. Colorado Shakespeare Festival hires AEA actors on two to three show contracts and non-AEA actors on one, two, or three show contracts. Live auditions or video submissions are held in October. Two contrasting monologues, no more than two minutes (each should be less than one minute).

Creede Repertory Theatre
Location: Creede, CO
Professional Positions:[7] Numerous positions are open for each summer form May – July, including stage management, technical, carpentry, costume, first hand, sound, lighting, electrician, artisan, paint, props, and stitcher.

CONNECTICUT

Goodspeed Musicals
Location: East Haddam, CT
Paid Production Apprenticeships: Positions are available in Stage Carpentry, Technical/Construction, Prop Run Crew, Costume Shop, Stitchers, Wardrobe, and Electrics. Most 2022 apprenticeship positions are paid minimum wage. To apply, submit cover letter, resume, availability and list of three references to jobs@goodspeed.org.[8]

---

5 Santa Cruz Shakespeare, "Internship," *Santa Cruz Shakespeare*, n.d., https://santacruzshakespeare.org/internship/

6 Will Geer's Theatricum Botanicum, "Internships," *Will Geer's Theatricum Botanicum*, n.d., https://theatricum.com/internships/

7 Creede Repetory Theatre, "Work With Us," *Creede Repetory Theatre*, n.d., https://creederep.org/work-with-us/

8 Goodspeed Musicals, "Job Opportunities," *Goodspeed Musicals*, n.d., https://www.goodspeed.org/about/career-opportunities

Actors – Equity video submissions for three musicals. All principal roles will be understudied ($1,008 weekly minimum). Video audition, headshot, resume.

IDAHO

Idaho Shakespeare Festival
Location: Boise, ID
Volunteer/Paid/Apprenticeship Positions: Production & Technical Positions, Volunteers, Apprenticeship Program, Workshops, Residences, Casting, Directors & Designers, and Acting Company.

Actors may submit headshots, resumes, and video auditions (include Shakespeare and contemporary monologues and a song if you sing) at any time of the year. EQUITY and non-EQUITY actors are considered.

ILLINOIS

Illinois Shakespeare Festival
Location: Bloomington, IL (Illinois State University)
Internships: Acting, Company Management, Lighting/Electrics, Prop Shop, Scenic Artist/Paint Shop, Scene Shop/Carpentry, Sound Shop, and Stage Management. "Interns will participate in an internship class once a week for professional development and education. Interns will be registered for THE 398 - Professional Practice in Theatre at Illinois State University…The Illinois Shakespeare Festival will pay for the tuition and fees for up to six credit hours of THE 398 and assist students in transferring this credit to their home academic institution.

"Our summer 2022 course will be facilitated by Dr. Ann Haugo and Dr. Derek R. Munson. Interns will meet with their mentor and the production manager every three weeks. Mentorship meeting goals are to provide structured feedback for each individual, discuss any programmatic challenges they are having, and to set goals for the internship experience.

"Current enrollment in a college program with an anticipated graduation date of August 2022 or later. Ability to commit to the full summer season. All internships are full-time commitments."

MAINE

Theater at Monmouth
Location: Monmouth, ME
Internships: "Each year, early career theatre artists, technicians, and administrators start their professional journey at Theater at Monmouth. Members of the intern and apprentice company work alongside artists and professionals to produce the summer season at one of the nation's only classical repertory theatres."[10]

MASSACHUSETTS

Barrington Stage Company
Location: Pittsfield, MA
Internships/Jobs:[11] The listing in early 2022 included these positions: Lighting and Sound Technician, Scene Shop Operations Manager, Scenic Carpenter/Welder, Scenic Carpenter, Charge Scenic Artist, Scenic Artist, Stitcher, Associate Wardrobe Supervisor, Wardrobe Technician, Light Board Operator, Electrician, Audio Supervisor, Sound Board Operator (A1), Sound Technician (A2), Properties Supervisor, Assistant Properties Supervisor, Properties Artisan, Stage Crew Chief, Stage Crew.

Berkshire Theater Festival
Location: Pittsfield/Stockbridge, MA
Internships and Jobs: https://www.berkshiretheatregroup.org/Join%20Our%20Team/#Year-Round_Job_Opps

Shakespeare & Company
Location: Lenox, MA
Internships: In addition to exclusive lectures, career guidance, and the possibility of a capstone project, "Interns receive one-on-one mentoring from within their department and experience with professional artists and staff…Internships are

---

9 Illinois Shakespeare Festival, "Internship Program," *Illinois Shakespeare Festival,* n.d., https://illinoisshakes.com/employment/internships/

10 Theater at Monmouth, "Work With Us," *Theater at Monmouth,* n.d., http://theateratmonmouth.org/about-us/work-with-us/

11 Barrington Stage Company, "Job Opportunities," *Barrington Stage Company,* n.d., https://barringtonstageco.org/about-the-company/jobs/

available year-round, typically 15- or 16-week duration, but if one of the tracks below is not perfect for an applicant, programs of custom duration or areas of interest can be developed as well."[12]

Actors are sought for the season. All roles will be understudied. Virtual auditions (may change). Auditions are for Equity actors, no non-union acting roles are available. Auditions include a Vimeo submission with contrasting monologues, a headshot, and a resume.

Williamstown Theatre Festival
Location: Williamstown, MA (Williams College)
Internships: "Tony Award-winning Williamstown Theatre Festival's summer season offers a variety of career opportunities for theatre professionals at all levels of experience.... In the summer of 2021, salaried positions will be compensated at a range of $684 to $750 per week. Hourly positions will be compensated at a rate of $13.50 to $15.00 per hour."[13]

NEW YORK

Adirondack Theatre Festival
Location: Glen Falls, NY
Internships: "ATF's professional internship program offers rigorous, hands-on educational opportunities for current students and early career professionals seeking an introduction to careers in the professional theatre. Our goal is to provide interns with practical experience in the shop, rehearsal room, backstage and in the front office as well as valuable networking opportunities with working theatre professionals."[14] Internships available in administration, artistic, production, carpentry, electrics, sound, props, paint, and wardrobe.

Apply by February 1st. Chorus roles are possible for interns as well. "While interns are assigned specific departments and mentors, they are also expected to learn and work outside their chosen area of expertise. We hope to provide the intern with a well-rounded experience designed to inform them of all the various jobs required to mount a professional production." Interns may receive either course credit or a weekly stipend.

Hudson Valley Shakespeare Festival
Location: Garrison, NY
Internships/Training: "While most theater training programs are unpaid (or charge tuition), we're proud to pay educational stipends to participants and, in most cases, offer local housing, reducing barriers to employment in the arts.

---

12 Shakespeare & Company, "Jobs and Volunteering," *Shakespeare & Company,* n.d., https://www.shakespeare.org/jobs-and-volunteering/interns

13 Williamstown Theatre Festival, "Work & Learn," *Williamstown Theatre Festival,* n.d., https://wtfestival.org/work-learn/

14 Adirondack Theatre Festival, "Professional Theatre Internships at Adirondack Theatre Festival," *Adirondack Theatre Festival,* 2021, https://www.atfestival.org/opportunities/internships/

Our Conservatory Company training program, Production and Administrative Internships and Directing Fellowships offer exceptional practical experience through collaboration, hands-on learning, and mentorship."[15]

Powerhouse Theater
Location: Poughkeepsie, NY (Vassar College)
Training Program: The summer 2022 training program is five weeks encompassing the theatre process while observing and participating in shows.[16]
Shakespeare in the Park
Location: New York, NY
Freelance Positions: Stitchers/Costume Department – stitching and finishes to costumes - $25/hour
Scenery Department – Hard-working carpenters, scenic artists, and props run crew. Construction/painting experience required - $25-$27/hour.[17]

OREGON

Oregon Shakespeare Festival
Location: Ashland, OR
Internships: "Internships are designed to provide participants with a learning opportunity within our artistic, production, and administration areas...Prior theatre experience is not required. This is a 2- to 4–month experience that is designed to provide a professional development opportunity for emerging artists and aspiring arts administrators. Recipients are paired with an OSF company member and receive mentorship in their respective discipline.

"Internships are unpaid learning opportunities. Housing and travel are not provided for Internships...Candidates for Internships must be a high school graduate or have at least one year of work experience. Applicants interested in an Internship in Stage Management and any of the production areas must have at least one year of experience in their specific area of interest, a year of experience in an academic environment will be considered."[18]

Actors – AEA required for auditions – Contact Oregon Shakespeare Festival in July for open call auditions for the following summer repertory season.

---

15 Hudson Valley Shakespeare Festival, "Professional Training," *Hudson Valley Shakespeare Festival,* n.d., https://hvshakespeare.org/education/training/

16 Vassar College, "Powerhouse Theater Training Program," *Vassar College,* n.d., https://www.vassar.edu/powerhouse/apprentices/

17 The Public, "Employment & Internships," *The Public,* n.d., https://publictheater.org/footer/employment--internships/

18 Oregon Shakespeare Festival, "Internships," *Oregon Shakespeare Festival,* n.d., https://www.osfashland.org/en/work-with-us/FAIR/Internships.aspx

PENNSYLVANIA

Pennsylvania Shakespeare Festival
Location: Center Valley, PA
The 2022 Season includes productions of A Chorus Line, Fences, Little Red, Every Brilliant Thing, The River Bride (reading) and Much Ado About Nothing.
Internships: There are numerous Stage Management (SM) tracks. Interns work alongside Equity SMs. Responsibilities include prop tracking, feeding lines, backstage deck, run crew, lifting, props, repairing, construction, carpentry, and foreman shadowing. Specialty skills will be learned on the job. SM and Carp interns must be go-getters in a fast-paced environment. Salary $300/week.
Costume Design – **First Hand Assistant** to the Cutter/Draper – Experienced in pattern layout/cutting/sewing. Salary $475/week. **Costume Shop Craftsperson** – assists with crafts, including millinery, footwear, jewelry, masks – must be self-motivated, manage multiple simultaneous projects. and able to read/ interpret sketches. Salary $425/week. **Stitcher** – Intermediate/Advanced sewing by hand/maching, including alterations, construction, and finishing. Salary $340/ week. **Costume Shop Intern** and **Costume Shop Management Intern** – Assists the costumer design staff while working following instructions and working independently. Salary $300/week. **Wardrobe Crafts** and **Wardrobe Stitcher**– Salary $340/week. **Wardrobe Intern** and **Wig and Makeup Dresser** – Salary $300/week

TEXAS

Texas Shakespeare Festival
Location: Kilgore, TX (Kilgore College)
Internships:[19]
Costume Intern / Wardrobe: May 20 - August 3 Salary: $1,500 / double occupancy dorm housing / 14 meals a week. Minimum Requirements: undergraduate costume technology training required and/or one year of professional experience. **Costume and Wig Stylist Intern:** May 20 - August 3 Salary: $1,500 / double occupancy dormitory housing / 14 meals a week. Minimum Requirements: undergraduate training in wigs and hairstyling preferred and/or one year of professional experience working on wigs and hairstyling. **Properties Intern:** May 20 - August 3 Salary: $1,500 stipend / double occupancy dorm housing / 14 meals a week Note: Properties Interns are assigned primarily to the properties department, but may also be reassigned, as needed, to other technical areas. **Scenic Carpenters:** May 16 - August 3 Salary: $4,400 stipend / up to $300 / double occupancy dorm housing / 14 meals a week Minimum Requirements: Experience with various scenic construction techniques and materials; strong woodworking skills. **Scene Painting Intern:** May 20 - August 3 Salary: $1,500 stipend / double occupancy dorm housing / 14 meals a week. Minimum Requirements: Fundamental experience in scenic treatments including, but not limited to, faux finish, carving, texturing, aging, and distressing. The candidate should also be comfortable working at heights above 16'. **Lighting Intern:** May 20 - August 3 Salary: $1,500 stipend / double occupancy dorm housing / 14 meals a week. Minimum Requirements: Assist with the hang, focus, and strike of electrics and special effects for all productions; program and run the lighting console for shows as assigned; assist with the maintenance and upkeep for all lighting inventory and systems. **Stage Management Intern**: May 20 - August 3 Salary: $1,500 stipend / double occupancy dorm housing / 14 meals a week. Minimum requirement: one year undergraduate stage management training. **Stage Management Intern:** May 20 - August 3 Salary: $1,500 stipend / double occupancy dorm housing / 14 meals a week. Minimum Requirement: minimum one year undergraduate stage management training.

Review the website for audition opportunities in the fall. Even though they have more than a thousand submissions, some of those who audition get a spot. Casting is completed in late February. The Texas Shakespeare Festival also has a fall Roadshow Educational Tour.

UTAH

Utah Shakespearean Festival
Location: Cedar City, UT
Inernships: May/June – July/September Draper:[20] May – July - Oversees all

19 Texas Shakespeare Festival, "Costume Department," *Texas Shakespeare Festival,* n.d., https://www.texasshakespeare.com/costumes

20 Utah Shakespeare Festival, "Employment," *Utah Shakespeare Festival*, n.d., https://www.bard.org/employment

construction of costumes for assigned show. Works in direct relationship with costume designer. **First Hand:** Works with the draper to construct and supervise construction of costumes. Supervises costume technicians. **Technician:** Constructs all costume pieces assigned by first hand. Contracts are May 2–July 2 or June 1–July 13. **Wardrobe:** Works on the run of assigned productions assisting in preparation and maintenance (laundry and repair) of costumes. **Assistant Costume Crafts Supervisor:** Assists with the operation of costume crafts including scheduling of fittings and attending fittings; helps interpret costume designer's sketches and ideas and assists with problem-solving and engineering of costume crafts items. **Crafts Technician:** Assists senior crafts technician in the construction of all accessories or special costume projects. **Junior Artisan/Stage Crew:** Responsible for the building and fabrication of stage and rehearsal properties for assigned productions. Works with the prop team to complete shop improvement and organizational projects as assigned. **Scenic Carpenter**: Constructs and loads in all scenic set elements for assigned productions. Completes shop improvement and organization projects as assigned. **Junior Carpenter/Stage Crew:** Constructs and loads-in all scenic set elements for assigned productions. Responsible for running, storage, and maintenance of scenery for assigned productions. **Scenic Artist:** Responsible for painting and finishing of all scenic elements for assigned productions. **Junior Painter/Stage Crew:** Responsible for painting and finishing of all scenic elements for assigned productions. Responsible for running, storage, and maintenance of paints for assigned productions. **Deck Carpenter:** Responsible for load in, running, organization of storage, and maintenance of scenery and props for a theatre (Engelstad, Randall, or Anes). Works with scenery director on stage crew schedule and necessary adjustments. **Junior Carpenters/Painters/Prop Interns:** Responsible for load in, running, storage, changeovers, and maintenance of scenery and props for assigned productions. **Stage Crew:** Responsible for load in, running, storage, and changeovers of scenery and props for assigned productions.

VIRGINIA

American Shakespeare Center
Location: Staunton, VA
Drama Club: "With Shakespeare's text as our touchstone and his technology as

our laboratory, the Drama Club meets once a week in 12-week terms to explore Shakespeare's wordcraft and stagecraft through play, building confidence and expanding creativity by working together to craft and rehearse a final performance of Shakespearean scenes at the Blackfriars Playhouse."[21]

American Shakespeare Center holds Equity auditions each year. Submit your headshot and resume to be considered for upcoming seasons.

Appalachian Festival of Plays and Playwrights
Location: Abingdon, VA (Emory & Henry College -10 min away)
Internships: The Association of the Barter Theatre with Emory & Henry College "offers theatre majors opportunities for professional internships, mentoring, workshops, and master classes throughout their college career. Barter staff members and artists often serve as adjunct faculty and guest artists in the Theatre Department. In addition, E&H theatre majors have the opportunity to attend professional rehearsals, participate in "talk backs" with the actors and crew after Barter performances, and serve as understudies in Barter Theatre productions. With this partnership, Emory & Henry Theatre Department offers students the combined strengths of a small liberal arts college and the type of pre-professional experiences often found only in large conservatories."[22]

WEST VIRGINIA

Contemporary American Theater Festival
Location: Shepherdstown, WV (Shepherd University)
Internships: "Apply for a specific department based on your strengths and passions as a theater artist. You may apply for no more than two departments [carpentry, costumes, electrics, props, scenic arts, sound] but if hired, you will only be assigned to one. Internships usually begin in late May and end in early August, running 8-10 weeks."[23]

WISCONSIN

American Players Theatre
Location: Spring Green, WI
Positions: Stitchers, Wigs, Stage Management, Carpentry, First Hand, Lighting, Production[24]

---

21 American Shakespeare Center, "Drama Club," *American Shakespeare Center,* n.d., https://americanshakespearecenter.com/education/drama-club/

22 Barter Theatre, "Emory & Henry College," *Barter Theatre,* n.d., https://bartertheatre.com/emory-henry/

23 Contemporary American Theater Festival, "Internships," *Contemporary American Theater Festival,* n.d., https://catf.org/internships/

24 American Players Theatre, "Employment," *American Players Theatre,* n.d., https://americanplayers.org/about/employment

INTERNATIONAL

ONTARIO, CANADA

Shaw Festival
Location: Niagara-On-The-Lake, Ontario, Canada
Camps and Training Programs: While there are no internships, per se, there is training, including a summer stage combat class.

Stratford Shakespeare Festival
Location: Stratford, Ontario, Canada
Camps and Training Programs: While there are no internships, per se, there are summer camps and training programs for students of all ages.

CHAPTER 5

UNIVERSITY OPTIONS: WHAT COLLEGE PROGRAMS ARE BEST FOR MUSICAL THEATRE?

"Great theatre is about challenging how we think and encouraging us to fantasize about a world we aspire to."

– **William Dafoe**

Everyone has heard about the top colleges for musical theatre and most students want to apply to NYU, Carnegie Mellon, Ithaca College, Penn State, and the University of Michigan, but there are so many more excellent musical theatre programs. Some offer students with greater opportunities for personalized training, smaller classes, wise faculty, performance roles in on-campus shows, and unique programs.

Some small colleges produce acclaimed successes. Lisa Kron, playwright and lyricist of the Tony Award-winning musical *Fun Home* graduated from Kalamazoo College, while Anaïs Mitchell, who wrote and composed *Hadestown,* which won eight Tony Awards, graduated from Middlebury College.

Since there are many excellent opportunities, here are fourteen schools you might consider that are not in New York City.

SPOTLIGHT ON 14 NON-NEW YORK CITY PROGRAMS

ILLINOIS, MICHIGAN, OHIO, AND PENNSYLVANIA

Baldwin Wallace University (Private, Cleveland Area)

Baldwin Wallace University presents three full musical theatre productions each year. Students take private voice lessons for four years, dance training, ballet boot camp, acting, and eight semesters of musical theatre workshops. Acclaimed for having the oldest collegiate Bach Festival in the Nation, Riemenschneider-Bach Institute, and Baldwin Wallace Conservatory of Music.

Carnegie Mellon University (private, Pittsburgh)

The less than 1% acceptance rate for CMU's conservatory-style program is daunting. However, the program is fantastic. Options for additional study include directing, stage/production management, video/media/scenic design, production technology, dramaturgy, and sound/lighting. Students can take wide-ranging courses like "Art of Cabaret" and study at Sydney's National Institute of Dramatic Art, The Moscow Art Theatre, London's Drama Centre, and famed programs worldwide.

University of Cincinnati (public, Cincinnati)

The four-year BFA in musical theatre includes a freshman showcase in Cincinnati and a senior showcase in New York City where students perform for agents and casting directors. With dozens of graduates throughout musical theatre in national and international touring productions, students are well situated to perform. Students undertake vocal coaching, rigorous acting, extensive dance training, and five musicals per year.

University of Michigan (public, Ann Arbor, MI)

With one of the top five musical theatre programs in the United States and one of the top ten in the world, U-M students have access to premier trainers, professors, and performers in an intense conservatory-style environment. Students must be book smart, people smart, and performance smart. With the possibility of a dual degree students are encouraged to explore their interests and collaborate with others. The University of Michigan's extensive network of alumni offers unparalleled connections.

Penn State University (public, State College, PA)

Penn State emphasizes academics, performance, and study abroad. From contemporary plays, film, and new media to classical plays, musicals, and Shakespeare numerous performance opportunities exist. With a student-faculty ratio of less than 4 to 1, students get individualized attention in a high-performing, dynamic environment. Penn State's musical theatre program commissions musical theatre writers through the unique New Musicals Initiative. Other opportunities include the Master Class Series, and Musical Theatre Wellness Center. Additionally, students are encouraged to spend a semester at the Theatre Academy London.

Point Park University (private, Pittsburgh area)

Point Park University is well-known for its leading performers, particularly in dance. Students not only gain acting and singing training, but some of the best dancers on Broadway come from Point Park University. Thus, graduating from Point Park gives students an extra edge through the university's conservatory dance program. Students perform at the Pittsburgh Playhouse where four theatre companies, the REP, Conservatory Theatre Company, Conservatory Dance Company, and Playhouse Jr. perform. Thus, students not only take part in university productions but have the opportunity to perform with professional artists, observing the work behind the scenes.

VIRGINIA AND NORTH CAROLINA

Elon University (private, Elon, NC)

Elon's professionalization in theatre begins from the start of the student's education with onstage opportunities from day one. Student auditions are held starting in the first semester with musicals, one-act plays, dance performances, vocal ensembles, and impromptu groups. BFA students can participate in classical studies in Greece and residencies in London while seeing shows and weekend travel to Spain, France, and Portugal. Seniors take a two-semester seminar on the "Business of Show" followed by opportunities to meet with agents and casting directors.

Shenandoah University (private, Winchester, VA)

Though a smaller conservatory school, its reputation for turning out some of the top musical theatre students is astounding. Shenandoah's program is the second-oldest in the country. Known as a "pop/rock school" whose performers earn roles in contemporary Broadway shows. While mastering storytelling, students also learn branding, marketing, web design for artists, the "Business of the Business", and "Prep for the Profession". The faculty are Broadway veterans and industry professionals.

MASSACHUSETTS AND NEW YORK (NOT NYC AREA)

Emerson College (private, Boston, MA)

Emerson College has its theatre right on Boston Common where thousands of people come for fresh air, peace of mind, and artistic performances. Emerson College's approach is to hone student's skills in musical theatre. Senior showcases in Boston and New York City allow students to perform for current industry leaders. Many students take summer theatre positions in New York, New England, and destinations across the country. Preparation includes self-reliance, audition training, teamwork, stamina, fitness, entrepreneurship, technique, and the nomenclature of the theatrical arts. Students are encouraged to attend combined auditions like SETC, NETC, StrawHats, IOC/Outdoor Drama, NHPTA, and UPTAs.

Ithaca College (private, Ithaca, NY)

Ithaca College is one of the top programs in the country for musical theatre with rigorous training and a focus on performance. Students participate in 20 hours of studio training per week along with classes, auditions, rehearsals, and performances. Students take private voice lessons and vocal repertoire classes while gaining skills in piano, scene study, movement, ballet, jazz, and modern dance. Students can study British drama and culture at Ithaca College's London Center and take workshops and masterclasses. During a one-week field studies trip to New York City, students connect with alumni working in the industry.

Syracuse University (private, Syracuse, NY)

Syracuse University partners with Syracuse Stage, a professional theatrical company. Syracuse University offers students training in all areas of musical theatre with shows produced by the university as well as opportunities to train professionally and earn points toward Equity membership through Syracuse Stage. In a thorough performance-oriented program, students gain opportunities to train and practice individually and in group settings in acting, dance, and voice. Students train to be artists, while also learning to read, analyze, and interpret a script and a score. Students master the entire theatrical and musical canon, learning how to vividly bring to life their individual piece of the puzzle while collaboratively working to perfect each show.

OKLAHOMA AND TEXAS

Oklahoma City College (public, Oklahoma City, OK)

Oklahoma City University is well known for coupling rigorous musical training with equally rigorous courses in dance, acting, performance, and stagecraft. Students audition for six annual Bass School of Music musical and opera productions. Students study musical theatre and opera with a junior recital in classical repertoire and a senior recital in musical theatre. Vocal cross-training offers greater versatility and strong vocal skillsets. Seniors audition for a New York City showcase and meet with agents and casting directors. Although a solid foundation in acting and singing is laid, students focus on vocal training and earn a Bachelor of Music in Musical Theatre.

Texas State University (public, San Marcos, TX)

With relationships with summer stock theatres nationwide, students gain significant experience. Furthermore, Texas State provides audition support and training for students after graduation. Nearly all of their graduates are working professionally in theatre, film, or television. A casting director at Telsey Casting produces the senior showcase in New York City. The university produces two musicals and 9 – 12 plays as well as other performance opportunities. Training is extensive with one-on-one coaching, weekly voice lessons, individual musical director sessions, and private work sessions, in acting and musical theatre. One reviewer exclaimed, “San Marcos has become a mecca for musicals.”

The University of Oklahoma (public, Norman, OK)

The University of Oklahoma at Norman’s A. Max Weitzenhoffer School of Musical Theatre offers conservatory-style training for fifty students in each cohort. After the rigorous selection process, students earn the opportunity to participate in conservatory-style training while studying at a major university. Award-winning theatre professionals serve as faculty who train selected students in a five-to-one student-teacher ratio. With this personalized approach students master the art of acting and theatre. Graduates perform on Broadway, national tours, international productions, regional theatre, and the television and film industry.

The Many Roads to Theatre Success

While about a quarter of the Tony Award winners never attended college, this was, in part, because in the middle of the last century, wars prevented many people from attending college. Furthermore, many famous actors served in the U.S. military.

An abbreviated list of military veterans who became successful actors include Alan Alda, Sunny Anderson, Bea Arthur, Harry Belafonte, Tony Bennett, Charles Bronson, Mel Brooks, Drew Carey, Kirk Douglas, Adam Driver, Robert Duvall, Clint Eastwood, Morgan Freeman, Gene Hackman, MC Hammer, Zulay Henao, Bob Hope, Ice-T, James Earl Jones, Buster Keaton, Harvey Keitel, Steve McQueen, Audie Murphy, Paul Newman, David Niven, Chuck Norris, Jack Palance, Sidney Poitier, Elvis Presley, Robin Quivers, Rob Riggle, Jason Robards, Tom Selleck, Sinbad, Robert Stack, Jimmy Stewart, and Oliver Stone.

Also, to show you that there are many roads to success, here are the top Tony Award winners and the colleges they attended. Some of the schools in which these actors went to were smaller programs where they gained a broader or more extensive liberal arts education.

Note that Juilliard is listed numerous times and does not appear in this book's profiles. The reason for this is that they do not have a specific undergraduate musical theatre major, though students studying acting can also study voice and dance to combine these skills. Very successful actors and actresses attended Juilliard and gained valuable skills that they later applied to the musicals in which they appeared.

TONY AWARD FOR BEST MALE ACTOR IN A MUSICAL OR PLAY

Frank A. Langella, Jr. – 7 nominations, 4 wins – Syracuse University

Boyd Payne Gaines – 5 nominations, 4 wins – Juilliard

Nathan Lane - 6 nominations, 3 wins – did not attend college

Mark Rylance – 5 nominations, 3 wins – Did not attend college

Kevin Kline – 4 nominations, 3 wins –University of Indiana, Bloomington

Zero Mostel – 4 nominations, 3 wins – City College of New York, New York University

Hinton Battle – 3 nominations, 3 wins – did not attend college

Christopher Plummer – 7 nominations, 2 wins – did not attend college

John Lithgow – 6 nominations, 2 wins – Harvard University, London Academy of Music and Dramatic Art

Michael Cerveris – 6 nominations, 2 wins – Yale University

George Hearn – 5 nominations, 2 wins – Rhodes College

George Rose – 5 nominations, 2 wins – Oxford University

John Cullum -- 5 nominations, 2 wins – University of Tennessee

Robert Morse – 5 nominations, 2 wins – did not attend college

Christian Borle – 4 nominations, 2 wins – Carnegie Mellon University

James Earl Jones – 4 nominations, 2 wins – University of Michigan

Norbert Leo Butz – 4 nominations, 2 wins – Webster University, University of Alabama

Richard Kiley – 4 nominations, 2 wins – Loyola University Chicago, Chicago's Barnum Dramatic School

Al Pacino – 3 nominations, 2 wins – Actors Studio

David Burns – 3 nominations, 2 wins – did not attend college

David Wayne – 3 nominations, 2 wins – Western Michigan University

Fredric March – 3 nominations, 2 wins – University of Wisconsin, Madison

Judd Hirsch – 3 nominations, 2 wins – City College of New York, American Academy of Dramatic Arts

Matthew Broderick – 3 nominations, 2 wins – HB Studio

Phil Silvers – 3 nominations, 2 wins – did not attend college

Rex Harrison – 3 nominations, 2 wins – Liverpool College

Robert Preston – 3 nominations, 2 wins – did not go to college

Stephen Spinella – 3 nominations, 2 wins – University of Arizona, New York University

Walter Matthau – 3 nominations, 2 wins – did not attend college

Alan Bates – 2 nominations, 2 wins – Royal Academy of Dramatic Art

Brian Dennehy – 2 nominations, 2 wins – Columbia University

Bryan Cranston – 2 nominations, 2 wins – Los Angeles Valley College

Harvey Fierstein – 2 nominations, 2 wins – Pratt Institute

Hiram Sherman – 2 nominations, 2 wins – did not attend college

James Naughton – 2 nominations, 2 wins – Brown University, Yale University

Jonathan Pryce – 2 nominations, 2 wins – Royal Academy of Dramatic Art

Jose Ferrer – 2 nominations, 2 wins – Princeton University

Russell Nype – 2 nominations, 2 wins – Lake Forest College

Tommy Tune – 2 nominations, 2 wins – Lon Morris College, University of Texas, Austin, University of Houston

Jason Robards – 8 nominations, 1 win – American Academy of Dramatic Arts

Brian Bedford – 7 nominations, 1 win – Royal Academy of Dramatic Art

Danny Burstein – 7 nominations, 1 win – City University of New York, UCSD

Philip Bosco – 6 nominations, 1 win – Catholic University

Brian F. O'Bryrne – 5 nominations, 1 win – Trinity College, Dublin

Hume Cronyn – 5 nominations, 1 win – Ridley College, McGill University

Jim Dale – 5 nominations, 1 win – did not attend college

TONY AWARD FOR BEST FEMALE ACTOR IN A MUSICAL OR PLAY

Audra McDonald – 9 nominations, 6 wins – Juilliard

Julie Harris – 10 nominations, 5 wins – Yale University

Angela Lansbury – 7 nominations, 5 wins – did not attend college

Gwen Verdon – 6 nominations, 4 wins – did not attend college

Zoe Caldwell – 4 nominations, 4 wins – did not attend college

Irene Worth – 5 nominations, 3 wins – UCLA

Jessica Tandy – 5 nominations, 3 wins – did not attend college

Glenn Close – 4 nominations, 3 wins – The College of William and Mary

Mary Martin – 4 nominations, 3 wins – did not attend college

Shirley Booth – 3 nominations, 3 wins – did not attend college

Chita Rivera – 10 nominations, 2 wins – did not attend college

Colleen Dewhurst - 8 nominations, 2 wins – Milwaukee-Downer College

Bernadette Peters - 7 nominations, 2 wins – did not attend college

Frances Sternhagen - 7 nominations, 2 wins – Vassar College, Catholic University

Patti LuPone - 7 nominations, 2 wins – Juilliard

Andrea Martin - 6 nominations, 2 wins – Emerson College

Laurie Metcalf - 6 nominations, 2 wins – Illinois State University

Maureen Stapleton - 6 nominations, 2 wins – did not attend college

Sutton Foster - 6 nominations, 2 wins – Carnegie Mellon University

Cherry Jones - 5 nominations, 2 wins – Carnegie Mellon University

Donna Murphy - 5 nominations, 2 wins – New York University

Swoosie Kurtz - 5 nominations, 2 wins – University of Southern California, London

Academy of Music and Dramatic Art

Christine Ebersole - 4 nominations, 2 wins – MacMurray College, American Academy of Dramatic Arts

Cynthia Nixon - 4 nominations, 2 wins – Barnard College

Judith Ivey - 4 nominations, 2 wins – Illinois State University

Judy Kaye - 4 nominations, 2 wins – UCLA

Margaret Leighton - 4 nominations, 2 wins – did not attend college

Mary-Louise Parker - 4 nominations, 2 wins – University of North Carolina School of the Arts

Anne Bancroft - 3 nominations, 2 wins – HB Studio, American Academy of Dramatic Arts, Actors Studio

Helen Gallagher - 3 nominations, 2 wins – did not attend college

Helen Hayes - 3 nominations, 2 wins – did not attend college

Jennifer Ehle - 3 nominations, 2 wins – University of North Carolina School of the Arts, University of London

Judith Light - 3 nominations, 2 wins – Carnegie Mellon University

Liza Minnelli - 3 nominations, 2 wins – did not attend college

Viola Davis - 3 nominations, 2 wins – Rhode Island College, Juilliard

Bebe Neuwirth - 2 nominations, 2 wins – Juilliard

Christine Baranski - 2 nominations, 2 wins – Juilliard

Katie Finneran - 2 nominations, 2 wins – Carnegie Mellon University, HB Studio

Lauren Bacall - 2 nominations, 2 wins – did not attend college

Sandy Dennis - 2 nominations, 2 wins – Nebraska Wesleyan University, University of Nebraska, HB Studio

Tammy Grimes - 2 nominations, 2 wins – Stephens College

Uta Hagen - 2 nominations, 2 wins – Royal Academy of Dramatic Art, University of Wisconsin–Madison

Rosemary Harris- 9 nominations, 1 win – Royal Academy of Dramatic Art

Jane Alexander - 8 nominations, 1 win – Sarah Lawrence College, University of Edinburgh

Stockard Channing - 8 nominations, 1 win – Radcliffe/Harvard University, HB Studio

Kelli O'Hara - 7 nominations, 1 win – Oklahoma City University

Linda Lavin - 6 nominations, 1 win – College of William and Mary

Glenda Jackson - 5 nominations, 1 win – Royal Academy of Dramatic Art

Laura Benanti - 5 nominations, 1 win – did not attend college

Marian Seides - 5 nominations, 1 win – did not attend college

Broadway

CHAPTER 6

WHAT IS THE DIFFERENCE BETWEEN AN AA, AS, BA, BS, BFA, AND MFA?

"I regard the theater as the greatest of all art forms, the most immediate way in which a human being can share with another the sense of what it is to be a human being. This supremacy of the theater derives from the fact that it is always "now" on the stage."

– **Thornton Wilder**

UNDERGRADUATE AND GRADUATE DEGREES

AA - Associate of Arts - 2-year degree

AS - Associate of Science - 2-year degree

BA - Bachelor of Arts - 4-year degree

BS - Bachelor of Science - 4-year degree

BFA - Bachelor of Fine Arts - 4-year degree with most classes focused on art

MFA - Master of Fine Arts - 1-2-year degree earned after the BA, BS, or BFA

Basically, BA and BS degrees are degrees that typically offer a liberal arts foundation along with a major or concentration in a specific subject. Meanwhile, a BFA is considered a professional arts-focused degree with fewer courses in English, science, math, social science, and the humanities. Thus, the BFA is a specialist qualification in the arts. A BA or BS degree in acting, theatre arts, or musical theatre is also valuable. The BFA is more focused on the specific area of art you choose.

The BA and BS degrees include significantly more liberal arts classes and thus are more general degrees. However, the intention of the BFA degree is for students to pursue an arts-focused curriculum, and thus there are fewer general subject courses.

Finally, while many AA or AS degrees are focused on providing technical or professional skills for acting, music or dance, an AA or AS in these areas are often interchangeable. Similarly, a BA or BS in theatre-oriented degrees are often interchangeable. However, a BFA may be seen as different since there is typically more coursework focused on your specific pursuit, and thus, you may have more technical experiences and knowledge than someone who has a BA or BS.

AA – ASSOCIATE OF ARTS

The Associate of Arts degree is typically a 2-year general studies degree offered online or in-person by a community college. However, some universities offer AA degrees as well. The Associate of Arts degree focused on liberal arts courses often has no barrier to entry, meaning that students can enter most AA programs with a high school diploma or the equivalent. Some students take a longer or shorter time to complete the AA based upon their skills upon entering the program, certainty about the direction they are heading, and the transfer requirements for the program they desire. For example, students majoring in business may have additional business, communication, accounting, and economics requirements and need to create an academic plan early in their program to finish in two years.

AS – ASSOCIATE OF SCIENCE

The Associate of Science degree is very similar to the AA. However, the AS degree frequently emphasizes science and math and often has additional requirements.

BA – BACHELOR OF ARTS

The Bachelor of Arts degree is typically a 4-year degree offered online or in-person by a college or university. However, a few community colleges offer BA degrees as well. Some students complete their BA in fewer years depending upon AP/IB credit, dual enrollment in high school, and summer/intersession classes. College programs have stricter or less stringent requirements depending upon the school. The Bachelor of Arts degree frequently requires students to take lower-division (first and second year) liberal arts courses before taking specialized courses focused around a major or concentration in their third and fourth years. Some students take a longer or shorter time to complete their BA based upon their skills upon entering the program, certainty about the direction they are heading, and their chosen major. According to the National Center for Educational Statistics, college advisors aid students in finishing "on time" though less than half of all students in the United States who start a BA program do not finish their degree in four years.[1]

---

1 IEC NCES, "Digest of Education Statistics, Table 326.10," IES NCES, n.d., https://nces.ed.gov/programs/digest/d20/tables/dt20_326.10.asp?referer=raceindica.asp

BS - BACHELOR OF SCIENCE

The Bachelor of Science degree is very similar to the BA. However, the BS degree frequently emphasizes science and math and often has additional requirements.[2]

BFA - BACHELOR OF FINE ARTS

The Bachelor of Fine Arts is a 4-year college degree focusing on the arts. BFA students are often not required to take as many English, science, math, social science, and humanities courses. However, they must still complete roughly the same number of credits as a person who earns a BA or BS, and the courses are not necessarily easier. BFA students frequently take general art requirements to lay a foundation in drawing, graphic design, and courses in their specialty area during their first two years, along with basic writing and quantitative skill-building.

BFA students are traditionally art-in-practice students who learn the technical craft of their art form while putting in enormous numbers of hours practicing their skill doing assignments and participating in internships and experiential learning. Students who know that they want a future in the arts often finds this avenue perfectly tailored for their pursuits. However, students who change their minds and transfer to a university in another degree program may require an additional year to make up for coursework they have not completed.

MFA - MASTER OF FINE ARTS

The Master of Fine Arts is a graduate degree for students who have completed their BA, BS, or BFA. This degree takes one to two years depending upon the program, coursework, and experiential component, which may be a capstone, practicum, internship, or thesis. While there are also MA and MS degrees, many art students who continue to earn their master's degree in the arts chose to focus on their field of interest. The MFA is an intensive immersion into a higher level of skill-building. However, students who graduate with an MFA have a broader range of talents and experiences than those who earn their bachelor's degrees. While admission into these programs is generally selective, with planning, preparation, and a good portfolio, there are options for you to pursue your interests.

---

2 IEC NCES, "Digest of Education Statistics, Table 326.10," IES NCES, n.d., https://nces.ed.gov/programs/digest/d20/tables/dt20_326.10.asp?referer=raceindica.asp

THE SEVEN MAJOR DIFFERENCES BETWEEN THE ASSOCIATE, BACHELORS, AND MASTER'S DEGREES

1. Starting Point
2. Academic Discipline
3. Time to Completion
4. Location of the Education
5. Educational Costs
6. Earning Power
7. Professional Opportunities

STARTING POINT

Most students who begin with an Associate of Arts (AA) or Associate of Science (AS) have no college credits. Starting from scratch with their college education, they accumulate their 60+ units beginning from this community college starting point. While most students earn AA or AS degrees at a community college, some earn this degree at a 4-year college or university.

The AA or AS is either a terminal degree, meaning that the student will not continue on with their bachelor's degree or just a steppingstone to their BA, BS, or BFA. The difference between the associate's and bachelor's degrees is just the starting point.

The starting point for students who pursue a bachelor's degree may be farther along the traditional 4-year pathway. Meanwhile, the starting point for the master's degree (MA, MS, or MFA) begins after obtaining a bachelor's degree.

ACADEMIC DISCIPLINE

Every degree encompasses different requirements. Requirements for the AA differ from an AS. Similarly, the requirements for the BA, BS, and BFA also differ. With two additional years of coursework, the BA, BS, and BFA are more thorough. The MA, MS, and MFA build upon the bachelor's degree and even deeper. Theatre arts students will not take the same classes as musical theatre, though a few may overlap. Though both are behind-the-scenes players in the dramatic arts, the essential skills for each career area are distinct; course requirements are also unique.

Furthermore, with the myriad of combinations, it is rare that any two undergraduate students have the same exact classes in the same exact order. Since the requirements for a chemistry degree are not the same as for biology and technical theatre differs from musical theatre, the various degrees not only include a different number of credits but different types of classes and program specifications.

TIME TO COMPLETION

Associate of Arts (AA) and Associate of Science (AS) degrees typically take two years, while most BA, BS, and BFA degrees are 4-year programs, depending upon full-time or part-time status. Students who transfer in credits or earn credits otherwise can reduce their time to completion.

Some students may choose to extend their education in acting, theatre arts, or musical theatre by earning a second bachelor's degree in another field. By cross-training in directing or dramaturgy, students open more doors. Additionally, a degree in business on the bachelor's level or Master's in Business Administration (MBA) may lead to alternative leadership positions.

Time in college can be reduced. Some students enter a BA, BS, or BFA program having already completed college credits because they were dual-enrolled or they took college classes directly through a college or university ahead of time. Some students have taken AP/IB tests from taking higher-level tests while in high school and earned qualifying scores to be granted credits by the college or university. Other ways students can enter at a different starting point are with credit-by-exam, CLEP tests, experiential credits, and those granted in the military.

Colleges and universities are keenly aware of the challenges students face today with work, illness, and family responsibilities. Thus, many schools of higher education offer flexible enrollment with opportunities for part-time, evening, weekend, and online classes.

LOCATION OF THE EDUCATION

The AA and AS are earned at colleges that grant 2-year degrees. The location may be at a local community college or a university. BA, BS, and BFA programs are offered at a 4-year college or university. However, with online classes, students have the flexibility to take classes from colleges farther away as well. Thus, the location in which a typical student studies is not as set as it once was. Nevertheless, the in-person internships are often situated in corporate hubs and thus require grounding to a specific location.

EDUCATIONAL COSTS

Since the AA or AS requires a shorter amount of time and is typically completed at a lower-cost community college, the cost for an associate's degree is typically less than a bachelor's degree. Master's degree programs cost more per credit but take less time than a bachelor's degree.

On the other hand, many students can obtain financial aid in the form of grants, loans, and both merit and need-based scholarships. This aid can pay for school and reduce debt after college.

EARNING POWER

Students with more education can earn more. According to the 2019 National Center for Educational Statistics (NCES) data for the median person,[3]

Master's Degree or Higher - $70,000

Bachelor's Degree - $55,700

Associate's Degree - $43,300

High School - $35,000

PROFESSIONAL OPPORTUNITIES

Earning a BA, BS, or BFA opens more doors than an AA or AS. Similarly, an MA, MS, or MFA opens more doors than a BA, BS, or BFA. Baccalaureate and master's degrees require more training. You can obtain this training through workshops or studio classes, but with a scholarship to pay for college, you might find that the training and opportunities are worth your time. Besides, you will gain additional skills that could prove valuable in your future.

3 IES NCES, "Annual Earnings by Educational Attainment," IEC NCES, May 2021, https://nces.ed.gov/programs/coe/indicator/cba

CHAPTER 7

COLLEGE ADMISSIONS: APPLICATIONS, ESSAYS, RECOMMENDATIONS, AND SCHOLARSHIPS

"A certain kind of magic is born when the curtain rises. Intoxicated by the smell of the greasepaint and powered by the glow of the footlights, lovers successfully elope, villains get their just deserts and people die in epic stunts and yet live to tell the tale. Thousands pay to sit and be fooled by illusions and still jump to their feet to applaud despite their gullibility. It's an inexplicable, delicious, addictive power that keeps people entranced and coming back for more, again and again."

– **Carrie Hope Fletcher, *When the Curtain Falls***

With amazing faculty, excellent facilities, and easy access to Broadway, NYU stands as one of the premier schools for musical theatre. Just a few of NYU's talented alumni are Broadway musical theatre performers include Jelani Alladin, De'Adre Aziza, Kristen Bell, Ato Blankson-Wood, Jere Burns, Kevin Cahoon, Raul Esparza, Lady Gaga, Jenn Gambatese, Gina Gershon, Lisa Gay Hamilton, Jessica Hecht, Christine Hope, Bryce Dallas Howard, Timothy Huang, Adam Jacobs, Nikki M. James, Molly Jobe, Keziah John-Paul, Brittney Johnson, Denis Jones, Stephanie Kurtzuba, Michael Longoria, Jesse L. Martin, Idina Menzel, Dimitri Moise, Matthew Morrison, Javier Muñoz, Anisha Nagarajan, Yianni Papadimos, Anthony Rapp, Steve Rosen, Paul Sparks, Bobby Steggert, Jason Tam, Juan Torres-Falcon, Brandon Uranowitz, Ryan Vandenboom, and Chandra Wilson.

Choices of programs, majors, and concentrations include:

NYU Steinhardt: Bachelor's in Music - Vocal Performance

Concentrations:

- Music Theatre
- Contemporary Voice
- Classical Voice

NYU Tisch: BFA in Drama (conservatory training)

Concentrations:

- Musical theatre
- Drama
- Dance
- Open Arts
- Performance Studies

NYU Tisch Drama's musical theatre program combines rigorous conservatory training in acting, singing, and dance with NYU's academic studies in the humanities and social sciences and the whole of New York's wide-ranging performance opportunities. Students combine performance, creativity, artistry, and intellectualism. Tisch's studio system offers a unique approach to studio training and the totality of theatre arts. You will learn to think broadly, pursue your craft creatively, tell stories, and ask questions. Moreover, you will be fully prepared for professional opportunities with lifelong connections to the musical theatre world.

NYU Steinhardt, BM (Musical Theatre)	NYU Tisch BFA (Musical Theatre)
Music Theatre History I and II	Primary Studio Training (32 credits)
Acting I and II for Singers	Advanced Studio/Internships (16 credits)
Vocal Coaching/Vocal Performance	Theatre Studies/Theatre Production
Music Theatre Workshop	Dramatic Literature
Tap, Jazz, Hip Hop, Music Theatre Dance	Theatre Theory
Vocal Production for Singers	Performance Studies

SCHOLARSHIPS

Nearly every school in the United States offers need-based scholarships. However, most schools offer merit scholarships. Many are listed in the profile section. Check it out.

Below are a couple of schools chosen at random to give you a sense of a few of the options listed in the profile section.

Baldwin Wallace University

- BWMT is a Bachelors of Music in the Baldwin Wallace Conservatory of Music

Merit scholarships are offered up to $21,000 per year. Additional monies for talent scholarships can be added to the merit scholarships are offered.

Chapman University

- BA Theatre Studies, BFA Theatre Performance; Musical Theatre Minor

First-year scholarships range in amounts up to $36,000 per year. Select admitted students will also be offered institutional awards. These include awards for first-generation and underrepresented students, as well as awards from departments and schools/colleges. The College of Performing Arts (CoPA) has a limited number of Talent Awards for incoming first-year and transfer students. Students must be theatre majors. Consideration is made at the audition/interview and notified afterward.

Columbia College Chicago

- BA Musical Theatre, BFA Musical Theatre Performance

Students are automatically considered for renewable scholarships upon admission. For need-based scholarship, submit a FAFSA. For talent-based scholarships, submit an audition that demonstrates your best creative work. First-year, international students may be considered for talent-based scholarships.

Florida State University

- BFA Musical Theatre (Joint program: College of Music and College of Theatre)

The School of Theatre awards scholarships to selected incoming and continuing students. BFA students can qualify based on academic ability and potential.

Long Island University Post

- BFA in Theatre Arts (Musical Theatre)

LIU Post awards over $100 million in scholarships & grants each year.

Marymount Manhattan University

- BFA Musical Theatre

Scholarships are available for successful candidates. Consideration for these competitive talent awards is made at the time of the audition. Scholarships are renewable for four years if the student remains academically successful and stays in the program.

Pace University

- BFA Musical Theatre

Students are considered for need-based scholarships. There are also Dyson College Scholarships specifically for each program. The average non-need-based scholarship awarded to first-year students is $24,996. There is also the Professor Chris Thomas Endowed Scholarship.

Pepperdine University

- BA Theatre Arts (Musical Theatre Emphasis)

Merit and need-based scholarships are available for Theatre/Musical Theatre students. Approximately 75% of theatre majors receive scholarships in varying amounts. Students must complete a FAFSA form.

COLLEGE ADMISSIONS:

Success in the Face of Uncertainty

There are no guarantees in college admissions. However, planning is essential for success. The most beneficial advice is to pursue your passions with gusto, train to be the best you can be, take advantage of internships and experiences, and meet lots of people along the way. Remember, "life is a journey, not a destination." Often the journey is more exciting, leading to lessons, friendships, and indelible moments. However, the fact is…in the end, if college is your goal, then you need to know a few action items to remember for success.

Should you worry about grades? Of course. You should also take classes that will challenge you. Colleges pick the best candidates from those who apply. Students must be academically prepared, socially conscious, and talented in a few different areas in which they are passionate (conceptual design, graphic arts, costumes, theatre, acting, singing, dance, musical instruments, debate, public speaking, leadership, athletics, community service, computer coding, robotics, construction, etc.).

This selection process is not that much different than companies picking employees. While colleges are more or less competitive, companies may have only one job and fifty resumes. Discover the unique drive and internal motivations within you that make you the very best you can be. Be exceptional at what you choose to do academically, personally, and professionally.

Most of all,

You Do You

TALENT FOCUSED

Not all schools require high grades and test scores. Many are simply interested in selecting students who are the most talented, most driven, and the most willing to be team players on the college campus. Thus, while you should take a solid set of courses and fulfill requirements, only the top schools emphasize completing a challenging curriculum, high grades, and standardized test scores.

FOR HIGHLY SELECTIVE COLLEGES, TALENT IS JUST THE BEGINNING

A few highly selective colleges seek extraordinary talent over academics, but most zero in on a student's challenging courses and high grades. To gain admission into the most highly selective colleges, you must take the most challenging course load you can manage and succeed. Highly selective colleges want disciplined scholars AND remarkably talented students.

Determine what you can handle, knowing that some colleges with extremely competitive admission will only take students who have completed more than ten AP, IB, or honors classes over the four years, including AP Calculus. AP Statistics is not of equal rigor in their eyes. Why, then, would these most competitive colleges require a class that is beyond the scope of what you need for your major? This situation is the $50,000 question. However, if this seems daunting, remember that most colleges accepting students for artistic fields do not need these types of classes.

College admissions can feel like a rollercoaster of energy and emotion. Creating a portfolio of talent, training, and experience is just the beginning. Meanwhile, some colleges want to see standardized test scores which are aided by practice. Applications and essays may seem easy at first, but managing the various requirements and deadlines can be difficult. Therefore, this application period is a good time to get a calendar and organize your tasks.

STANDARDIZED TESTING

A few schools require testing. Check first. Many colleges are test optional. This means that you are not required to take the SAT or ACT. However, if you do have a good score, it may make all the difference in accepting you. College admissions offices are studying this topic and considering their future policies. Much of their concern began with cancelations worldwide due to the pandemic. Schools did not want to let students into their site who may be infected. In addition, social distancing limited the number of students who could take a test at a site at a time.

Yet, college admissions decisions were once centered around grades and test scores. The change has rattled admissions departments. Meanwhile, colleges proclaim that test-optional truly means that the test is not required, but evidence proves otherwise. Thus, many students are still taking the test and working around the hurdles amid all of the confusion. Competition continues to drive students to present evidence to show that they are worthy candidates.

In the end, colleges need to make a final decision between very good candidates. If one student has a high score, that student may have a higher likelihood of admission depending upon the admissions committee's decision-making process. Data show that students who submitted scores within the college's range or higher were accepted at a higher rate than those without a score. Some schools are test blind in that they say that they do not consider your scores. A few of these colleges still provide a place for you to input your scores, thus, they are not truly blind. Nevertheless, this decision is yours. If the school does not require an admissions test, then you can choose to take the test. If your academics are solid and you are willing to prepare, you should take the test.

APPLYING EARLY

Early Action (EA), Restricted Early Action (REA), and Early Decision (ED)

With low acceptance rates, the chance to get more scholarship money, and chaos surrounding the cancellations and changes in AP, IB, SAT, and ACT testing, students clamor to apply early to schools. In addition, applications to top schools increased during the pandemic, resulting in colleges making difficult admissions decisions in their quest to build a diverse, talented, and engaged class of students. Furthermore, students applying early have access to many more scholarship options. This confluence sent students in droves to apply early and this trend is likely to continue.

Early Action (EA), Restricted Early Action (REA), and Early Decision (ED), students apply in late summer or early fall to college and generally find out around winter break, though some decisions come out earlier and a few arrive later. This advantage not only gives students the chance for more scholarship money in some cases but the benefit of finding out early reduces the tension of the long waiting period to find out about Regular Decision schools.

Early Action (EA) and Restricted Early Action (REA) are different. In restricted early action, a limitation is placed on either how many or what colleges you can apply to simultaneously. Many REA schools do not allow students to apply to other early action schools, though some will allow students to apply EA to public colleges. In addition, some schools like Georgetown will allow students to apply EA elsewhere but not apply to a binding Early Decision (ED) program where the student commits to attending if they are accepted. However, most EA schools do not have these restrictions, and some students apply to a handful of EA schools during the Admissions process.

Early Decision (ED) is a binding agreement between the student and college with signatures from the student's parents and the high school. Each of these parties acknowledges and agrees that, if granted admission, they will attend. There are incentives. Frequently, acceptance rates are higher with ED. Also, at some schools, a large percentage of their class is filled with students who profess their unequivocal love for their dream school. Students who know they have a top choice school, have the necessary admissions requirements, and are committed to accepting the binding agreement to attend, should apply ED.

COMMON APPLICATION, COALITION APPLICATION, OR COLLEGE-SPECIFIC APPLICATION

Every college's process is unique. However, there are a few commonalities. In 2022, approximately 900 colleges used the Common App; about 150 colleges used the Coalition Application. A few used both. The University of California system has its own application as do the California State Universities and the Texas schools. The Common App and Coalition App may be started early. In your junior year, consider getting a head start on reviewing what is required. The college-specific questions may change each year. However, the basic application is generally the same and can be created ahead of time. At the end of July, make a copy of everything you have completed just in case.

In August, most admissions applications are open and ready for you to dive into the college-specific questions. Some schools admit on a rolling basis. 'Rolling' means that periodically, after all of the materials are received, the admissions committee determines who they will accept, and they send the notification right away. Many students are accepted as early as August. The thrill of acceptance cannot be overstated.

Complete the application fully. Think carefully about optional sections. Typically, they offer you the chance to provide the school with just the right cherry on top of the ice cream sundae. If you have absolutely nothing to say, then leave it blank. There are often required essays on the main Common App and the supplemental applications for each school. Some include scholarship essays. Start early.

DECISIONS, DECISIONS: WAITING FOR A RESPONSE

The period between submitting your application and getting your results may not require a tremendous amount of work, but it does require patience and diligence. First, most schools will send you a link to a portal where you will check your results, though the most important reason for checking every couple of weeks is to ensure that they are not missing something or have not offered you the chance to apply for an extra scholarship. Check your portal regularly. Otherwise, read the correspondence that the school may send through your e-mail.

Waiting is difficult. This is a tough period because students want to know. However, on the portal, the college typically lists the date they will send out the results. You will find out soon.

CELEBRATING ACCEPTANCES AND DEALING WITH REJECTION

Acceptance is not guaranteed. The probabilities are low at the most highly selective schools. However, you just need to work to have what it takes and give this commitment all you have.

When you find out the results, you will celebrate your acceptances. Congratulations! These go on your list of wins. Check your financial aid and scholarship package. Money is often an important factor in making your decision. Consider visiting the school. Many students apply by only looking at pictures and profiles on a website or book. There is nothing that replaces the actual visit. After all, you will be spending a few years there.

However, you may not be accepted everywhere you apply. The pandemic's uncertainty added more question marks to an already complicated set of admissions processes. The buzzword for the 2020s is resillience. It is never easy to be rejected. However, rejection happens, and you will survive this. Note that many colleges still accept applications in April, May, and June. Look up those colleges if you did not get accepted or if you want to see what other schools might be good options for you. You will be surprised to see the colleges on the list.

WAITLISTS: THE ART OF WAITING

Confirm immediately if you are given a waitlist spot and still want to attend. There is often a deadline, and you do not want to miss this. If you are no longer interested or have selected another school, go into the portal and turn down the offer. Someone else is bound to be thrilled by your anonymous gift.

Next, if you are highly interested, find the location on the portal or site designated by the college to update them on what you have done – accomplishments, awards, extra class, honors, art, shows, or films. You only want to add what they have not yet seen, but if you have taken the initiative to do something more than what you originally stated on the application, by all means, tell them. You could just wait for their decision, but you are better off being proactive and showing that you really want to be at their school.

Students do get off of the waitlists at most schools. Meanwhile, you will have to deposit somewhere else before the May 1st deadline. Stay hopeful. This next year will be a significant step along your journey. Relax!

DETERMINING FINANCIAL AID

You do not need to complete the FAFSA (Free Application for Federal Student Aid) or CSS Profile (College Scholarship Service) if you do not need aid. However, a handful of schools want to see one or both of these forms to obtain scholarships. Check now since there are deadlines.

If you completed the FAFSA (and CSS profile, if required), the financial aid package you receive would be viewable on your portal. The college will delineate the amounts you will receive for grants, loans, and work-study. Some students turn down work-study, but I caution against that. There are jobs on campus where you conduct research, work with a professor, work in the library, or assist an athletic team. Some of these jobs pay well, and you might have even done them as a volunteer.

If your financial situation changed since you applied, you may be able to renegotiate the amount they offered.

CHOOSING THE RIGHT SCHOOL FOR YOU

Once you have acceptances, you need to make a decision. With the turmoil of the pandemic, disruption in clubs, sports, and experiential activities, and serious family health concerns, access to some opportunities has been non-existent. Most training and practice have been virtual. Furthermore, few students have traveled to visit colleges due to the crisis. However, with college costs for four years around $300,000 at some schools, college is the most significant investment some families will ever make. Furthermore, student loans can saddle a student in debt for a decade or more.

Financial decisions are key. However, there are many variables in deciding which school to choose. Will I be able to afford my education? Will classes be online or in-person? Will I be able to continue my training? Will I get to visit the colleges first? Can I live through the repercussions of stressful decision-making? Should I defer my admissions and take a year off?

Once you make your decision, focus on your future. What is trending? What do people want? How can you deliver?

You've Got This!

CHAPTER 8

MUSICAL THEATRE: SUPPLEMENTAL MATERIALS, AUDITIONS, AND OTHER REQUIREMENTS

"The life of a play begins and ends in the moment of performance. This is where author, actors and directors express all they have to say. If the event has a future, this can only lie in the memories of those who were present and who retained a trace in their hearts. This is the only place for our Dream. No form nor interpretation is forever. A form has to become fixed for a short time, then it has to go. As the world changes, there will and must be new and totally unpredictable Dreams."

– **Peter Brook, The Quality of Mercy:**
Reflections on Shakespeare

At the top schools, Carnegie Mellon, University of Michigan, University of Cincinnati, NYU, and Ithaca, a BFA in musical theatre is one of the most intense and most demanding degrees students can earn in college. Mastering the trifecta of acting, singing, and dance requires students to be on the ball, multitalented, and extremely focused. Students must be literally and figuratively brilliant and unstoppable. With that kind of multitasking intensity and vigorous competition, admissions officers and program directors are as interested in the applicant's personality as they are in their talent. After prescreening, most of the student candidates who audition are talented or show significant potential.

THOUSANDS OF APPLICANTS – MULTITUDES OF ROADS

The number of applicants is astounding with schools like Carnegie Mellon having 2,000 to 2,500 applicants for 12 – 14 spots. CMU is not alone, other schools like the University of Michigan and the University of Cincinnati also have tremendously high applications to these programs. The process is literally daunting. Of course, students will apply to 10-30 schools, but that takes a ton of dedicated time and money for coaching, preparation, application fees, and travel to auditions. Other options might include applying to colleges to study writing, dramatic literature, or another area of your interest.

Although BFA training is often exceptional and the contacts made through the faculty, alumni, and NYC showcases are valuable, being cast in a show is more about whether your talent, look, and personality fit the show. Thus, a BFA is not necessary to be selected. Many amazing performers never went to college or studied in a completely different degree area. However, if you have a passion to perform and train for your own enjoyment, commitment, and desire, you could land a fabulous part.

You only have to read a few blogs or threads on *Broadway World* or other sites to grasp the stories of students who discussed their journey, found their niche, or decided upon alternative paths to their future in musical theatre. As Euclid once said, "There is no royal road." The journey from trainee to the stage takes mental and physical stamina with its ups and down, but anything is possible.

DEFYING GRAVITY

In 2015, there were more than 73,000 people who worked in live performance venues in the United States. This number dropped to less than 54,000 in 2020 and 2021. The drop of approximately 20,000 jobs, a function of quarantines and the pandemic, marked a sad period in our history. However, if the enthusiastic reactions of audiences who attended the theatre in 2022 are any indication, new shows will be added and the excitement will return. Old and new actors will take to the stage and patrons will buy tickets for shows. No doubt some exciting new musicals were written during the pandemic with upbeat, contemporary themes to bring more people out for a wonderful impassioned show.

Normal may not happen until 2025, but the 20,000 jobs will return, and possibly new venues for musical theatre will open as well. People want to feel empowered again. The theatre is an unlimited place where dreams can come true and regular people can defy gravity as Glinda and Elphaba sing, "There's no fight we cannot win. Just you and I, defying gravity."

PRESCREENS

The first entry point for most musical theatre programs is the prescreen. College BFA programs require prescreening to determine each applicant's skill level and compare students to select the best and the ones that they feel are moldable. Prescreens also eliminate about half of the applicants who do not have the mix of required skills. The University of Cincinnati and Juilliard will require the highest level of vocal skills while Point Park, Pace University, and the University of Hartford will want performers to be talented in dance.

ACCEPTD

There was once a time when each musical theatre program had a different set of requirements for prescreening and auditions. Students who wanted to apply for musical theatre programs needed to prepare a wide array of songs, monologues, and choreography. This problem was resolved with a common set of prescreen requirements.

Acceptd resolved this problem with its prescreen platform in which each participating school had the same requirements. In conjunction with Paper Mill Playhouse, Acceptd created a unified set of prescreen requirements across participating schools. Universities came together to determine a unified set of requirements which eliminated some of the anxiety applicants experienced in the preparation of their materials.

COMMON REQUIREMENTS

The MTCP (Musical Theatre Common Prescreen) offers a set of criteria for songs, monologues, slating, dance, and wild cards that colleges agree to follow in the musical theatre application process so that the efforts may be streamlined for both applicants and schools. Colleges choose which option makes the most sense for their school. College cannot change the common prescreen requirements since the goal is to avoid confusion and simplify the processes.

There is no MTCP fee, though each college has its own application fee. The common prescreen is not affiliated with the Common App. The MTCP was designed to unify prescreening processes for admissions. Nevertheless, the actual live, on-campus auditions and callbacks do not follow common practices. Each is likely to vary between programs depending on the university's focus, culture, and institutional differences. Colleges and conservatories in the U.S. and abroad may sign on to participate in this process. The MTCP is, thus, a set of guidelines for schools that choose to participate.

REQUIREMENTS FOR THE MTCP PRESCREEN

Each piece should be filmed and uploaded as separate media. Continuous videos are not acceptable. Students are encouraged to use standard technology and recording devices (i.e. smartphones, tablets, etc).

SLATES

At the beginning of each piece of media, students should introduce that performance with the following information within the allotted time. No extra time is allowed for the slate introduction. Note: there should not be a separate "slate" video.

- For songs, include your name, song title, and show in which the song appears.
- For monologues, include your name, the title of the play, and the playwright.

PRESCREEN SONG REQUIREMENTS

- Students must prepare two contrasting pieces (one ballad, one up-tempo). Check each college to determine which are accepted.
- Each song file should be 60-90 seconds, which should include the slate at the beginning. Media files longer than 90 seconds are not accepted.
- All songs should be sung with a musical accompanist – live or pre-recorded. "A cappella" singing is not accepted.
- Songs should be filmed so that the top of the head down to the knees is visible in the frame.
- Universities may require or prefer one of the following song options. Check with each university.

Option A

- One song should be written before 1970. This song may be either the up-tempo or the ballad.
- One song should be written after 1970 and present the opposite style as the first selection.

Option B

- Both songs should be from contemporary musicals written after 1970 with one ballad and one up-tempo.

PRESCREEN MONOLOGUE REQUIREMENTS

- Students may be asked to prepare one or two monologues. Check with each university for the specific requirement.
- Monologues must be from a published play.
- Monologues cannot be from musicals, television shows, or movies.
- Each monologue should be 60-90 seconds in length counting the introductory slate. Media files longer than 90 seconds are not accepted.
- Universities may require or prefer one of the following monologue options. Check with each university.

Option A

- 1 contemporary monologue written after 1900
- The contemporary monologue should be filmed showing only the top of the head down to the chest in the frame.

Option B

- 2 contrasting monologues - one contemporary monologue written after 1900 and one classical written before 1900.

PRESCREEN DANCE REQUIREMENTS

- Students may be asked to perform one or both of the following. Check with each university for the specific requirement.
- All dance media should be filmed with the entire body in the frame at all times.
- No slate is required for dance media.
- Regardless of the style of dance you choose, the choreography and movements should be story-driven, purposeful, meaningful, and connected to the musical accompaniment.
- Universities may also ask for a required dance option or offer an optional ballet submission.

Dance Option

- Choose the type of dance (ballet, jazz, modern, tap, hip hop, lyrical, contemporary, cultural, etc.) in which you feel most confident (30-60 seconds).
- Do not submit "barre work". However, for ballet, check to see if the university offers an optional ballet submission.
- Use well-executed steps, movement, and physical vocabulary.
- Dances should be a solo performance and may be self-choreographed. If you have a solo dance in a show, competition, or other performance, be sure that you are clearly featured.
- All choreography must be performed to music. A cappella dances are not accepted.

Ballet Option

- Ballet media should be no more than 30 seconds.
- Execute a brief series of plié, tendu, and grande battement.
- Execute pirouette en déhors (to both sides).
- Execute one or more grand jeté across the floor.

PRESCREEN WILD CARD REQUIREMENTS

Students may be asked to execute a "Wild Card" submission. Some colleges allow students to present a free choice submission in an area they want to highlight or display. Check with each university to see if they allow this submission.

- Submissions should be no more than 60 seconds.
- No slate is required on wild card media.
- The wild card can be anything - a special skill, an interesting story, a passionate speech, an instrumental composition, or what you want to communicate that makes you unique.

EIGHT SUGGESTIONS TO CREATE YOUR VIDEOS

The Acceptd website made some of the following suggestions to set up your home studio for filming.

1. Find a creative space where you have freedom of movement without impediments or distractions.
2. Ensure your camera is placed at eye level to record naturally as others see you. You might use a tripod, bookcase, stack of books on a desk, or stand that is 60 - 70 inches high.
3. Solid-colored walls are ideal to avoid visual distractions considering your possible clashes with your outfit and desire to focus on your performance.
4. Check the lighting. Adequate lighting is important for reviewers to see you clearly. Lamps and windows behind you are likely to cast a shadow

over your face. Thus, it is best for the lighting to emanate from behind your recording device to provide lighting to your face.

5. For songs, accompaniment tracks for musical theatre are available on YouTube and other websites. A live accompanist is not required. If the music is not available elsewhere, some apps, like Harmony Helper, will generate a piano track when you photograph and upload your sheet music.
6. Place the accompaniment music near you so the sounds of your voice and the music reach the recording device together in a smoother, more natural way.
7. For monologues, the Acceptd website suggests that you only perform Shakespeare if you feel comfortable. Other monologue options are available before 1900 that you can find in the public domain. Shakespeare is commonly used and, with seasoned performers, is often very well done.
8. For dance, you might consider having a full-length mirror behind the camera so that you can visually see yourself as you deliver your choreography.

For more information, review the following website - https://getacceptd.com/musical-theater-common-prescreen

NATIONAL UNIFIED AUDITIONS

Auditions were held in January and February 2022 in New York City, Chicago, and Anaheim. These months are likely to be the same in 2023 and 2024 though they may be held in different cities or with different universities participating.

Twenty-six universities participated, including, University of the Arts, Ball State University, Boston Conservatory at Berklee, University of Cincinnati, Cornish College of the Arts, Emerson College, the University of Evansville, Florida State University, University of Hartford, Ithaca College, University of Miami, Montclair State University, Northern Illinois University, Ohio University, University of Oklahoma, Otterbein University, Penn State University, Point Park University, Rider University, Roosevelt University, Savannah College of Art and Design, Southern Methodist University, Texas Christian University, The University of Utah, Viterbo University, and Webster University.

MOONIFIED AND COLLEGEAUDITIONCOACH

November 17th – 20th, 2022, registered participants will audition for 35 colleges. These private, individual, in-person auditions will be held in Dallas with representatives from the following schools. Students will meet with professors, admissions representatives, and former students appearing on Broadway and on national tours.

Baldwin Wallace, Ball State, Cal State Fullerton, Coastal Carolina, Florida State, The Hartt School, Howard University, Indiana University, James Madison, Missouri State, Molloy/CAP 21, Montclair State, Oakland University, Ohio Northern, Ohio University, Otterbein, Pace, Penn State, Point Park, Rider, Shenandoah Conservatory, Texas Christian University, Texas State, Texas Tech, University of the Arts, University of Arizona, University of Central Oklahoma, University of Miami, University of Oklahoma, University of Southern California, Viterbo, and Wright State.

OTHER PRESCREEN AND AUDITION METHODS

Some colleges use their own platforms and methods for students to upload content and audition candidates for their programs. Nevertheless, while they may not have students post their videos on Acceptd, they often require the same types of songs, monologues, and dance videos prepared in the same way. This uniformity aids in simplifying the process. However, a few schools do not participate in the prescreening process because they are looking for unique elements.

Best wishes you each of you as you prepare your prescreen and audition materials.

MUSICAL THEATER COMMON PRESCREEN 2021/2022 CYCLE

PARTICIPATING SCHOOLS as of October 15th, 2021

*Institutions with an asterisk do not require a digital prescreen. Please review the school website

Adapted from https://papermill.org/wp-content/uploads/2021/11/2021_2022-MTCP-Website-Update-OCT-15.pdf

SCHOOL NAME	SONG	MONOLOGUE	DANCE	BALLET	WILD CARD
Abilene Christian University	A: 2 Songs; 1 - Prior to 1970; 1 - Post 1970	A; 1 Monologue - Contemporary Post 1900	Required	Optional	Optional
Auburn University	Either A or B	Either A or B	Required	Optional	Optional
Baldwin Wallace University*	Either A or B	Either A or B	Required	Not Accepted	Required
Boston Conservatory at Berklee	A: 2 Songs; 1 - Prior to 1970; 1 - Post 1970	A; 1 Monologue - Contemporary Post 1900	Not Accepted	Not Accepted	Optional
California State University, Fullerton*	Either A or B	A; 1 Monologue - Contemporary Post 1900	Required	Optional	Optional
Carnegie Mellon University	A: 2 Songs; 1 - Prior to 1970; 1 - Post 1970	B; 2 Monologues; 1 - Contemporary Post 1900	Not Accepted	Not Accepted	Not Accepted
Circle in the Square Theatre School	A: 2 Songs; 1 - Prior to 1970; 1 - Post 1970	B; 2 Monologues; 1 - Contemporary Post 1900	Optional	Optional	Optional
Eckerd College	A: 2 Songs; 1 - Prior to 1970; 1 - Post 1970	B; 2 Monologues; 1 - Contemporary Post 1900	Optional	Optional	Optional
Coastal Carolina University	A: 2 Songs; 1 - Prior to 1970; 1 - Post 1970	A; 1 Monologue - Contemporary Post 1900	Required	Optional	Required
East Carolina University	A: 2 Songs; 1 - Prior to 1970; 1 - Post 1970	A; 1 Monologue - Contemporary Post 1900	Required	Not Accepted	Optional

SCHOOL NAME	SONG	MONOLOGUE	DANCE	BALLET	WILD CARD
Elon University	Either A or B	A; 1 Monologue - Contemporary Post 1900	Required	Not Accepted	Not Accepted
Emerson College	A: 2 Songs; 1 - Prior to 1970; 1 - Post 1970	A; 1 Monologue - Contemporary Post 1900	Required	Not Accepted	Not Accepted
Fairleigh Dickinson University	Either A or B	Either A or B	Optional	Optional	Optional
Florida Southern College	A: 2 Songs; 1 - Prior to 1970; 1 - Post 1970	A; 1 Monologue - Contemporary Post 1900	Required	Optional	Optional
Florida State University	Either A or B	A; 1 Monologue - Contemporary Post 1900	Required	Required	Optional
Hartt / The University of Hartford	A: 2 Songs; 1 - Prior to 1970; 1 - Post 1970	A; 1 Monologue - Contemporary Post 1900	Required	Optional	Required
Hussian College Los Angeles	Either A or B	Either A or B	Required	Optional	Required
Illinois Wesleyan University	A: 2 Songs; 1 - Prior to 1970; 1 - Post 1970	A; 1 Monologue - Contemporary Post 1900	Optional	Optional	Optional
Indiana University Bloomington	A: 2 Songs; 1 - Prior to 1970; 1 - Post 1970	A; 1 Monologue - Contemporary Post 1900	Required	Optional	Required
Indiana University South Bend*	A: 2 Songs; 1 - Prior to 1970; 1 - Post 1970	A; 1 Monologue - Contemporary Post 1900	Not Accepted	Not Accepted	Not Accepted
Ithaca College	A: 2 Songs; 1 - Prior to 1970; 1 - Post 1970	B; 2 Monologues; 1 - Contemporary Post 1900	Required	Optional	Optional
James Madison University*	Either A or B	A; 1 Monologue - Contemporary Post 1900	Required	Optional	Optional
Marymount Manhattan College*	Either A or B	A; 1 Monologue - Contemporary Post 1900	Not Accepted	Not Accepted	Required
Millikin University	A: 2 Songs; 1 - Prior to 1970; 1 - Post 1970	A; 1 Monologue - Contemporary Post 1900	Required	Optional	Optional
Missouri State University*	Either A or B	Either A or B	Required	Optional	Optional

SCHOOL NAME	SONG	MONOLOGUE	DANCE	BALLET	WILD CARD
Molloy College/ CAP21	A: 2 Songs; 1 - Prior to 1970; 1 - Post 1970	A; 1 Monologue - Contemporary Post 1900	Optional	Optional	Optional
Montclair State University*	A: 2 Songs; 1 - Prior to 1970; 1 - Post 1970	A; 1 Monologue - Contemporary Post 1900	Required	Optional	Optional
Nazareth College*	A: 2 Songs; 1 - Prior to 1970; 1 - Post 1970	A; 1 Monologue - Contemporary Post 1900	Required	Optional	Required
Ohio Northern University*	A: 2 Songs; 1 - Prior to 1970; 1 - Post 1970	A; 1 Monologue - Contemporary Post 1900	Required	Optional	Optional
Ohio University*	A: 2 Songs; 1 - Prior to 1970; 1 - Post 1970	A; 1 Monologue - Contemporary Post 1900	Optional	Optional	Optional
Oklahoma City University	A: 2 Songs; 1 - Prior to 1970; 1 - Post 1970	B; 2 Monologues; 1 - Contemporary Post 1900	Required	Not Accepted	Required
Oklahoma State University*	Either A or B	A; 1 Monologue - Contemporary Post 1900	Optional	Optional	Optional
Otterbein University	A: 2 Songs; 1 - Prior to 1970; 1 - Post 1970	B; 2 Monologues; 1 - Contemporary Post 1900	Required	Optional	Optional
Ouachita Baptist University*	A: 2 Songs; 1 - Prior to 1970; 1 - Post 1970	A; 1 Monologue - Contemporary Post 1900	Required	Optional	Optional
Pace University	Either A or B	A; 1 Monologue - Contemporary Post 1900	Required	Not Accepted	Optional
Penn State Musical Theatre	A: 2 Songs; 1 - Prior to 1970; 1 - Post 1970	A; 1 Monologue - Contemporary Post 1900	Required	Not Accepted	Optional
Point Park University	A: 2 Songs; 1 - Prior to 1970; 1 - Post 1970	A; 1 Monologue - Contemporary Post 1900	Required	Optional	Optional
Rider University	Either A or B	Either A or B	Required	Not Accepted	Optional
Roosevelt University	Either A or B	A; 1 Monologue - Contemporary Post 1900	Required	Optional	Optional

SCHOOL NAME	SONG	MONOLOGUE	DANCE	BALLET	WILD CARD
San Diego State University	A: 2 Songs; 1 - Prior to 1970; 1 - Post 1970	A; 1 Monologue - Contemporary Post 1900	Not Accepted	Not Accepted	Not Accepted
Shenandoah University	Either A or B	A; 1 Monologue - Contemporary Post 1900	Optional	Not Accepted	Optional
Siena Heights University*	Either A or B	A; 1 Monologue - Contemporary Post 1900	Optional	Optional	Optional
Slippery Rock University	Either A or B	A; 1 Monologue - Contemporary Post 1900	Optional	Optional	Required
Southeast Missouri State University	Either A or B	Either A or B	Required	Optional	Optional
Southern Illinois University	A: 2 Songs; 1 - Prior to 1970; 1 - Post 1970	A; 1 Monologue - Contemporary Post 1900	Required	Optional	Optional
Stephens College	Either A or B	Either A or B	Required	Optional	Optional
SUNY Fredonia	Either A or B	Either A or B	Required	Optional	Optional
Syracuse University	A: 2 Songs; 1 - Prior to 1970; 1 - Post 1970	A; 1 Monologue - Contemporary Post 1900	Required	Optional	Required
Temple University	A: 2 Songs; 1 - Prior to 1970; 1 - Post 1970	A; 1 Monologue - Contemporary Post 1900	Required	Optional	Required
Texas Christian University	B: 2 Songs; Both Post 1970	A; 1 Monologue - Contemporary Post 1900	Required	Optional	Optional
Texas State University	Either A or B	A; 1 Monologue - Contemporary Post 1900	Required	Optional	Required
Texas Tech Univesity	A: 2 Songs; 1 - Prior to 1970; 1 - Post 1970	B; 2 Monologues; 1 - Contemporary Post 1900	Required	Optional	Required
University of Alabama	Either A or B	A; 1 Monologue - Contemporary Post 1900	Required	Optional	Optional
University of Alabama at Birmingham	Either A or B	A; 1 Monologue - Contemporary Post 1900	Required	Optional	Required

SCHOOL NAME	SONG	MONOLOGUE	DANCE	BALLET	WILD CARD
University of Arizona	A: 2 Songs; 1 - Prior to 1970; 1 - Post 1970	A; 1 Monologue - Contemporary Post 1900	Required	Not Accepted	Required
University of Central Florida	A: 2 Songs; 1 - Prior to 1970; 1 - Post 1970	A; 1 Monologue - Contemporary Post 1900	Required	Optional	Optional
University of Cincinnati College	A: 2 Songs; 1 - Prior to 1970; 1 - Post 1970	A; 1 Monologue - Contemporary Post 1900	Required	Not Accepted	Optional
University of Florida	Either A or B	Either A or B	Required	Not Accepted	Optional
University of NC at Greensboro	A: 2 Songs; 1 - Prior to 1970; 1 - Post 1970	A; 1 Monologue - Contemporary Post 1900	Required	Optional	Required
University of New Hampshire	A: 2 Songs; 1 - Prior to 1970; 1 - Post 1970	B; 2 Monologues; 1 - Contemporary Post 1900	Required	Optional	Optional
University of Oklahoma	A: 2 Songs; 1 - Prior to 1970; 1 - Post 1970	B; 2 Monologues; 1 - Contemporary Post 1900	Required	Not Accepted	Optional
University of Texas at Arlington*	A: 2 Songs; 1 - Prior to 1970; 1 - Post 1970	A; 1 Monologue - Contemporary Post 1900	Optional	Not Accepted	Optional
Viterbo University	Either A or B	A; 1 Monologue - Contemporary Post 1900	Required	Optional	Required
Western Connecticut State University	A: 2 Songs; 1 - Prior to 1970; 1 - Post 1970	A; 1 Monologue - Contemporary Post 1900	Optional	Optional	Optional
Wright State University*	A: 2 Songs; 1 - Prior to 1970; 1 - Post 1970	B; 2 Monologues; 1 - Contemporary Post 1900	Optional	Optional	Optional

CHAPTER 9

POST-PANDEMIC EMPLOYMENT OUTLOOK: STATISTICS AND ECONOMIC PROJECTIONS

"The curtain rises even on an actor's worst day."

– Stewart Stafford

ECONOMIC OUTLOOK FOR THEATRE, MUSICAL THEATRE, AND THE PERFORMING ARTS

Actors portray characters in all forms of media, stages, and venues, interpreting a script to entertain or inform. According to the Occupational Outlook Handbook, most actors struggle to find steady work and often have long periods of unemployment between roles, often holding other jobs to make a living. Some actors teach classes, sing, dance, work as "extras", do voiceover/narration for animated feature stories, audiobooks, or electronic media.

In acting, there are typically more applicants than positions. With the volume of people choosing this direction, acting spots tend to go to those whose talent and experience fit the company's needs. Also, the more competitive markets, like New York City, will require additional skills and extraordinary ambition. On the Texas Shakespeare Festival site where you are to upload your headshot and resume, Artistic Director, Meaghan Simpson's note to actors states,

> At this time, we have closed our online submissions for the TSF 2022 season. I want to say thank-you for the time and effort you put into learning a new monologue, stacking books under your iPhone, or perfecting the ideal 32-bar cutting. The energy and devotion to your craft is incredible and admirable.
>
> Each year, we receive approximately 1500 submissions to fill 22 tracks in our summer acting company. Suffice it to say, the odds are not in your favor. That said, we promise to view your audition and to contact you to inform you of your status once the casting process has completed.

Furthermore, do not let the number of people applying for undergraduate or graduate degree programs or an internship or a job stop you. If acting is the field you want to pursue, pave the road in front of you and drive. An internship or apprenticeship or two would not hurt you in your pursuit. Although most internships are unpaid, you will find that most applicants will have one or more.

If you are serious, you can make a fantastic career out of your pursuit. Initiative-taking persistence, talent, creativity, and moxie can get you into your desired college program and career. You may have to start at the very bottom of the ladder, but you can climb the rungs methodically one by one.

Acting companies want to know the work ethic, personality, and professionalism of the employees they choose. An internship allows you to get to know their corporate climate better and allows them to get to know you better too. Thus, many companies hire the interns they feel are the best fit rather than choosing candidates from the piles of resumes, headshots, and audition tapes that have been submitted.

Education unlocks doors. In the dramatic arts, this is also true. Persistence and showmanship are invaluable tools in this career pursuit. Your education, highlighted on your resume, can move your audition materials to the top of the pile.

Those who perform on stage do so on Broadway, Off-Broadway, and in touring companies, summer stock, and resident companies. Approximately two-thirds of all actors are men with 23% LGBTQ+. Nearly 60% are White, 15.6% Hispanic, 13.9% African American, and 6% Asian. The average age of employed actors is 37 years old.

ECONOMIC OUTLOOK FOR ACTORS

Bureau of Labor Statistics – Actors

2020 Median Pay: $21.88 per hour

Bachelor's Degree: Theatre, Drama, Musical Theatre

Number of Jobs in 2020: 51,600

Job Growth: 32% Increase (much higher than average)

Location of Most Positions: New York and Los Angeles

According to the Bureau of Labor Statistics, the growth rate of 32% for acting is much higher than the average for jobs in the United States. Furthermore, the growth in jobs from 2020 – 2030 is expected to be 16,700 new jobs in theatre, film, television, and other performing arts media. Work assignments tend to be short contract work.

As for education,

Master's Degree – 6%

Bachelor's Degree – 61%

Associate's Degree – 12%

HS Diploma – 16%

Another degree/certificate – 5%

Actors with a bachelor's degree or higher earn on average approximately $13,000 per year more. Most actors live in New York or Los Angeles.

Alternative jobs related to acting:

Actor
Anchor
Audio Engineer
Audition Coach
Background Actor
Bartending
Carpenter
Cast Member
Catering
Character Performer
Comedian
Company Manager
Costume Assistant
Crafts Technician
Debate Teacher
Drama Coach
Dramaturg
Entertainer
First Hand
Host
Lighting Technicians
Magician
Makeup Artists
Marketing
Modeling
Musical Theatre
Painter
Personal Assistant
Production Studios
Promo Work
Scare Actor
Scenic Carpenter
Seamstress
Set Dresser
Stage Crew
Stitcher

Stunt Double
Teacher
Theatre
Theatre Arts Educator
Theatre Camp Counselor
Theme Parks
Trade Shows
Video Editor
Voice Actor
Voice-Over Artist
Wardrobe

Whatever direction you pursue, if you lay a foundation, undaunted by the competition, and are unafraid of starting at the bottom, you will do fine. Hard work and creativity go a long way in this industry. Start by getting a solid education.

MANAGEMENT AND EMPLOYEE RETENTION

Skills to Know: *Management, Human Resources, Social Consciousness, Ethics*

One of the most significant challenges facing the years from 2022 - 2030 will be locating and retaining talent. The pandemic slowed education and learning with online classes, reduced access to faculty/advising, limited access to labs, inability to attend workshops, retail closures, and fewer conferences, meetings, and shows. Health concerns rose to the top of importance as did financial stress, job uncertainty, and social consciousness. Many students chose to work rather than study and start online stores when they could not access locations for community service or continue with their sport, instrument, or hobbies. With the changes in lifestyle and fears about health, safety, and wellness, many bright and talented students developed a fearless sense of autonomy and independence, while for others, the necessary skills ordinarily developed in school were fraught by limitations.

Finding talent within the changing hiring atmosphere will require new skills to retain staff. Employees are increasingly looking elsewhere for a better opportunity. This development will require managers to earn and harness employee trust and loyalty.

The digital workforce has also placed demands on human resources. While many companies want their employees to work in-person, the convenience of working at home and the drudgery of commuting to work have created an environment where employees seek greater flexibility. Changes are coming. The employee talent challenge is likely to create a more global workforce where companies look for less expensive online talent from a pool of eager workers in other countries.

STAGE DOOR

CHAPTER 10

NEXT STEPS: PREPARATION AND REAL-WORLD SKILLS

"I think drama has to push things to extremes so that we can understand what we are doing in our society."

– Edward Bond

While you do not need a college education, a Bachelor of Fine Arts from a respected school certainly helps you get noticed. Connections through your professors, classmates, and alumni are excellent ways to discover opportunities. Performances in school, out of school, in the summer, or through social media can help you get noticed. Also, throughout your varied experiences, you will meet other actors who can recommend you or let you know of auditions, even some that are not publicly announced. Many schools have a senior showcase in front of agents and casting directors where you can put your best foot forward.

Exposure to agents and industry professionals helps. Interacting with people online or in-person allows you to maintain those connections. You could wait for the phone to ring or for you to be discovered, however, you will have to be out and about for that to happen. Some pine away hoping to be signed or reading scripts deciding which would be a perfect fit. However, the reason why so many actors work in New York restaurants is to get out and see what is happening outside of their apartment.

BOLD NETWORKING

Networking takes social skills and a bit of moxie. From elevator speeches and restaurant encounters to auditions, masterclasses, and workshops, your job is to find a way to get in front of people. How can you be recognized? Meet people, hand out your resume, give them your business card, ask for their business card, follow up, ask if you can call or meet them, even when the instance may be uncomfortable. Stay in touch with people you meet, even if it is just happenstance or serendipity. Keep a log with each person's phone, e-mail, identifying information, and both date and location where you met. You never know when you will need it.

If you meet people professionally at a masterclass or workshop, even if you do not exchange information, you will recognize them. They may recognize you in a future event too. Keep training. You should always want to improve no matter how good you are, though you should not train just for the sake of meeting people. Your focus will not be on improvement and you may appear insincere. However, this forum can allow others to see you too. Big-ticket training does not always mean better trainers or opportunities. See shows, film premieres, and engage in all things theatre.

STAY IN TOUCH

Do not annoy busy people, but you can keep in touch every couple of months. Communicating more frequently is overwhelming. However, life is long, and people who grow with their craft in this industry, transitioning through career phases of their life often perform until they are in their 60s and 70s. In this industry, contacts are important in all phases of your career.

Also, do not be surprised. Many go-getters auditioning with you could become lifelong colleagues and friends and may also turn out to be very successful. People tend to only want to stay in touch with the "important" people. Note: your contemporaries or peers are important people...although possibly not yet. Remember that as you form your lists of contacts, you are likely to stay in touch with them throughout your career.

Be audacious, while also being authentic. Networking can sometimes appear fake or forced, as if you are going out on a hunt to find people for your own benefit. Worse, the act of networking in theatre can reach the verge of stalking as a young actor follows an agent or casting director to connect. The mental image this type of 'networking' conjures up the image of people congregating at stage doors, smiling broadly and blatantly flirting.

Friendships and mutual support of allies can be enormously helpful, 20,000 or even 200,000 followers on your website does not mean you are popular. However, you can have unexpected meaningful exchanges if you get out and live life. I once had a fascinating and memorable conversation with Matthew Perry in Palm Desert, CA for more than an hour where we talked about life, culture, and world affairs. I was not trying to network, nor was he, and we did not exchange information. We live in very different worlds. Nevertheless, there are times when deeply moving, casual conversations in non-professional settings could also turn into connections.

Do not lose touch with people or burn bridges along the way. This industry is not that big, and you will continually see movers and shakers on all levels of the acting and performance world. You never know. They may contact you to collaborate one day or meet for coffee at an event. Networking is a two-way street, and the best networkers know this.

Elphaba has some great advice to energize you into action. For an uplifting feeling, sing this part from Wicked in the shower.

Something has changed within me

Something is not the same

I'm through with playing by the rules

Of someone else's game

Too late for second-guessing

Too late to go back to sleep

It's time to trust my instincts

Close my eyes and leap!

It's time to try defying gravity

I think I'll try defying gravity

And you can't pull me down.

Although college theatre managers, program directors, and conservatory coordinators often do what they can to help you get acting roles, summer stock opportunities, and auditions, you might also go to your campus career center. They often have interesting prospects that you might not get elsewhere. There may be a specific career liaison for the dramatic arts.

Connect with them for help in your search process. Besides, you might just want to get a related job that utilizes your presentation skills. Companies that hold tradeshows often hire theatre majors. Marketing companies also appreciate people who can tell more about their products. These jobs may not be your ideal, but sometimes you just need a position to earn money and get yourself on your feet. Career center coordinators often have excellent ideas.

Furthermore, they can assist you with creating a professional resume and cover letters for specific industries that are different from the ones you have for acting, voice, or dance. They may also connect you with past graduates in the industry who make excellent connections. Some of them may have been in your program and have been through the ropes, know a few people, and may be able to get you an interview or invite you to an industry event. Any contact may be able to get your foot into the door or a job to make money in the meantime.

LINKEDIN

LinkedIn is especially helpful for career searches. You can find numerous influential contacts on LinkedIn. After each audition, connect with each person you met on LinkedIn. Keep a contact list of individuals you know in the theatre and performing arts world. Do not constantly try to connect with people you do not really know. However, if you have made the connection, occasionally keep in touch.

While some LinkedIn message boxes may be full and you may not get a reply, you can try. Occasionally, you hit on a lucky break. Though I do not have time to communicate with everyone, I have connected with some of my most inspiring authors, advisors, and intellectual leaders through LinkedIn.

FINALLY

Most people are willing to help you. Five percent will not. Thus, you have a 19 out of 20 chance of interacting with decent people who have the time and will give you advice. Don't lose faith in humanity just because you ran into a few people who are too busy to stop for you or are too self-absorbed that they cannot answer your question.

- Work ethic is everything.
- Excellence is expected.
- Learn what you do not know on your own time.
- Come to work prepared.
- Take constructive criticism well.
- Keep your cool under pressure.
- Avoid being timid.
- Stay on task.
- Come early.
- Stay late.
- Take your work seriously.
- Do more than expected.
- Read your e-mail/texts after hours in case something is important.
- Ask questions. No question is too stupid.
- Maintain a clean workspace.
- Dress and act professionally.
- Don't gossip or complain.
- Avoid frustrating your phenomenally busy supervisor.
- Be straightforward, and don't beat around the bush.

See you on Broadway!

4
Regions

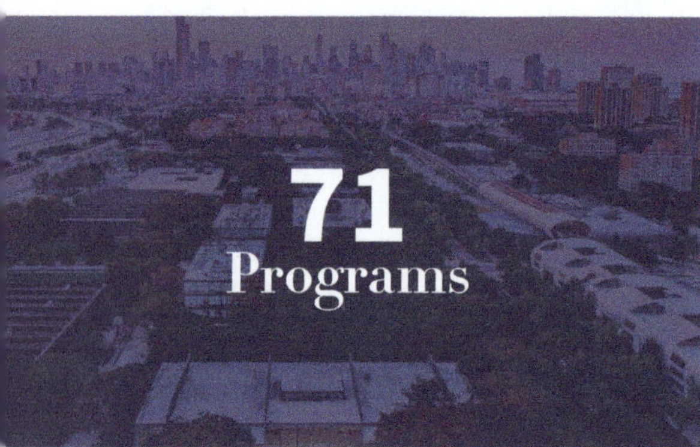
71
Programs

COLLEGE PROFILES AND REQUIREMENTS

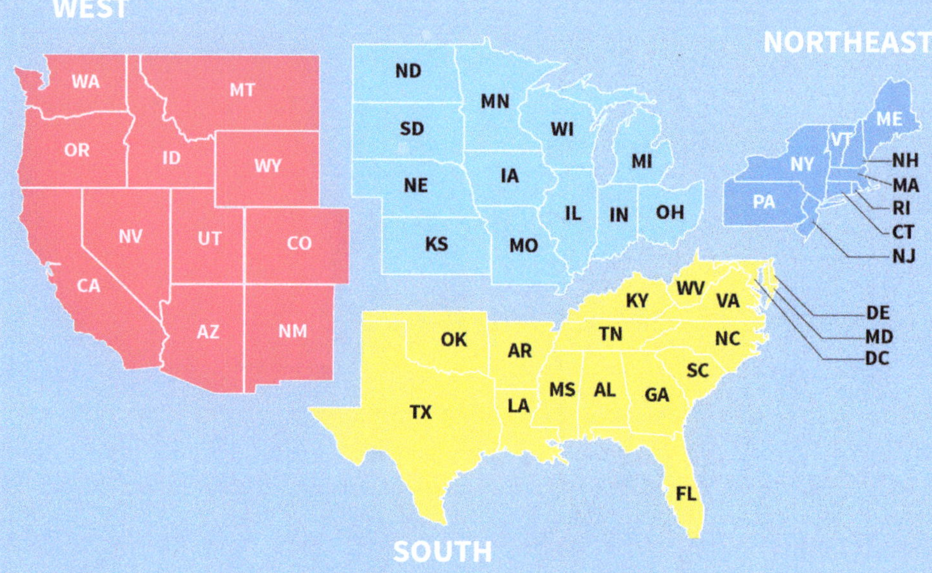

PROGRAMS BY REGION

U.S. CENSUS BUREAU CLASSIFICATIONS

REGION 1 – NORTHEAST

Connecticut, Maine, Massachusetts, New Hampshire, New Jersey, New York, Pennsylvania, Rhode Island, and Vermont

REGION 2 – MIDWEST

Illinois, Indiana, Iowa, Kansas, Michigan, Minnesota, Missouri, Nebraska, North Dakota, Ohio, South Dakota, and Wisconsin

REGION 3 – SOUTH

Alabama, Arkansas, Delaware, District of Columbia, Florida, Georgia, Kentucky, Louisiana, Maryland, Mississippi, North Carolina, Oklahoma, South Carolina, Tennessee, Texas, Virginia, and West Virginia

REGION 4 – WEST

Alaska, Arizona, California, Colorado, Hawaii, Idaho, Montana, Nevada, New Mexico, Oregon, Utah, Washington, and Wyoming

LIST OF MUSICAL THEATRE PROGRAMS

The programs listed in the following pages include top musical theatre programs. In addition, this book also lists the top theatre, costume design, and technical theatre programs. Many students interested in musical theatre are also interested in the artistic side of dance, voice, costume design, and theatre arts.

Thus, this book aims to provide you with a more comprehensive set of lists so that you can explore your options. Keep the book handy. Even after you begin college, you may find the additional programs in the back are helpful for connections or summer programs.

Creating lists is often tedious and cumbersome. These lists were gathered to help you with this task. Acceptance rates for musical theatre programs were often unavailable. Thus, university acceptance rates were provided.

These descriptions of the college programs, tuition, requirements, and deadlines are accurate as of March 2022. The requirements may have changed somewhat by the time you purchase this book, but this information is a great place to start!

Note: To simplify the text and fit information into the charts and descriptions, abbreviations were used as well as shortened sentences and acronyms. Also, note that theater and theatre are spelled differently depending upon the school or program. While "theatre" was used throughout the text, if a school or program used 'theater', we attempted to leave that name as they chose.

CHAPTER 13

REGION ONE
NORTHEAST

CONNECTICUT

MAINE

MASSACHUSETTS

NEW HAMPSHIRE

NEW JERSEY

NEW YORK

PENNSYLVANIA

RHODE ISLAND

VERMONT

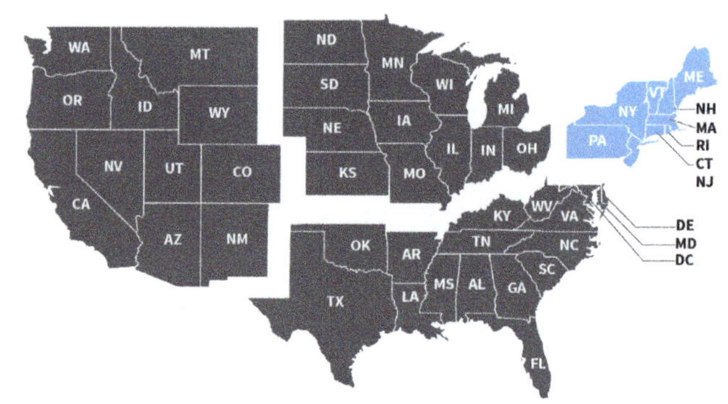

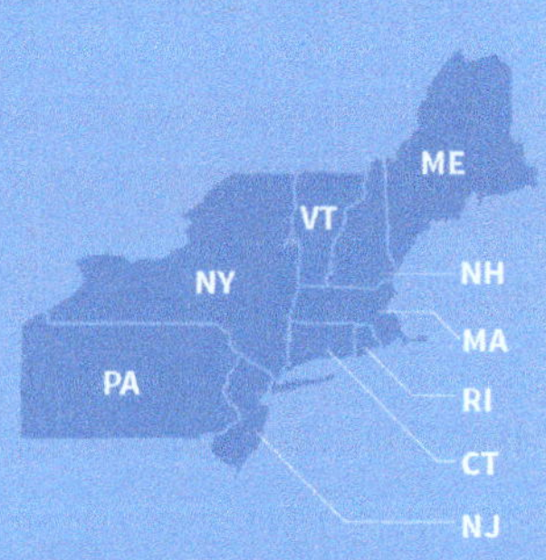

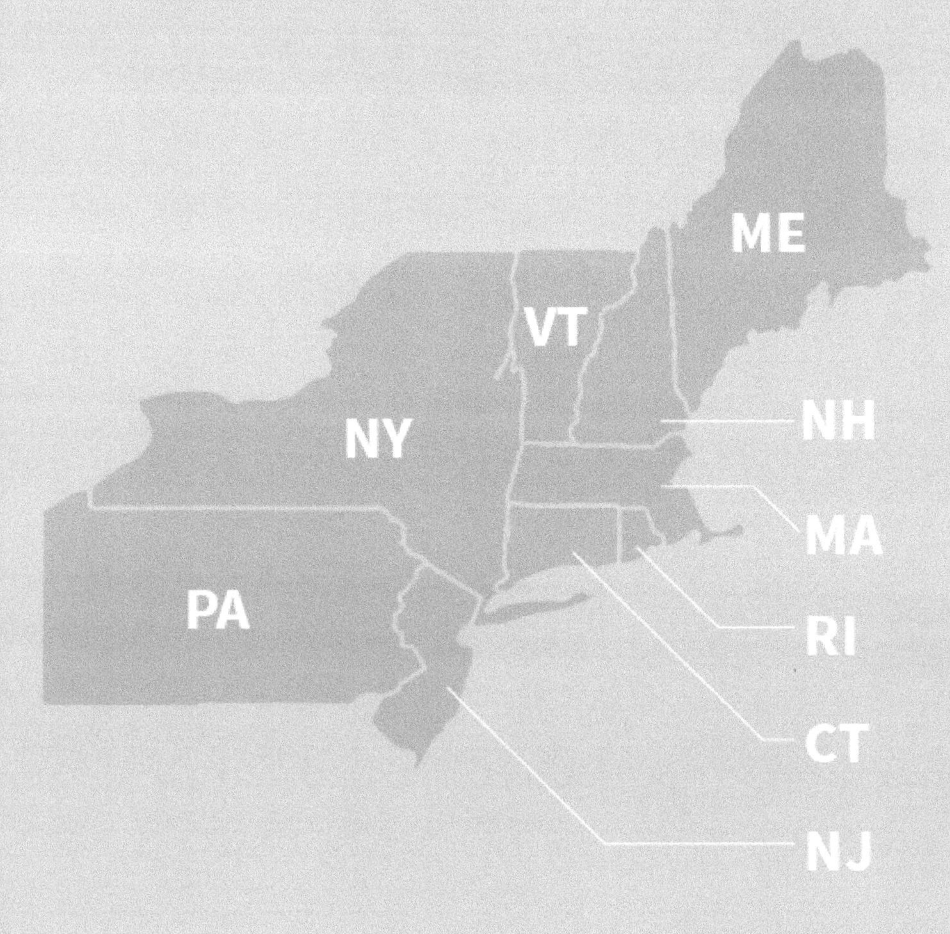

23 Programs | 9 States

1. *CT – University of Hartford - Hartt School*
2. *MA - Boston Conservatory at Berklee*
3. *MA - Emerson College*
4. *NJ - Montclair State University*
5. *NJ - Rider University*
6. *NY - American Musical & Dramatic Academy (AMDA)*
7. *NY - Ithaca College*
8. *NY - The Juilliard School*
9. *NY - Long Island University Post*
10. *NY - Manhattan School of Music*
11. *NY - Marymount Manhattan College*
12. *NY - Molloy College*
13. *NY - The New School*
14. *NY - New York University*
15. *NY - Pace University*
16. *NY - SUNY Cortland*
17. *NY - Syracuse University*
18. *NY - University at Buffalo*
19. *PA - Carnegie Mellon University*
20. *PA - Pennsylvania State University*
21. *PA - Point Park University*
22. *PA - Temple University*
23. *PA - University of the Arts*

MUSICAL THEATRE PROGRAMS

School	Avg. GPA, SAT Evidence-Based Reading Writing (ERW), SAT Math (M), and ACT Composite (C) Early Decision (ED): Yes/No	Admission Statistics	Program(s)	Pre-Screen and/or Audition Required (Req.)
University of Hartford - Hartt School 200 Bloomfield Avenue, West Hartford, CT 06117	GPA: N/A SAT (ERW): 510-610 SAT (M): 510-600 ACT (C): 22-29 ED: No	Overall College Admit Rate: 77% Undergrad Enrollment: 4,521 Total Enrollment: 6,493	BFA Music Theatre Degrees Awarded in the Program(s) (2020): N/A	Pre-screen req. Audition req.
Boston Conservatory at Berklee 8 Fenway, Boston, MA 02215	GPA: N/A SAT (ERW): N/A* SAT (M): N/A* ACT (C): N/A* *Test-optional ED: No	Overall College Admit Rate: 52% Undergrad Enrollment: 6,004 Total Enrollment: 6,631	BFA Theatre: Musical Theatre Degrees Awarded in the Program(s) (2020): 48	Pre-screen req. Audition req.
Emerson College 120 Boylston St., Boston, MA 02116	GPA: 3.5 SAT (ERW): 610-690 SAT (M): 580-690 ACT (C): 27-31 ED: Yes	Overall College Admit Rate: 41% Undergrad Enrollment: 3,708 Total Enrollment: 5,115	BFA Musical Theatre Degrees Awarded in the Program(s) (2020): 12	Pre-screen req. Audition req.
Montclair State University 1 Normal Ave., Montclair, NJ 07043	GPA: N/A SAT (ERW): N/A* SAT (M): N/A* ACT (C): N/A* *Test-optional ED: No	Overall College Admit Rate: 83% Undergrad Enrollment: 16,374 Total Enrollment: 21,005	BFA Musical Theatre Degrees Awarded in the Program(s) (2020): 71	Pre-screen req. Audition req.

School	Avg. GPA, SAT Evidence-Based Reading Writing (ERW), SAT Math (M), and ACT Composite (C) Early Decision (ED): Yes/No	Admission Statistics	Program(s)	Pre-Screen and/or Audition Required (Req.)
Rider University 2083 Lawrenceville Rd, Lawrenceville, NJ 08648	GPA: N/A SAT (ERW): 510-620 SAT (M): 510-600 ACT (C): 20-26 ED: No	Overall College Admit Rate: 76% Undergrad Enrollment: 3,630 Total Enrollment: 4,636	BFA Musical Theatre BA Theatre, concentration in Musical Theatre Degrees Awarded in the Program(s) (2020): N/A	Pre-screen req. Audition req.
American Musical & Dramatic Academy (AMDA) 211 W 61st St., New York, NY 10023	GPA: N/A SAT (ERW): N/A* SAT (M): N/A* ACT (C): N/A* *Test-optional ED: No	Overall College Admit Rate: 44% Undergrad Enrollment: 1,395 Total Enrollment: 1,399	BFA Music Theatre BFA Performing Arts: Music Theatre BFA Performing Arts: Music Theatre & Creative Content Development Degrees Awarded in the Program(s) (2020): 213	Pre-screen not req. Audition req.

MUSICAL THEATRE PROGRAMS

School	Avg. GPA, SAT Evidence-Based Reading Writing (ERW), SAT Math (M), and ACT Composite (C) Early Decision (ED): Yes/No	Admission Statistics	Program(s)	Pre-Screen and/or Audition Required (Req.)
Ithaca College 953 Danby Road, Ithaca, NY 14850	GPA: N/A SAT (ERW): 600-680 SAT (M): 580-670 ACT (C): 27-31 ED: Yes* *ED and EA are not available to MT applicants due to the audition process.	Overall College Admit Rate: 76% Undergrad Enrollment: 4,957 Total Enrollment: 5,354	BFA Musical Theatre Degrees Awarded in the Program(s) (2020): 12	Pre-screen req. Audition req.
The Juilliard School 60 Lincoln Center Plaza, New York, NY 10023	GPA: N/A SAT (ERW): N/A* SAT (M): N/A* ACT (C): N/A* *Test-optional ED: No	Overall College Admit Rate: 67% Undergrad Enrollment: 589 Total Enrollment: 961	BFA Acting Degrees Awarded in the Program(s): 9	Pre-screen req. Audition req.
Long Island University Post 720 Northern Blvd, Greenvale, NY 11548	GPA: N/A SAT (ERW): 540-640 SAT (M): 540-650 ACT (C): 22-29 ED: No	Overall College Admit Rate: 85% Undergrad Enrollment: 10,403 Total Enrollment: 15,066	BFA in Theatre Arts (Musical Theatre) Degrees Awarded in the Program(s): N/A	Pre-screen not req. Audition req.

School	Avg. GPA, SAT Evidence-Based Reading Writing (ERW), SAT Math (M), and ACT Composite (C) Early Decision (ED): Yes/No	Admission Statistics	Program(s)	Pre-Screen and/or Audition Required (Req.)
Manhattan School of Music 130 Claremont Ave, New York, NY 10027	GPA: N/A SAT (ERW): N/A* SAT (M): N/A* ACT (C): N/A* *Test-optional ED: No	Overall College Admit Rate: 42% Undergrad Enrollment: 497 Total Enrollment: 939	BM Musical Theatre Degrees Awarded in the Program(s) (2020): 38	Pre-screen req. Audition req.
Marymount Manhattan College 221 East 71st Street New York, NY 10021	GPA: N/A SAT (ERW): 500-580 SAT (M): 460-620 ACT (C): 20-28 ED: Yes	Overall College Admit Rate: 88% Undergrad Enrollment: 1,722 Total Enrollment: 1,722	BFA Musical Theatre Degrees Awarded in the Program(s) (2020): 23	Pre-screen not req. Audition req.
Molloy College 1000 Hempstead Ave, Rockville Centre, NY 11570	GPA: N/A SAT (ERW): 540-620 SAT (M): 540-630 ACT (C): 21-28 ED: No	Overall College Admit Rate: 74% Undergrad Enrollment: 3,510 Total Enrollment: 5,115	BFA Theatre Arts Degrees Awarded in the Program(s) (2020): 29	Pre-screen req. Audition req.

MUSICAL THEATRE PROGRAMS

School	Avg. GPA, SAT Evidence-Based Reading Writing (ERW), SAT Math (M), and ACT Composite (C) Early Decision (ED): Yes/No	Admission Statistics	Program(s)	Pre-Screen and/or Audition Required (Req.)
The New School 66 West 12th Street, New York, NY 10011	GPA: N/A SAT (ERW): 580-680 SAT (M): 560-680 ACT (C): 26-30 ED: No	Overall College Admit Rate: 69% Undergrad Enrollment: 6,399 Total Enrollment: 9,047	BFA Musical Theatre* Degrees Awarded in the Program(s) (2020): 21	Pre-screen not req.* Audition not req.* *This program is only open to graduates of the AMDA integrated program.
New York University 721 Broadway, New York, NY 10003	GPA: 3.71 SAT (ERW): 670-740 SAT (M): 700-800 ACT (C): 31-34 ED: Yes	Overall College Admit Rate: 21% Undergrad Enrollment: 27,444 Total Enrollment: 52,775	Degrees Awarded in the Program(s) (2020): N/A	Pre-screen not req. Audition req.
Pace University 1 Pace Plaza, New York, NY 10038	GPA: N/A SAT (ERW): 540-630* SAT (M): 520-610* ACT (C): 22-28* *Test-optional ED: Yes	Overall College Admit Rate: 83% Undergrad Enrollment: 7,994 Total Enrollment: 12,835	BFA Musical Theatre Degrees Awarded in the Program(s) (2020): 19	Pre-screen req. Audition req.
SUNY Cortland 22 Graham Ave, Cortland, NY 13045	GPA: N/A SAT (ERW): 550-610 SAT (M): 550-610 ACT (C): 22-26 ED: No	Overall College Admit Rate: 52% Undergrad Enrollment: 6,256 Total Enrollment: 6,832	BFA Musical Theatre Degrees Awarded in the Program(s) (2020): 14	Pre-screen not req. Audition req.

School	Avg. GPA, SAT Evidence-Based Reading Writing (ERW), SAT Math (M), and ACT Composite (C) Early Decision (ED): Yes/No	Admission Statistics	Program(s)	Pre-Screen and/or Audition Required (Req.)
Syracuse University 200 Crouse College, Syracuse, NY 13244	GPA: 3.67 SAT (ERW): N/A SAT (M): N/A ACT (C): N/A ED: Yes	Overall College Admit Rate: 69% Undergrad Enrollment: 14,479 Total Enrollment: 21,322	BFA Musical Theatre Degrees Awarded in the Program(s) (2020): 23	Pre-screen req. Audition req.
University at Buffalo University at Buffalo, Buffalo, NY 14260	GPA: 3.7 SAT (ERW): 560-640 SAT (M): 580-670 ACT (C): 23-29 ED: No	Overall College Admit Rate: 37% Undergrad Enrollment: 22,306 Total Enrollment: 32,347	BFA Music Theatre Degrees Awarded in the Program(s) (2020): 6	Pre-screen not req. Audition req.
Carnegie Mellon University 5000 Forbes Avenue, Pittsburgh, PA 15213	GPA: 3.85 SAT (ERW): 700-760 SAT (M): 760-800 ACT (C): 33-35 ED: Yes	Overall College Admit Rate: 17% Undergrad Enrollment: 7,073 Total Enrollment: 14,189	BFA Drama, option: Music Theater Degrees Awarded in the Program(s) (2020): N/A	Pre-screen req. Audition req.

MUSICAL THEATRE PROGRAMS

School	Avg. GPA, SAT Evidence-Based Reading Writing (ERW), SAT Math (M), and ACT Composite (C) Early Decision (ED): Yes/No	Admission Statistics	Program(s)	Pre-Screen and/or Audition Required (Req.)
Pennsylvania State University 124 Borland Building, University Park, PA 16802	GPA: N/A SAT (ERW): 580-670 SAT (M): 580-700 ACT (C): 25-30 ED: No	Overall College Admit Rate: 49% Undergrad Enrollment: 40,639 Total Enrollment: 47,223	BFA Musical Theatre Degrees Awarded in the Program(s) (2020): N/A	Pre-screen req. Audition req.
Point Park University 201 Wood Street, Pittsburgh, PA 15222	GPA: 3.46 SAT (ERW): 483-610 SAT (M): 470-570 ACT (C): 18-26 ED: No	Overall College Admit Rate: 70% Undergrad Enrollment: 2,791 Total Enrollment: 3,591	BFA Musical Theatre Degrees Awarded in the Program(s) (2020): 24	Pre-screen req. Audition req.
Temple University 1801 N Broad St, Philadelphia, PA 19122	GPA: 3.48 SAT (ERW): N/A* SAT (M): N/A* ACT (C): N/A* *Test-optional ED: No	Overall College Admit Rate: 71% Undergrad Enrollment: 27,306 Total Enrollment: 37,236	BFA Musical Theatre Degrees Awarded in the Program(s) (2020): 8	Pre-screen req. Audition req.
University of the Arts 320 S. Broad Street, Philadelphia, PA 19102	GPA: N/A SAT (ERW): N/A* SAT (M): N/A* ACT (C): N/A* *Test-optional ED: No	Overall College Admit Rate: 76% Undergrad Enrollment: 1,380 Total Enrollment: 1,530	BFA Theatre: Musical Theatre Degrees Awarded in the Program(s) (2020): 31	Pre-screen not req. Audition req.

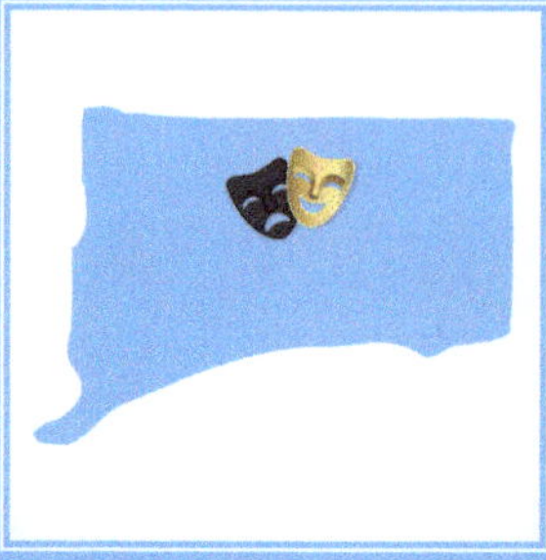

CONNECTICUT

MAINE

MASSACHUSETTS

NEW HAMPSHIRE

NEW JERSEY

NEW YORK

PENNSYLVANIA

RHODE ISLAND

VERMONT

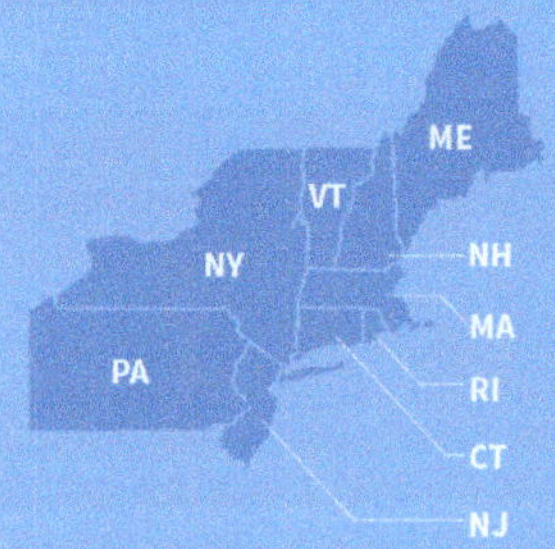

UNIVERSITY OF HARTFORD - HARTT SCHOOL

Address: 200 Bloomfield Avenue, West Hartford, CT 06117
Website: *https://www.hartford.edu/academics/schools-colleges/hartt/academics/theatre/music-theatre.aspx*
Contact: *https://www.hartford.edu/contact.aspx*
Phone: (860) 768-4100
Email: uofhart@hartford.edu

COST OF ATTENDANCE:

Tuition & Fees: $44,885 | **Additional Expenses:** $17,667
Total: $62,552

Financial Aid: https://www.hartford.edu/admission/financial-aid/default.aspx

ADDITIONAL INFORMATION:

Available Degree(s)

- BFA Music Theatre

Freshman Audition Requirement

University of Hartford participates in the Paper Mill Playhouse Common Pre-Screen. For more information, please refer to Chapter 8. Submit via Acceptd.

- Songs (Option A)
- Monologues (Option A)
- Dance Option (Required)
- Ballet Option (Optional)
- Wild Card (Required)

If you pass the Pre-Screen, you will be invited to a callback where you must demonstrate singing ability, a monologue, and dance exercises.

Scholarships Offered

The Hartt School offers aid to students based on the audition process and academic achievement. Awards go up to full tuition and are renewable for four years. In addition, all students may be eligible for institutional scholarships. Scholarships go up to full tuition. Students are automatically considered for academic scholarships when they apply to the University of Hartford.

Special Opportunities

At the Hartt School, fourth-year students are in residence at Goodspeed Musicals in January. Additionally, many students are members of the Equity Membership Candidate Program. This program allows actors-in-training to credit their theatrical work in certain theaters towards future membership in the Actor's Equity Association.

Notable Alumni

Keisha Gilles, Riza Takahashi, and Orin Wolf

BOSTON CONSERVATORY AT BERKLEE

Address: 8 Fenway, Boston, MA 02215
Website: *https://bostonconservatory.berklee.edu/musical-theater*
Contact: *https://bostonconservatory.berklee.edu/about/contact*
Phone: (617) 912-9153
Email: conservatoryadmissions@berklee.edu

COST OF ATTENDANCE:

Tuition & Fees: $48,512 | **Additional Expenses:** $21,054
Total: $69,566

Financial Aid: https://bostonconservatory.berklee.edu/financial-aid

ADDITIONAL INFORMATION:

Available Degree(s)

- BFA Theatre: Musical Theatre

Freshman Audition Requirement
Boston Conservatory at Berklee participates in the Paper Mill Playhouse Common Pre-Screen. For more information, please refer to Chapter 8.

- Songs (Option A)
- Monologues (Option A)
- Dance or Wild Card (optional, but recommended)

Students who pass the pre-screen may proceed to the live audition.

- Headshot & resume
- 2 contrasting monologues
- 2 contrasting songs
- 90-minute live dance class
- Virtual dance option: live improv. class
- Students may request a fully recorded audition but must contact admissions

Scholarships Offered
All students are automatically considered for merit-based, institutional scholarships when they apply to the Conservatory. There are many donor scholarships and endowed funds available to all students. In addition, Boston Conservatory at Berklee students are automatically considered for the Thrive Scholarship.

Special Opportunities
Students gain foundational knowledge in musical theatre, ear training, audition techniques. Boston Conservatory presents five stage productions and six faculty-directed studio productions, a dozen senior-directed shows, cabaret-style shows, and plays. In Boston, where there are more than 100 theatre companies, musical theatre opportunities abound. With rigorous training and successful graduates, students' possibilities are limitless.

Notable Alumni
Nick Adams, David Benoit, Adam Berry, Jennifer R. Blake, Angela Christian, Erin Davie, Kimiko Glenn, Josie de Guzman, Chad Kimball, Eddie Korbich, Victoria Livengood, Rachael MacFarlane, Constantine Maroulis, Katharine McPhee, Shoba Narayan, Travis Nesbitt, Jack Noseworthy, Hayley Podschun, Reva Rice, Drew Sarich, Keesha Sharp, Nikki Snelson, Lin Tucci, and Stephanie Umoh

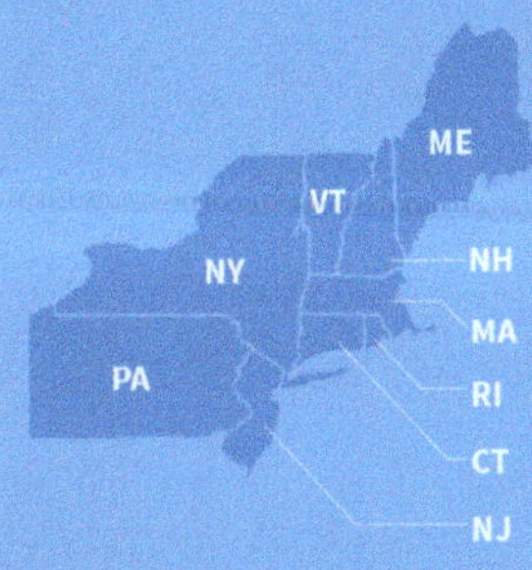

CONNECTICUT

MAINE

MASSACHUSETTS

NEW HAMPSHIRE

NEW JERSEY

NEW YORK

PENNSYLVANIA

RHODE ISLAND

VERMONT

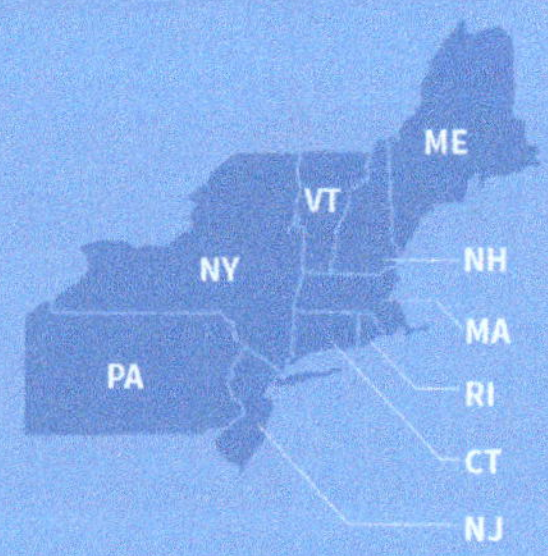

EMERSON COLLEGE

Address: 120 Boylston St., Boston, MA 02116
Website: *https://www.emerson.edu/programs/musical-theatre-bfa*
Contact: *https://www.emerson.edu/contact*
Phone: (617) 824-8500
Email: admission@emerson.edu
Other locations: Los Angeles, CA

COST OF ATTENDANCE:

Tuition & Fees: $51,264 | **Additional Expenses:** $19,644
Total: $70,908

Financial Aid: https://www.emerson.edu/admissions-aid/undergraduate-admission/financial-aid-scholarships

ADDITIONAL INFORMATION:

Available Degree(s)

- BFA Musical Theatre

Freshman Audition Requirement

Emerson College participates in the Paper Mill Playhouse Common Pre-Screen. However, you may follow either the Emerson College Musical Theatre Requirements or the Paper Mill Playhouse Common Pre-Screen. For more information, please refer to Chapter 8. Submit via Acceptd. Students who pass the pre-screen move on to the audition.

Emerson College Musical Theatre Prescreen Requirements

- 1 contemporary monologue
- 1 song with accompaniment

OR

Paper Mill Playhouse Common Pre-Screen:

- Songs (Option A)
- Monologues (Option A)
- Dance and Wildcard not accepted

Audition:

- 2 contrasting monologues
- 2 contrasting songs
- Dance Call
- Resume and Headshot

Scholarships Offered

The Trustees Scholarship is awarded to students who are accepted into the Honors Program. The award amount is $28,000 per year. An Honors Program essay is required with the admission application for consideration. The Aspire Scholarship is merit-based and awards $10,000-$40,000 annually. No additional essay is required for the Aspire Scholarship.

Special Opportunities

Boston's Theater District offers the perfect location to be coached by a distinguished faculty. Performing at Emerson Stage, students gain studio experience to project your personality. Emerson also has the art deco Robert J. Orchard Stage at the Paramount Center and the magnificent 1,200-seat Cutler Majestic Theatre. Students bring their years of experience to the New York City stage for a senior showcase and a second senior showcase in Boston.

Notable Alumni

Joseph Leo Bwarie, Andrea Martin, Betsy Morgan, and Henry Winkler

MONTCLAIR STATE UNIVERSITY

Address: 1 Normal Ave., Montclair, NJ 07043
Website: *https://www.montclair.edu/theatre-and-dance/academic-programs/undergraduate/bfa-musical-theatre/*
Contact: *https://www.montclair.edu/admissions/contact-us/*
Phone: (973) 655-4000
Email: msuadm@montclair.edu

COST OF ATTENDANCE:

In-State Tuition & Fees: $13,293 | **Additional Expenses:** $16,388
Total: $29,681

Out-of-State Tuition & Fees: $21,418 | **Additional Expenses:** $16,388
Total: $37,806

Financial Aid: https://www.montclair.edu/admissions/cost-and-financial-aid/

ADDITIONAL INFORMATION:

Available Degree(s)

- BFA Musical Theatre

Freshman Audition Requirement

Montclair State University participates in the Paper Mill Playhouse Common Pre-Screen. For more information, please refer to Chapter 8. Submit via Acceptd.

- Songs (Option A)
- Monologues (Option A)
- Dance (Required) – choose Dance or Ballet
- Wild Card (Optional)

Students who pass the pre-screen will be notified to submit a full audition via Zoom or in person. Applicants may instead choose to participate in a Partner Organization audition alternative.

Scholarships Offered

The Presidential Scholars Program is available to high school students who have high academic achievement. The award amount depends on the level of achievement. Montclair State also offers the Performing Arts Scholarship to all BFA Musical Theatre students who maintain a 3.0+ GPA. This award allows out-of-state and international students to pay in-state tuition rates.

Special Opportunities

This program is located 30 minutes away from Manhattan. Students often intern at on- and off-Broadway productions. Students also may perform in Montclair's fully-staged main stage, workshops, recitals, operas, and more.

Notable Alumni

Erick Avari, Stephen Bienskie, Kevin Carolan, Gerard McIntyre, Wilson Mendietta, Allison Strong, Michele Tauber, and Stuart Zagnit

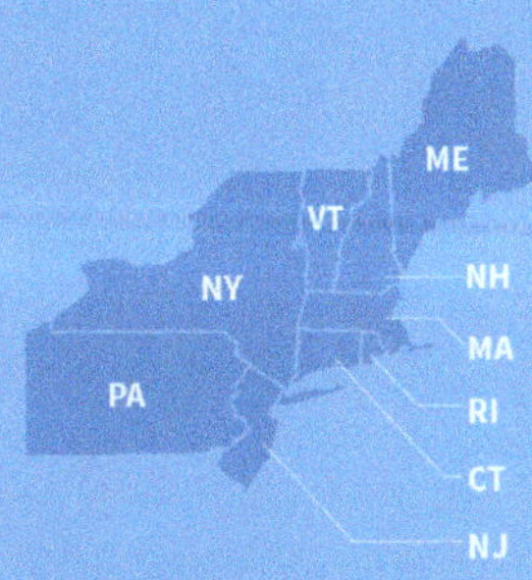

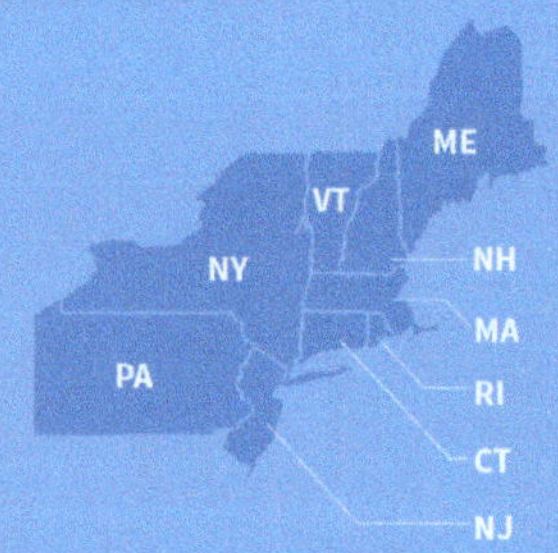

RIDER UNIVERSITY

Address: 2083 Lawrenceville Rd, Lawrenceville, NJ 08648
Website: *https://www.rider.edu/academics/colleges-schools/westminster-college-arts/sfpa/programs/musical-theatre*
Contact: *https://www.rider.edu/about/contact-us*
Phone: (609) 896-5000
Email: admissions@rider.edu

COST OF ATTENDANCE:

Tuition & Fees: $37,050 | **Additional Expenses:** $15,710
Total: $52,760

Financial Aid: https://www.rider.edu/tuition-aid/financial-aid

ADDITIONAL INFORMATION:

Available Degree(s)

- BFA Musical Theatre
- BA Theatre, concentration in Musical Theatre

Freshman Audition Requirement

Montclair State University participates in the Paper Mill Playhouse Common Pre-Screen. For more information, please refer to Chapter 8. Submit via Acceptd.

- Songs (Option A or B)
- Monologues (Option A or B)
- Dance (Required)
- Wild Card (Optional)

Students who pass the pre-screen move on to the live audition.

- 1-2 songs
- Monologue from pre-screen
- Resume & headshot

Scholarships Offered

Rider University offers numerous merit-based scholarships ranging from $12,000 to full tuition. Applicants that are test-optional are eligible for any of these scholarships. Students are automatically considered for all scholarships when they submit their application, however the Trustee Scholarship requires an additional essay.

Special Opportunities

At Rider University, all students are required to meet the Engaged Learning graduation requirement. This consists of taking coursework/experiences in six categories: leadership and mentorship, study abroad, guided research, civic and community engagement, arts, media, & creativity, and internships/fieldwork. This approach allows students to become well-rounded global citizens. Furthermore, Rider University's close proximity to New York City allows students greater opportunities to supplement their training with professional experiences.

Notable Alumni

Matt Cook, William Mastrosimone, James Morgart, Joanne Nosuchinsky, and Gerald Peary

AMERICAN MUSICAL & DRAMATIC ACADEMY (AMDA)

Address: 211 W 61st St., New York, NY 10023
Website: *https://www.amda.edu/programs/bfa-mt*
Contact: *https://www.amda.edu/contact-us*
Phone: (800) 367-7908
Email: admissionsteam@amda.edu
Other locations: Los Angeles, CA

COST OF ATTENDANCE:

Tuition & Fees: $44,260 | **Additional Expenses:** $19,560
Total: $63,820

Financial Aid: https://www.amda.edu/scholarships-financial-aid

ADDITIONAL INFORMATION:

Available Degree(s)

- BFA Music Theatre
- BFA Performing Arts: Music Theatre
- BFA Performing Arts: Music Theatre & Creative Content Development

Freshman Audition Requirement

Complete an audition in-person at AMDA

- 60-90 sec. song from the Musical Theatre repertoire
- Monologue
- Accompanist provided for you
- Interview

Scholarships Offered

Institutional scholarships are need- and/or merit-based. These awards are based on the audition and other factors seen during the application process. Furthermore, the AMDA accepts scholarship nominations for students.

Special Opportunities

The BFA programs in Music Theatre or Performing Arts: Music Theatre are all offered on AMDA's Los Angeles campus by default. However, students have the opportunity to combine the NY Integrated Certificate Program with the LA BFA Music Theatre degree program. This program is referred to as the Study in NY + LA: Integrated Certificate to BFA and is unique to the Musical Theatre, Acting, and Dance majors. Students in this program spend 4 semesters in Los Angeles and 4 semesters in New York. There is also an accelerated option that allows students to complete this special program track in 2.5 years.

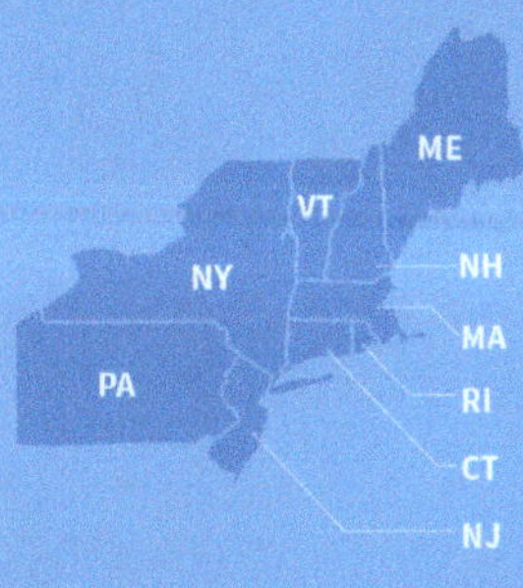

Notable Alumni

Nina Arianda, Tyne Daly, Jason Derulo, Jesse Tyler Ferguson, Christopher Jackson, Caissie Levy, Jeremy Pope, Anthony Ramos, Paul Sorvino, Sarah Stiles

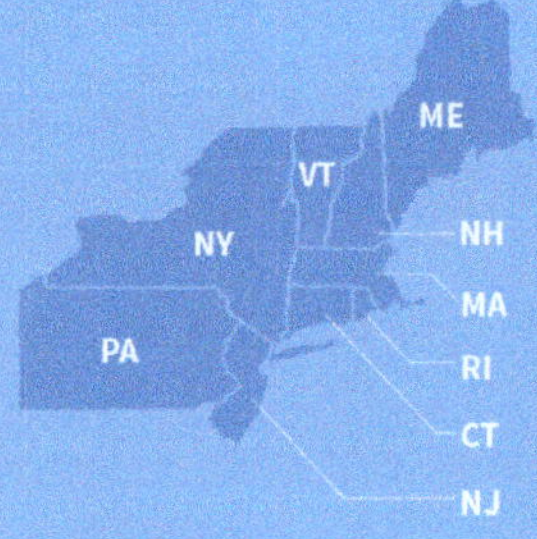

ITHACA COLLEGE

Address: 953 Danby Road, Ithaca, NY 14850
Website: *https://www.ithaca.edu/academics/school-humanities-and-sciences/theatre-arts/academic-programs/bfa-musical-theatre*
Contact: *https://www.ithaca.edu/contact/*
Phone: (607) 274-3011
Email: admission@ithaca.edu

COST OF ATTENDANCE:

Tuition & Fees: $46,610 | **Additional Expenses:** $18,989
Total: $65,599

Financial Aid: https://www.ithaca.edu/tuition-financial-aid

ADDITIONAL INFORMATION:

Available Degree(s)

- BFA Musical Theatre

Freshman Audition Requirement

Ithaca College participates in the Paper Mill Playhouse Common Pre-Screen. For more information, please refer to Chapter 8. Submit via Acceptd.

- Songs (Option A)
- Monologues (Option B)
- Dance Option (Required) – choose Ballet or Dance
- Wild Card (Optional)

If you pass the pre-screen, you will be offered a chance to audition virtually, or in-person in Ithaca, NY and Chicago, IL.

- Prepare same materials as pre-screen

Scholarships Offered

The Ithaca College Scholarship is awarded to students with exceptional academic achievements and/or talent. No separate application is required. The Ithaca Leadership Scholar Program Award requires a separate application and awards students $7,000 based on demonstrated leadership and superior academic performance. In addition, musical theatre majors may apply for the Ithaca Premier Talent Scholarship.

Special Opportunities

Students participate in extensive weekly training in acting, dance, and voice, including private lessons. Classes include scene study, movement for the stage, audition techniques, and masterclasses. Students can study drama for a semester at Ithaca College's London Center. On-campus, Ithaca College produces two musicals annually, two plays, an opera, a dance concert, and studio shows. Students are encouraged to audition at local professional theatres. Furthermore, a one-week alumni network field studies trip is offered in New York City.

Notable Alumni

Jerad Bortz, Kerry Butler, Matt Cavenaugh, Michelle Federer, Ben Feldman, Jeremy Jordan, Megan Ort, Caesar Samayoa, Q. Smith, and Aaron Tveit

THE JUILLIARD SCHOOL

Address: 60 Lincoln Center Plaza, New York, NY 10023
Website: *https://www.juilliard.edu/drama*
Contact: *https://www.juilliard.edu/admissions/connect-us*
Phone: (212) 799-5000
Email: admissions@juilliard.edu

COST OF ATTENDANCE:

Tuition & Fees: $51,230 | **Additional Expenses:** $22,714
Total: $73,944

Financial Aid: https://www.juilliard.edu/campus-life/financial-aid

ADDITIONAL INFORMATION:

Available Degree(s)

- BFA Acting

Freshman Audition Requirement

Applicants who currently live outside of the US and Canada are required to do a pre-screen regardless of citizenship status or permanent address. Pre-screens are optional for applicants living in Alaska, Hawaii, Puerto Rico, US Virgin Islands, or Canada.

Audition requirements:

- 4 monologues
- 1 song a capella

Callback requirements:

- Repeat audition pieces
- Cold readings
- Group exercises and improv.

Scholarships Offered

Juilliard Scholarship award amounts vary based on individual need and merit. According to Juilliard, approximately 85% of their students receive institutional aid. Applicants are encouraged to use the net price calculator for estimating potential aid amount.

Special Opportunities

Students do not audition for roles in school productions but are cast by faculty. In their first and second years, roles are assigned to serve the needs of individual students. Students participate in a different play each quarter. In the fall of the third year, students have 2 performance opportunities. In the spring, they participate in a musical cabaret and a heightened-language play. By the fourth year, students participate in Playwrights Festival workshops.

Notable Alumni

Adam Driver, Patti LuPone, Elizabeth Marvel, Tim Blake Nelson, Phillipa Soo, Michael Stuhlbarg, Michael Urie and Benjamin Walker

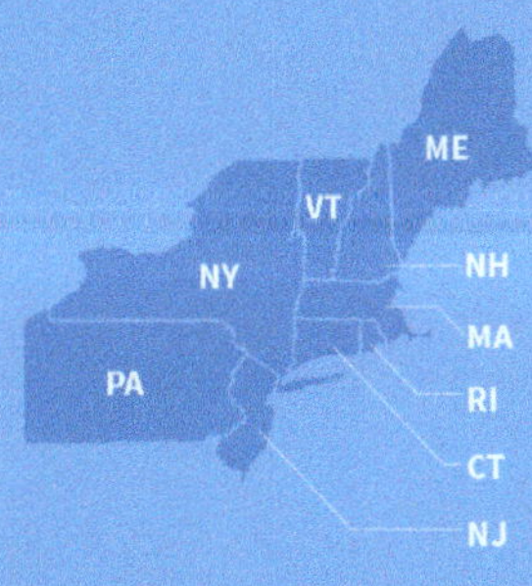

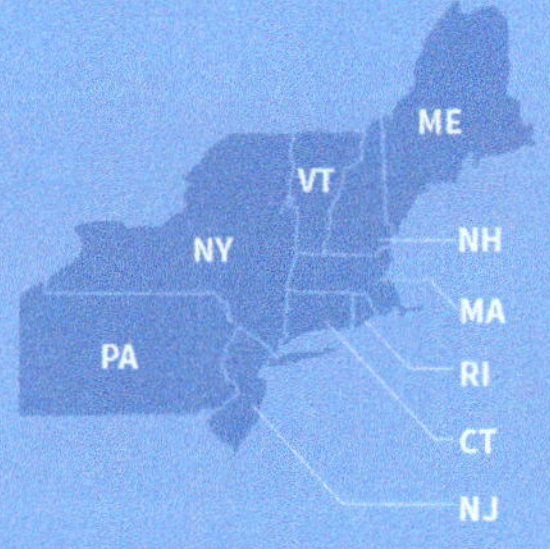

LONG ISLAND UNIVERSITY POST

Address: 720 Northern Blvd, Greenvale, NY 11548
Website: *https://www.liu.edu/post/academics/~/link.aspx?_id=9CCC4554117A47EA91EFE801134CE8D9&_z=z*
Contact: *https://apply.liu.edu/form/inquiry.aspx?id=1*
Phone: (516) 299-2900
Email: post-enroll@liu.edu

COST OF ATTENDANCE:

Tuition & Fees: $37,926 | **Additional Expenses:** $15,258
Total: $53,184

Financial Aid: https://www.liu.edu/enrollment-services/financial-aid

ADDITIONAL INFORMATION:

Available Degree(s)

- BFA Theatre Arts (Musical Theatre)

Freshman Audition Requirement

All applicants must audition and interview by appointment only. Students are strongly encouraged to audition via the National Unified Auditions. Auditions may be completed live or online.

- 1 short monologue
- 1 song
- Resume and headshot

Scholarships Offered

LIU Post awards over $100 million in scholarships & grants each year.

Special Opportunities

Rigorous grounding in history, literature, theories, and methodologies of Suzuki, Stanislavsky, Chekhov, and Linklater techniques, and work with professional musicians, actors, and playwrights. Taught by professional theatre artists and coordinated with the Post Theatre Company, students develop a riveting stage presence, dynamic physicality, emotional authenticity, and a commanding voice. Individual and ensemble training in stage, television, and film acting. The program culminates with a senior showcase before agents, managers, and directors in New York City. Students intern on and off-campus and travel to festivals in the U.S. and abroad.

Notable Alumni

Ed Lauter, Dina Meyer, Nicholas Pileggi, Michael Tucci, Denise Vasi

MANHATTAN SCHOOL OF MUSIC

Address: 130 Claremont Ave, New York, NY 10027
Website: *https://www.msmnyc.edu/programs/musical-theatre/*
Contact: *https://www.msmnyc.edu/contact-us/*
Phone: (917) 493-4436
Email: admissions@msmnyc.edu

COST OF ATTENDANCE:

Tuition & Fees: $49,130 | **Additional Expenses:** $21,795
Total: $70,925

Financial Aid: https://www.msmnyc.edu/admissions/scholarships-financial-aid/

ADDITIONAL INFORMATION:

Available Degree(s)

- BM Musical Theatre

Freshman Audition Requirement

Manhattan School of Music requires a pre-screen submitted online.

- 2 contrasting songs
- 1 monologue
- 1-minute dance

Applicants who pass the pre-screen are invited to audition in person or virtually.

- 2 contrasting songs
- 1 monologue
- Dance call (1 hour)

Scholarships Offered

MSM offers scholarships to students based on demonstrated financial need and merit. The President's Award is also available to students with no financial need but high academic achievement/ talent.

Special Opportunities

As stated on their website, MSM's Musical Theatre Program is, "the only stand-alone conservatory program in New York City." Faculty in this program include Broadway performers and creators. Students may participate any of their yearly productions.

Notable Alumni

Ahmed Best, Shuler Hensley, Sara Hershkowitz, Lisa Hopkins, Max Kuenzer, Catherine Malfitano, Nellie McKay, Simon O'Neill, Jarrett Winters Morley, Dolora Zajick, and Zane Zapata

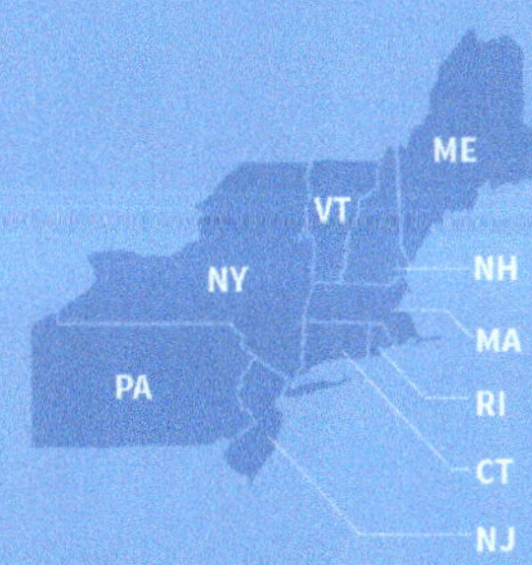

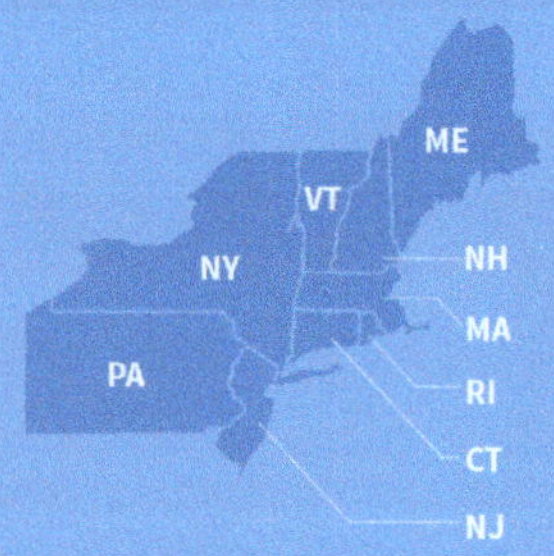

MARYMOUNT MANHATTAN COLLEGE

Address: 221 East 71st Street New York, NY 10021
Website: *https://www.mmm.edu/academics/theatre-arts/musical-theatre-major/*
Contact: *https://www.mmm.edu/admissions/contact-us/*
Phone: (212) 517-0430
Email: admissions@mmm.edu

COST OF ATTENDANCE:

Tuition & Fees: $37,410 | **Additional Expenses:** $26,880
Total: $64,290

Financial Aid: https://www.mmm.edu/admissions/financial-aid-scholarships.php

ADDITIONAL INFORMATION:

Available Degree(s)

- BFA Musical Theatre

Freshman Audition Requirement
An audition is required for the BFA in Musical Theatre. No pre-screen is required. Once you submit your application, you will have access to the Theatre Audition form. Applicants may complete their audition live (virtually through Acceptd) or digitally through pre-recorded videos.

Live Virtual Audition
- Headshot
- Resume
- 2 contrasting songs
- 1 monologue

Digital Audition
- 2 contrasting songs
- 1 monologue
- Wild Card Video Required

Scholarships Offered
Scholarships are available for successful candidates. Consideration for these competitive talent awards is made at the time of the audition. Scholarships are renewable for four years if the student remains academically successful and stays in the program.

Special Opportunities
Students take courses in cabaret, songwriting, pop/rock, camera work, and Shakespeare. Students dance five days a week, take master classes with top professionals, and work in an intimate setting. Students perform in musicals, off-site Studio Workshop productions at the National Dance Institute or York Theatre Company. Students can minor in music, music industry, or communication and media arts. Students study The Musical Theatre Song Portfolio and Professional Preparation: Musical Theatre. Given MMC's location, students often get free tickets to Broadway and Off-Broadway shows and gain professional internships in casting offices and theatre companies.

Notable Alumni
Annaleigh Ashford, Candace Bailey, Maddie Baillio, Laverne Cox, Alexandra Daddario, Abby Elliott, Spencer Grammar, Mimi Imfurst, Moire Kelly, Erik Palladino, Andrew Rannells, Melissa Rauch, Emmy Raver-Lampman, Alexander Skarsgard, Paige Spara, Chris Stafford, Tika Sumpter, Vanessa Trump, Jenna Ushkowitz, and Adrienna Warren

MOLLOY COLLEGE

Address: 1000 Hempstead Ave, Rockville Centre, NY 11570
Website: *https://www.molloy.edu/academics/undergraduate-programs/molloy-cap21-theatre-arts-program*
Contact: *https://www.molloy.edu/about-molloy-college/contact-molloy*
Phone: 1-800-4-MOLLOY
Email: info@molloy.edu

COST OF ATTENDANCE:

Tuition & Fees: $32,900 | **Additional Expenses:** $17,575
Total: $50,475

Financial Aid: https://www.molloy.edu/admissions/financial-aid

ADDITIONAL INFORMATION:

Available Degree(s)

- BFA Theatre Arts

Freshman Audition Requirement

Molloy College participates in the Paper Mill Playhouse Common Pre-Screen. For more information, please refer to Chapter 8. Submit via Acceptd.

- Songs (Option A)
- Monologues (Option A)
- Dance Option (Optional)
- Wild Card (Optional)

If you pass the pre-screen, you will be offered a chance to audition online or in person.

Scholarships Offered

Molloy College offers numerous need-based and merit-based scholarships. Rewards range from $1,000-$20,000. Musical Theatre students may qualify for Molloy's Fine Arts and Performing Arts Scholarships, which range up to full tuition. Students are considered for these scholarships on the basis of their audition, documented experience, or a portfolio.

Special Opportunities

Students in the Molloy College/CAP21 program enjoy the benefits of Molloy's campus experience along with the professional musical theatre experience via the Collaborative Arts Project 21 (CAP21) in New York City. Students split their time between the two campuses.

Notable Alumni

Maddy Apple, Sosie Bacon, Kristen Bell, Alex Brightman, Lady Gaga, Adam Jacobs, Matthew Morrison, Javier Munoz, Ali Stroker, and Jason Tam

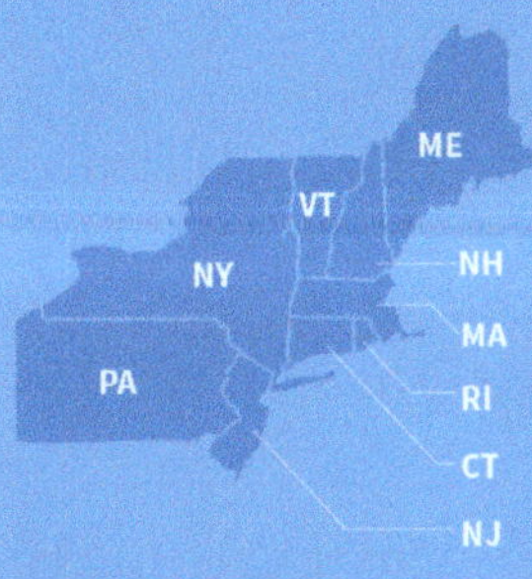

CONNECTICUT
MAINE
MASSACHUSETTS
NEW HAMPSHIRE
NEW JERSEY
NEW YORK
PENNSYLVANIA
RHODE ISLAND
VERMONT

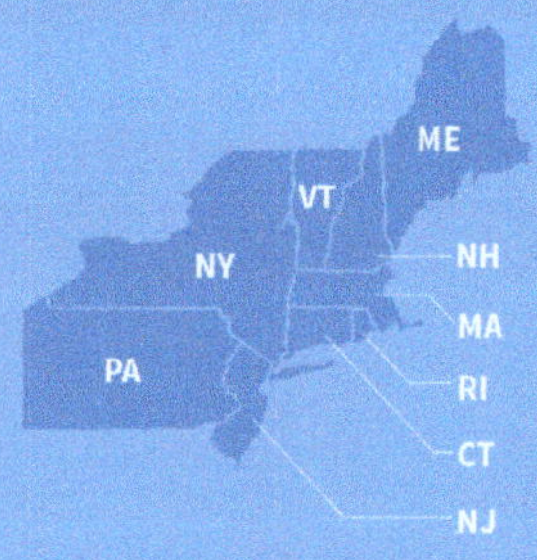

THE NEW SCHOOL

Address: 66 West 12th Street, New York, NY 10011
Website: *https://www.newschool.edu/bachelors-program/musical-theater-bfa/*
Contact: *https://www.newschool.edu/about/contact/*
Phone: (212) 229-5150
Email: finish@newschool.edu

COST OF ATTENDANCE:

Tuition & Fees: $51,722 | **Additional Expenses:** N/A
Total: $51,722

Financial Aid: https://www.newschool.edu/admission/financial-aid/how-to-apply/

ADDITIONAL INFORMATION:

Available Degree(s)

- BFA Musical Theatre*

*This program is only open to graduates of the American Musical and Dramatic Academy (AMDA). AMDA students may transfer credits to the Bachelor's Program for Adults and Transfer Students.

Audition Requirement

AMDA students must have completed 60 transfer credits from the AMDA Integrated program. 60 additional credits are required, 48 of which are in liberal arts. An audition is not required.

Scholarships Offered

The New School offers merit-based and need-based aid to students. Students are automatically considered for merit-based scholarships. These are based on the strength of the application and portfolio. Need-based aid is available to students who are eligible and submit the FAFSA.

Special Opportunities

Graduates of AMDA's studio program may finish their degree at The New School, earning a BFA in Musical Theatre.

Notable Alumni

Bea Arthur, Sherri Eden Barber, Harry Belafonte, Marlon Brando, Julia Chan, Andreas Damm, Mashup Deen, Nick Gandiello, Lorraine Hansberry, Walter Matthau, Janine Nabers, Victoria Pike, Rod Steiger, Elaine Stritch, Hadi Tabbal, Benjamin Thys, Kirya Traber, Tennessee Williams, and Shelley Winters

NEW YORK UNIVERSITY

Address: 721 Broadway, New York, NY 10003
Website: *https://tisch.nyu.edu/drama*
Contact: *https://tisch.nyu.edu/drama/contact-us*
Phone: (212) 998-1850
Email: tisch.drama.ug@nyu.edu

COST OF ATTENDANCE:

Tuition & Fees: $56,500 | **Additional Expenses:** $24,378
Total: $80,878

Financial Aid: https://tisch.nyu.edu/admissions/financial-aid

ADDITIONAL INFORMATION:

Available Degree(s)

- BFA Drama, studio in Musical Theatre

Freshman Audition Requirement
All drama major applicants must undergo an artistic review. When submitting their application, students are asked to choose consideration for "All Studios" or "Musical Theatre Only". Please note, when choosing "All Studios", you will be considered for Musical Theatre however if you do not pass, you will be placed in one of the acting studios. If you choose "Musical Theatre Only", and do not pass the review, you will be denied admission to NYU.

Submit all materials to the NYU Drama Artistic Review portal. Applicants may choose a live artistic review or a digital submission.

- 2 contrasting monologues
- 2 contrasting songs
- Dance evaluation
- Interview

Digital submissions
- 2 monologues
- Singing videos (uploaded) and live on Zoom
- Dance video

Scholarships Offered
NYU offers various need-based and/or merit-based scholarships to students in any major. Some examples include the AnBryce Scholarships (GPA 3.5+), the Martin Luther King, Jr. Scholarships, and several others. NYU Tisch recommends students apply for outside funding. The Tisch Scholarship Guide is a resource that includes various scholarship opportunities.

Special Opportunities
High school students may join the Summer High School Program, where they can showcase their work, grow as performers, and learn about what NYU's theatre department has to offer. High school students may also join the free Future Theatre Artists Workshop.

Notable Alumni
Jelani Alladin, Rachel Bloom, Lady Gaga, Adam Jacobs, Nikki M. James, Denis Jones, Moisés Kaufman, Idina Menzel, Matthew Morrison, Javier Muñoz, Donna Murphy, Anthony Rapp, Ali Stroker, Shaina Taub, and Brandon Uranowitz

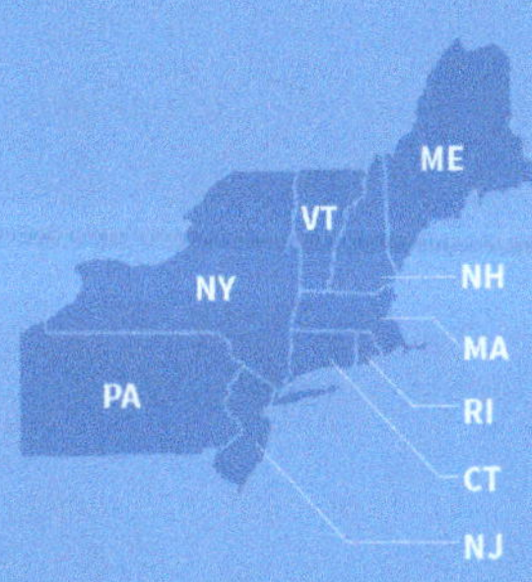

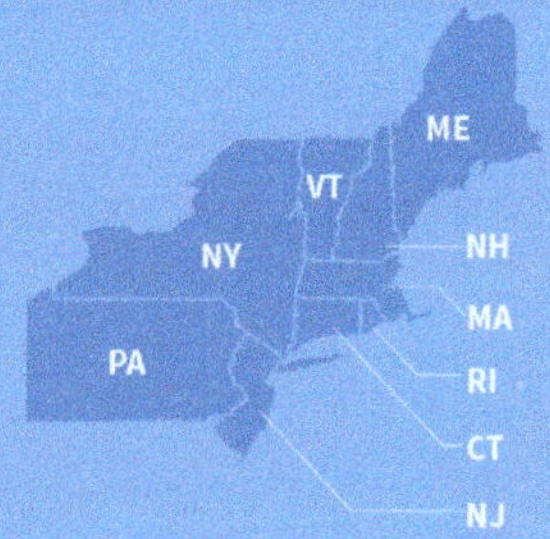

PACE UNIVERSITY

Address: 1 Pace Plaza, New York, NY 10038
Website: *http://performingarts.pace.edu/bfa-musical-theater*
Contact: *https://www.pace.edu/contact-us*
Phone: (866) 722-3338
Email: undergradadmission@pace.edu

COST OF ATTENDANCE:

Tuition & Fees: $48,830 | **Additional Expenses:** $23,270
Total: $72,100

Financial Aid: https://www.pace.edu/financial-aid/

ADDITIONAL INFORMATION:

Available Degree(s)

- BFA Musical Theatre

Freshman Audition Requirement

Pace University participates in the Paper Mill Playhouse Common Pre-Screen. For more information, please refer to Chapter 8. Submit via Acceptd.

- Songs (Option A or B)
- Monologues (Option A)
- Dance Option A (Required)
- Wild Card (Optional)
- Headshot and resume

Students who pass the pre-screen are invited for a callback audition.

- 1 monologue
- Up to 3 contrasting songs

Scholarships Offered

Pace offers two institutional grants: The Pace Grant and the Trustee Tuition Grant ($500). They also offer several merit scholarships that are renewable so long as students maintain a certain GPA, which depends on the type of scholarship. Students are also considered for need-based scholarships. There are also Dyson College Scholarships specifically for each program. The average non-need-based scholarship awarded to first-year students is $24,996.

Special Opportunities

Pace offers conservatory-style focused training, synthesizing acting, singing, and dancing taught by industry professionals. Masterclasses and members of the Artist-in-Residence program. Private voice lessons. Freshmen perform in a cabaret show during spring semester. Musical theatre students take 9 required dance classes. Advanced dancers may become part of the Commercial Dance minor with dances in the BFA Commercial Dance Program. Students organize a senior showcase for agents, directors, managers, and designers from NYC and LA.

Notable Alumni

Ailee, Michelle Borth, Trevor Braun, Kate Bristol, Bradley Cooper, Paul Dano, Dominique Fishback, Jordan Scott Gilbert, Matthew Humphreys, Tommy Nelson, Vincent Pastore, Diana Scarwid, Rafael L. Silva, and Glenn Taranto

SUNY CORTLAND

Address: 22 Graham Ave, Cortland, NY 13045
Website: *https://www2.cortland.edu/departments/performing-arts/musical-theatre-bfa*
Contact: *https://www2.cortland.edu/about/contact-us.dot*
Phone: (607) 753-2811
Email: admissions@cortland.edu

COST OF ATTENDANCE:

In-State Tuition & Fees: $8,815 | **Additional Expenses:** $13,200
Total: $22,015

Out-of-State Tuition & Fees: $18,725 | **Additional Expenses:** $13,200
Total: $31,925

Financial Aid: https://www2.cortland.edu/cost-aid/financial-aid/

ADDITIONAL INFORMATION:

Available Degree(s)

- BFA Musical Theatre

Freshman Audition Requirement

SUNY Cortland does not require a pre-screen. Auditions are required either in person or virtually. Email videos to PerformingArtsDepartment@cortland.edu.

- 2 contrasting songs
- 1 monologue
- Dance (Virtual: 30-60 sec., In-Person: Class)
- Headshot

Scholarships Offered

Students are automatically considered for SUNY Cortland grants and merit scholarships when they submit their general application. Rewards range from $2,500-$7,500 per year. Students are also welcome to apply for endowed scholarships.

Special Opportunities

SUNY Cortland's program emphasizes studio training, including 7 semesters fo ballet training, work with a voice teacher, and coursework in various forms of dance, acting, spoken voice, and more. Additionally, students may enjoy the recently renovated Dowd Fine Arts Center. This center houses a 400-seat theatre, private practice rooms, and other amenities for musical theatre students.

Notable Alumni

Hailey Aviva, Will Rivera, and Chloe Solan

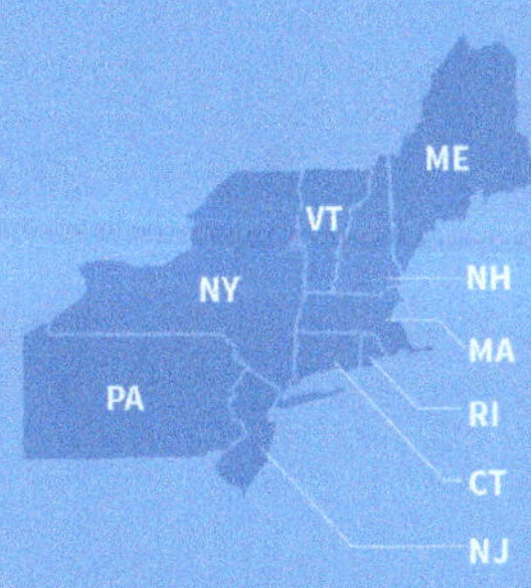

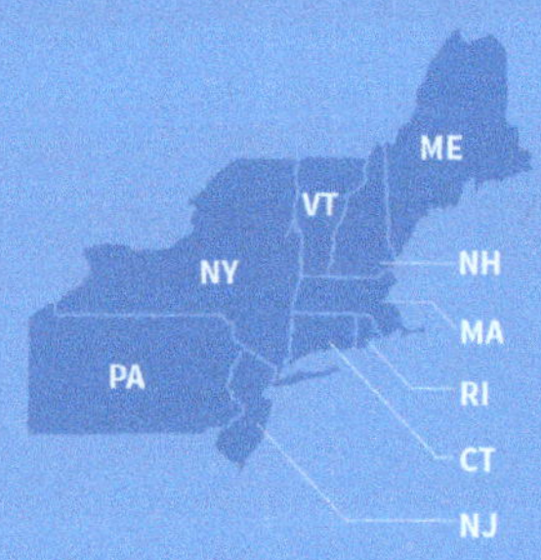

SYRACUSE UNIVERSITY

Address: 200 Crouse College, Syracuse, NY 13244
Website: *https://vpa.syr.edu/academics/drama/degree-programs/musical-theater-bfa/*
Contact: *https://vpa.syr.edu/about/contact/*
Phone: (315) 443-2769
Email: admissu@syr.edu

COST OF ATTENDANCE:

Tuition & Fees: $55,920 | **Additional Expenses:** $24,119
Total: $80,039

Financial Aid: https://www.syracuse.edu/admissions/cost-and-aid/

ADDITIONAL INFORMATION:

Available Degree(s)

- BFA Musical Theatre

Freshman Audition Requirement
Syracuse University allows applicants to opt in for "Musical Theater consideration only" or for Both Acting and Musical Theater. The requirements below are only for applicants interested in the Musical Theater program alone. Syracuse University participates in the Paper Mill Playhouse Common Pre-Screen. For more information, please refer to Chapter 8. Submit via Acceptd.

- Songs (Option A)
- Monologues (Option A)
- Dance Option (Required)
- Ballet Option (Optional)
- Wild Card (Required)
- Resume, statement, & headshot

Applicants with a successful pre-screen are invited for an in-person or virtual audition. Both formats require 2 contrasting monologues, 2 contrasting songs, a theatrical resume, and a headshot. The in-person audition will include a dance class while the virtual audition requires submission of a dance video.

Scholarships Offered
Syracuse University offers various merit-based and need-based scholarships and grants. Artistic Scholarships are awarded to students based on talent and a maintained cumulative GPA of 2.75+. The Distinguished Drama Performance Award offers $10,000 annually.

Special Opportunities
Syracuse University's conservatory-style, intensive training includes acting, dancing, and voice along with five mainstage productions and opportunities to perform with Syracuse Stage, a professional theatre company where students can earn points toward Equity membership candidacy. Syracuse offers musical theatre students a semester of study in New York City along with masterclasses to transition into acting with performers, agents, casting directors, and directors. Additionally, Syracuse offers networking opportunities and classes in auditioning where students have mock auditions with guest artists.

Notable Alumni
Taye Diggs, Peter Falk, Vera Farmiga, Jessie Mueller, Patti Murin, Julia Murney, Suzanne Pleshette, Aaron Sorkin, Jerry Stiller, Vanessa Williams, and Josh Young

UNIVERSITY AT BUFFALO

Address: University at Buffalo, Buffalo, NY 14260
Website: *https://arts-sciences.buffalo.edu/theatre-dance/undergraduate/bfa-music-theatre.html*
Contact: *https://arts-sciences.buffalo.edu/theatre-dance/about/contact-us.html*
Phone: (716) 645-6897
Email: td-theatredance@buffalo.edu

COST OF ATTENDANCE:

In-State Tuition & Fees: $10,724 | **Additional Expenses:** $18,142
Total: $28,866

Out-of-State Tuition & Fees: $28,444 | **Additional Expenses:** $18,142
Total: $46,586

Financial Aid: https://financialaid.buffalo.edu/

ADDITIONAL INFORMATION:

Available Degree(s)

- BFA Music Theatre

Freshman Audition Requirement

University at Buffalo requires an in-person audition.

- 2 contrasting songs
- 1 monologue
- Dance call
- Resume & headshot

Scholarships Offered

University at Buffalo offers various merit-based and need-based scholarships and grants including the Presidential Scholarship, Provost Scholarship, and Daniel Acker Scholarship.

Special Opportunities

The Department of Theatre and Dance puts together full productions that students may audition for, including two musicals, two plays, four dance concerts, and numerous student-directed plays per year. Students may also participate in workshops and masterclasses hosted by guest artists and professionals.

Notable Alumni

Brad Grey and Harvey Weinstein

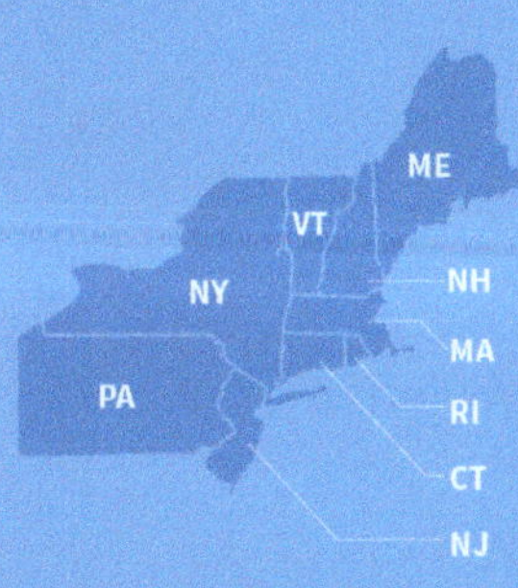

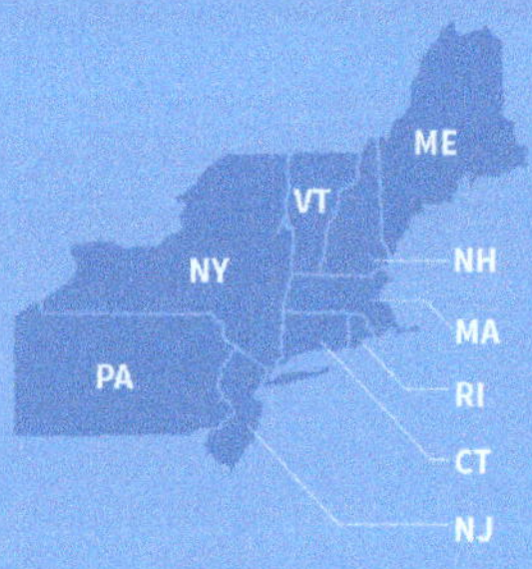

CARNEGIE MELLON UNIVERSITY

Address: 5000 Forbes Avenue, Pittsburgh, PA 15213
Website: *https://www.drama.cmu.edu/programs/undergraduate/acting-music-theater/*
Contact: *https://admission.enrollment.cmu.edu/pages/contact-us*
Phone: (412) 268-2082
Email: admission@andrew.cmu.edu

COST OF ATTENDANCE:

Tuition & Fees: $57,560 | **Additional Expenses:** $19,914
Total: $77,474

Financial Aid: https://www.cmu.edu/sfs/financial-aid/index.html

ADDITIONAL INFORMATION:

Available Degree(s)

- BFA Drama, option: Music Theater

Freshman Audition Requirement

Carnegie Mellon University (CMU) participates in the Paper Mill Playhouse Common Pre-Screen. For more information, please refer to Chapter 8. Submit via Acceptd.

- Songs (Option A)
- Monologues (Option B)
- Dance Option (Not Required)
- Wild Card (Not Required)

Scholarships Offered

CMU offers a need-based grant and endowed scholarships. The Presidential and Carnegie Scholarship programs are no longer available to incoming students.

Special Opportunities

This conservatory-style program offers seniors the chance to study at the Moscow Art Theatre or Sydney's NIDA. Students can assist theatre professionals to create a new musical with the Pittsburgh Civic Light Opera. Students showcase their talent by performing songs and monologues in New York, Los Angeles, and Pittsburgh.

Notable Alumni

Christian Borle, Eduardo Castro, Ted Danson, Cote de Pablo, Peggy Eisenhauer, Barbara Feldon, Sutton Foster, Josh Gad, Jeff Goldblum, Megan Hilty, Peter Hylenski, Cherry Jones, Jack Klugman, Kara Lindsay, Aaron Staton, Telly Leung, Joe Manganiello, Leslie Odom, Jr., Pablo Schreiber, Tamara Tunie, and John Wells

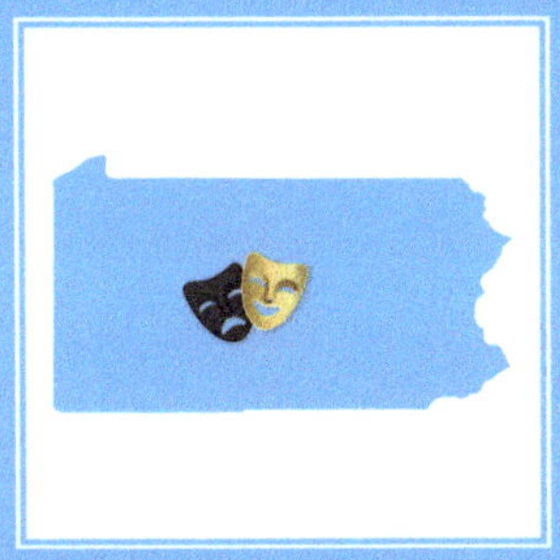

PENNSYLVANIA STATE UNIVERSITY (PENN STATE)

Address: 124 Borland Building, University Park, PA 16802
Website: *https://theatre.psu.edu/programs/musical-theatre*
Contact: *https://admissions.psu.edu/contact/*
Phone: (814) 865-2591
Email: admissions@psu.edu

COST OF ATTENDANCE:

In-State Tuition & Fees: $18,898 | **Additional Expenses:** $14,158
Total: $33,056

Out-of-State Tuition & Fees: $36,476 | **Additional Expenses:** $14,158
Total: $50,634

Financial Aid: https://studentaid.psu.edu/

ADDITIONAL INFORMATION:

Available Degree(s)

- BFA Musical Theatre

Freshman Audition Requirement
Penn State participates in the Paper Mill Playhouse Common Pre-Screen. For more information, please refer to Chapter 8. Submit via Acceptd.

- Songs (Option A)
- Monologues (Option A)
- Dance Option (Required)
- Wild Card (Optional)

Applicants with a successful pre-screen are invited for an in-person or virtual audition.

- Dance audition
- 2 vocal selections
- 1 monologue

Scholarships Offered
Penn State offers various university scholarships including the Discover Penn State Award ($6,000-6,500 annually) and the Provost's Award ($5,000 annually) as well as campus and college scholarships.

Special Opportunities
Students train in acting, voice, and dance. A class called Musical Theatre Styles offers Broadway dance and choreography. Penn State produces three musicals each year, along with new musical theatre works written by students on campus. Guest artists offer workshops on class in a program called the Master Class Series. Other opportunities include an annual trip to New York City and a course entitled "Business of the Business" that focuses on casting, agents, and budgeting. Students receive help creating a website, headshot, resume, video shoot, New York City showcase, and funding to audition and explore opportunities.

Notable Alumni
Caroline Bowman, Dan Gleason, Matthew Hydzik, Adam Jepsen, Nathan Lucrezio, Laurie Veldheer, and Alan Wiggins

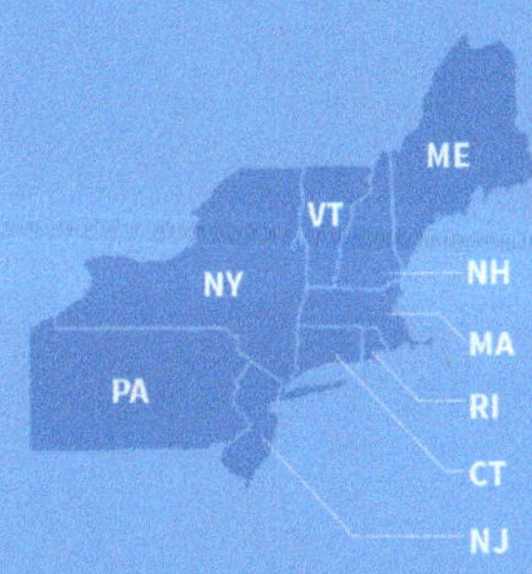

POINT PARK UNIVERSITY

Address: 201 Wood Street, Pittsburgh, PA 15222
Website: *https://www.pointpark.edu/Academics/Schools/COPA/COPADeptsMajors/Theatre/MusicalTheatre*
Contact: *https://www.pointpark.edu/contact*
Phone: (412) 391-4100
Email: enroll@pointpark.edu

COST OF ATTENDANCE:

Tuition & Fees: $44,420 | **Additional Expenses:** N/A
Total: $44,420

Financial Aid: https://www.pointpark.edu/Admissions/FinancialAid/index

ADDITIONAL INFORMATION:

Available Degree(s)

- BFA Musical Theatre

Freshman Audition Requirement

Point Park University participates in the Paper Mill Playhouse Common Pre-Screen. For more information, please refer to Chapter 8. Submit via Acceptd.

- Songs (Option A)
- Monologues (Option A)
- Dance Option (Required)
- Ballet Option (Optional)
- Wild Card (Optional)

Applicants with a successful pre-screen are invited to register for an in-person audition. Audition slots are available on a first-come, first served basis.

Scholarships Offered

Point Park University offers scholarships specific to the students in the Conservatory of Performing Arts. Some of these include the Artistic Achievement Scholarship ($5,000-$28,000) and the Dean's Academic Freshmen Scholarship ($5,000-$8,000).

Special Opportunities

Point Park University's BFA Musical Theatre Conservatory offers students some of the best training in acting, voice, speech, dance, music theory, sight-singing, ensemble singing, repertoire, script and score analysis, stage makeup, stagecraft, and production. This rigorous 131-credit program offers rigorous training, senior showcase in New York, and intensive training in dance. Students have the opportunity to audition for the Conservatory Theatre Company.

Notable Alumni

Stephanie Lynn Bissonnette, Maya Bowles, Viveca Chow, Jeff Gorti, Benjamin Mapp, Sarah Meahl, Ahmad Simmons, Lamont Walker II, and Tony Yazbeck

TEMPLE UNIVERSITY

Address: 1801 N Broad St, Philadelphia, PA 19122
Website: *https://www.temple.edu/academics/degree-programs/musical-theater-major-ca-must-bfa*
Contact: *https://www.temple.edu/contact/*
Phone: (215) 204-7000
Email: askanowl@temple.edu

COST OF ATTENDANCE:

In-State Tuition & Fees: $18,168 | **Additional Expenses:** $17,880
Total: $36,048

Out-of-State Tuition & Fees: $31,440 | **Additional Expenses:** $19,944
Total: $51,384

Financial Aid: https://admissions.temple.edu/costs-aid-scholarships/financial-aid-scholarships

ADDITIONAL INFORMATION:

Available Degree(s)

- BFA Musical Theatre

Freshman Audition Requirement
Penn State participates in the Paper Mill Playhouse Common Pre-Screen. For more information, please refer to Chapter 8. Submit via Acceptd.

- Songs (Option A)
- Monologues (Option A)
- Dance Option (Required)
- Ballet Option (Optional)
- Wild Card (Required)

Applicants with a successful pre-screen are invited for an in-person or virtual audition.

- 2 contrasting songs
- 1 monologue
- Dance call
- Resume & headshot

Scholarships Offered
All students who submit their application by February 1 are automatically considered for merit scholarships. Award amounts range from $1,000 to full tuition.

Special Opportunities
Students in Temple University's program build their technical skills, participate in hands-on coursework, and gain knowledge in the history of musical theatre. The musical theatre program is interdisciplinary. Students study in the Theatre Department as well as refine their musicianship through coursework in the Boyer College of Music and Dance. Additionally, faculty individually mentor students throughout the program.

Notable Alumni
Keith Andes, David Brenner, Bill Cosby, Cody Calafiore, Colman Domingo, Norman Fell, Jason Winston George, Johnny Ray Gill, Kunal Nayyar, Hugh Panaro, Robert Prosky, James Riordan, Herbert Rudley, Bob Saget, Michael Schoeffling, Tom Sizemore, Paul F. Tompkins, Jesse Williams, Danny Woodburn, and Alicia Woods

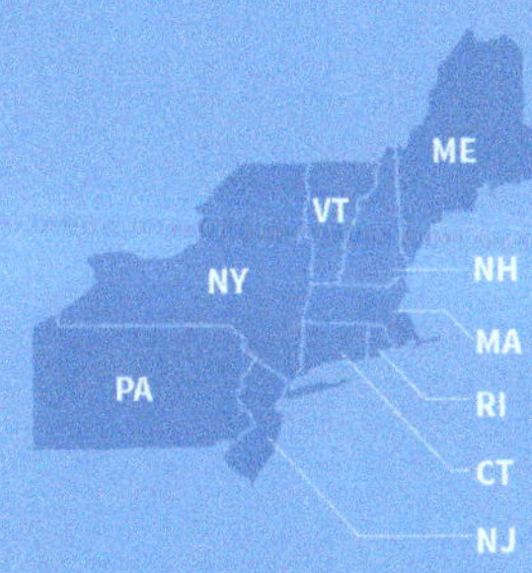

CONNECTICUT
MAINE
MASSACHUSETTS
NEW HAMPSHIRE
NEW JERSEY
NEW YORK
PENNSYLVANIA
RHODE ISLAND
VERMONT

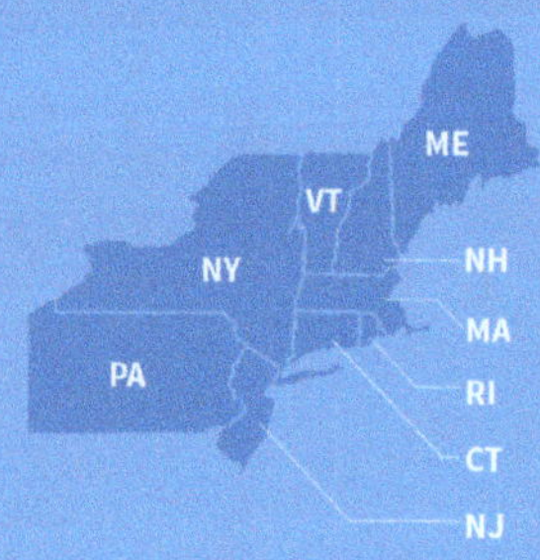

UNIVERSITY OF THE ARTS

Address: 320 S. Broad Street, Philadelphia, PA 19102
Website: *https://www.uarts.edu/academics/musical-theater*
Contact: *https://www.uarts.edu/about/contact-us*
Phone: (215) 717-6049
Email: admissions@uarts.edu

COST OF ATTENDANCE:

Tuition & Fees: $48,350 | **Additional Expenses:** $20,600
Total: $68,950

Financial Aid: https://www.uarts.edu/tuition-and-financial-aid

ADDITIONAL INFORMATION:

Available Degree(s)

- BFA Theatre: Musical Theatre

Freshman Audition Requirement

There is no pre-screen. Applicants may audition in person or virtually. Virtual auditions are submitted via Acceptd.

In-Person:

- Part 1: initial presentation of repertoire, of which you may receive a callback
- Part 2 (Callback): perform prepared work a second time; participate in an ensemble, a dance call and an interview.

Virtual:

- Wild Card video
- Dance call video

Musical Theater requirements:

- 2 contrasting songs
- 1 monologue
- Dance call video (virtual auditions only)

Scholarships Offered

Various named scholarships are available to all students for varied award amounts. Some scholarships are available to all University of the Arts students, such as the W.W. Smith Scholarship, the James M. Cresson, Scholarship, the Arnold A. Bayard Scholarship, and more. The School of Theater offers a few scholarships for theater students as well.

Special Opportunities

The Ira Brind School of Theater Arts within the University of the Arts holds five public performance venues and many facilities.

Notable Alumni

Sarah Bolt, Elana Boulos, Jennifer Childs, Rory Donovan, Jacob Jarrett, Aimé Donna Kelly, Jillian Keys, Elaina Di Monaco, Brad Pouliot, Matteo Scammell, and Lucas Steele

THEATRE

CHAPTER 14
REGION TWO
MIDWEST

ILLINOIS
INDIANA
IOWA
KANSAS
MICHIGAN
MINNESOTA
MISSOURI
NEBRASKA
NORTH DAKOTA
OHIO
SOUTH DAKOTA
WISCONSIN

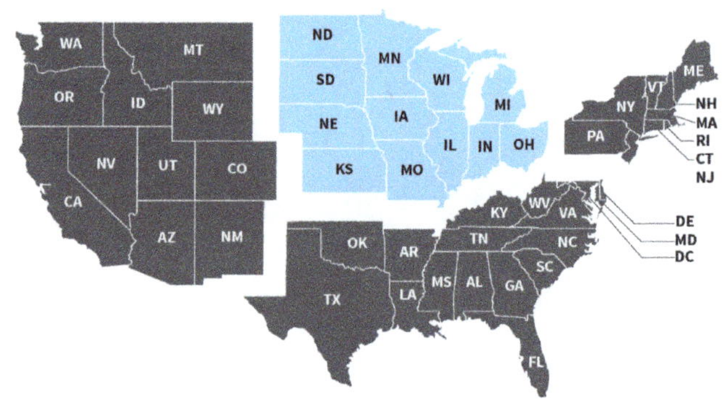

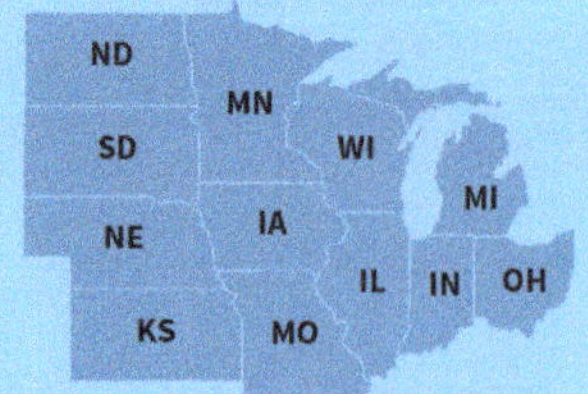

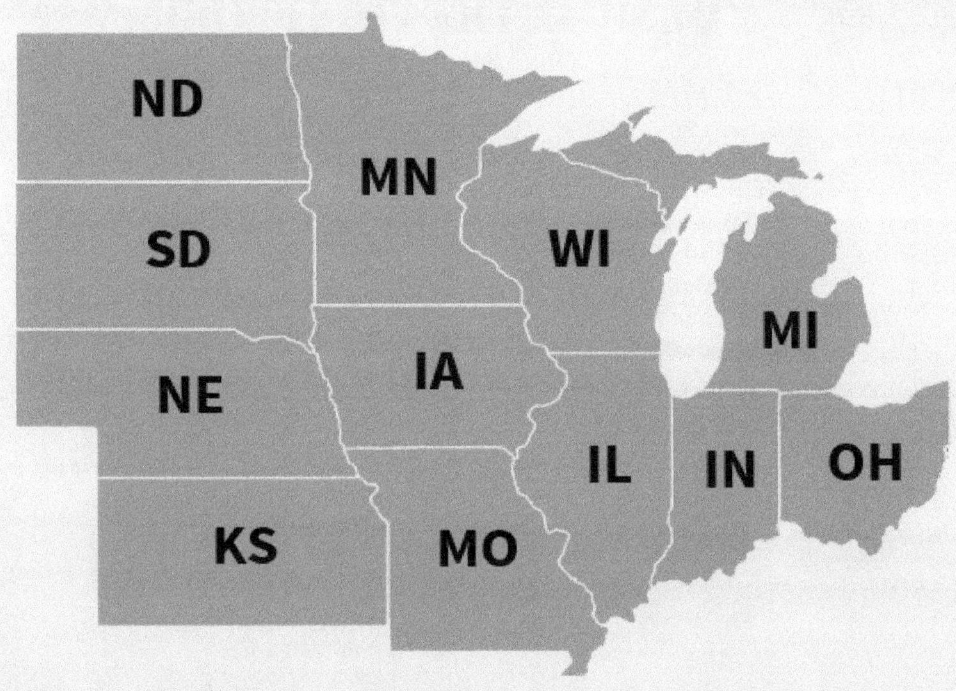

22 Programs | 12 States

1. IL - Columbia College Chicago
2. IL – Illinois Wesleyan University
3. IL - Millikin University
4. IL - Northwestern University
5. IL - Roosevelt University
6. IN - Ball State University
7. IN - Indiana University Bloomington
8. MI - University of Michigan
9. MI - Western Michigan University
10. MO - Southeast Missouri State University
11. MO - Stephens College
12. MO - University of Central Missouri
13. MO - Webster University
14. NE - Creighton University
15. NE - Nebraska Wesleyan University
16. OH - Baldwin Wallace University
17. OH - Kent State University
18. OH - Ohio University
19. OH - Otterbein University
20. OH - University of Cincinnati
21. OH - Wright State University
22. WI - Viterbo University

MUSICAL THEATRE PROGRAMS

School	Avg. GPA, SAT Evidence-Based Reading Writing (ERW), SAT Math (M), and ACT Composite (C) Early Decision (ED): Yes/No	Admission Statistics	Program(s)	Pre-Screen and/or Audition Required (Req.)
Columbia College Chicago 600 S Michigan Ave, Chicago, IL 60605	GPA: N/A SAT (ERW): N/A* SAT (M): N/A* ACT (C): N/A* *Test-optional ED: No	Overall College Admit Rate: 90% Undergrad Enrollment: 6,542 Total Enrollment: 6,769	BA Musical Theatre BFA Musical Theatre Performance Degrees Awarded in the Program(s) (2020): 29	Pre-screen req. Audition req.
Illinois Wesleyan University 1312 Park Street, Bloomington, IL 61701	GPA: 3.8 SAT (ERW): 550-640 SAT (M): 550-660 ACT (C): 24-29 ED: No	Overall College Admit Rate: 57% Undergrad Enrollment: 1,636 Total Enrollment: 1,636	BFA Music Theatre Degrees Awarded in the Program(s) (2020): 12	Pre-screen req. Audition req.
Millikin University 1184 W Main St, Decatur, IL 62522	GPA: N/A SAT (ERW): 470-590 SAT (M): 470-570 ACT (C): 20-27 ED: No	Overall College Admit Rate: 71% Undergrad Enrollment: 1,875 Total Enrollment: 1,982	BFA Musical Theatre Degrees Awarded in the Program(s) (2020): 29	Pre-screen req. Audition req.
Northwestern University 633 Clark St, Evanston, IL 60208	GPA: N/A SAT (ERW): 700-760 SAT (M): 730-790 ACT (C): 33-35 ED: Yes	Overall College Admit Rate: 9% Undergrad Enrollment: 8,194 Total Enrollment: 22,072	BA Theatre, Musical Theatre Certificate Degrees Awarded in the Program(s) (2020): N/A	Pre-screen not req. Musical Theatre Supplement optional

MUSICAL THEATRE PROGRAMS

School	Avg. GPA, SAT Evidence-Based Reading Writing (ERW), SAT Math (M), and ACT Composite (C) Early Decision (ED): Yes/No	Admission Statistics	Program(s)	Pre-Screen and/or Audition Required (Req.)
Roosevelt University 430 S Michigan Ave, Chicago, IL 60605	GPA: N/A SAT (ERW): 450-580 SAT (M): 440-550 ACT (C): 18-26 ED: No	Overall College Admit Rate: 77% Undergrad Enrollment: 3,068 Total Enrollment: 4,680	BFA Musical Theatre BFA Musical Theatre, concentration: Dance Degrees Awarded in the Program(s) (2020): 35	Pre-screen req. Audition req.
Ball State University 2000 W University Ave, Muncie, IN 47306	GPA: 3.52 SAT (ERW): N/A* SAT (M): N/A* ACT (C): N/A* *Test-optional ED: No	Overall College Admit Rate: 87% Undergrad Enrollment: 15,780 Total Enrollment: 21,597	BFA in Theatre, option: Musical Theatre Degrees Awarded in the Program(s) (2020): 70	Pre-screen not req. Audition req.
Indiana University Bloomington 107 S Indiana Ave, Bloomington, IN 47405	GPA: 3.74 SAT (ERW): 580-700 SAT (M): 560-680 ACT (C): 26-32 ED: No	Overall College Admit Rate: 85% Undergrad Enrollment: 34,253 Total Enrollment: 45,328	BFA Musical Theatre Degrees Awarded in the Program(s) (2020): 14	Pre-screen req. Audition req.

MUSICAL THEATRE PROGRAMS

School	Avg. GPA, SAT Evidence-Based Reading Writing (ERW), SAT Math (M), and ACT Composite (C) Early Decision (ED): Yes/No	Admission Statistics	Program(s)	Pre-Screen and/or Audition Required (Req.)
University of Michigan 500 S. State St., Ann Arbor, MI 48109	GPA: 3.87 SAT (ERW): 660-740 SAT (M): 680-780 ACT (C): 31-34 ED: No	Overall College Admit Rate: 26% Undergrad Enrollment: 31,329 Total Enrollment: 47,907	BFA Musical Theatre Degrees Awarded in the Program(s) (2020): 21	Pre-screen req. Audition req.
Western Michigan University 1903 W Michigan Ave, Kalamazoo, MI 49008	GPA: 3.47 SAT (ERW): 500-610 SAT (M): 510-610 ACT (C): 20-27 ED: No	Overall College Admit Rate: 85% Undergrad Enrollment: 15,969 Total Enrollment: 19,887	BFA Theatre: Music Theatre Performance Degrees Awarded in the Program(s) (2020): 16	Pre-screen req. Audition req.
Southeast Missouri State University 1 University Plaza, Cape Girardeau, MO 63701	GPA: 3.54 SAT (ERW): 500-600 SAT (M): 500-590 ACT (C): 19-25 ED: No	Overall College Admit Rate: 93% Undergrad Enrollment: 8,929 Total Enrollment: 10,001	BFA Theatre: Musical Theatre Degrees Awarded in the Program(s) (2020): N/A	Pre-screen req. Audition req.
Stephens College 1200 E Broadway, Columbia, MO 65215	GPA: N/A SAT (ERW): 480-540 SAT (M): 470-580 ACT (C): 20-24 ED: No	Overall College Admit Rate: 64% Undergrad Enrollment: 443 Total Enrollment: 622	BFA Musical Theatre Degrees Awarded in the Program(s) (2020): 8	Pre-screen req. Audition not req.

MUSICAL THEATRE PROGRAMS

School	Avg. GPA, SAT Evidence-Based Reading Writing (ERW), SAT Math (M), and ACT Composite (C) Early Decision (ED): Yes/No	Admission Statistics	Program(s)	Pre-Screen and/or Audition Required (Req.)
University of Central Missouri 116 W South St, Warrensburg, MO 64093	GPA: 3.44 SAT (ERW): N/A* SAT (M): N/A* ACT (C): N/A* *Test-optional ED: No	Overall College Admit Rate: 64% Undergrad Enrollment: 7,629 Total Enrollment: 9,959	BFA Musical Theatre Degrees Awarded in the Program(s) (2020): 6	Pre-screen not req. Audition req.
Webster University 470 E Lockwood Ave, Webster Groves, MO 63119	GPA: N/A SAT (ERW): 548-650 SAT (M): 530-610 ACT (C): 20-27 ED: No	Overall College Admit Rate: 53% Undergrad Enrollment: 2,563 Total Enrollment: 8,197	BFA Musical Theatre Degrees Awarded in the Program(s) (2020): 11	Pre-screen req. Audition req.
Creighton University 2500 California Plaza, Omaha, NE 68178	GPA: N/A SAT (ERW): N/A SAT (M): N/A ACT (C): N/A ED: No	Overall College Admit Rate: 64% Undergrad Enrollment: 4,458 Total Enrollment: 8,770	BFA Musical Theatre Degrees Awarded in the Program(s) (2020): 2	Pre-screen not req. Audition not req.
Nebraska Wesleyan University 51st and Huntington Ave., Lincoln, NE 68504	GPA: N/A SAT (ERW): 490-640 SAT (M): 500-610 ACT (C): 22-29 ED: No	Overall College Admit Rate: 70% Undergrad Enrollment: 1,773 Total Enrollment: 1,924	BFA Musical Theatre Degrees Awarded in the Program(s) (2020): 12	Pre-screen not req. Audition req.

MUSICAL THEATRE PROGRAMS

School	Avg. GPA, SAT Evidence-Based Reading Writing (ERW), SAT Math (M), and ACT Composite (C) Early Decision (ED): Yes/No	Admission Statistics	Program(s)	Pre-Screen and/or Audition Required (Req.)
Baldwin Wallace University 275 Eastland Rd, Berea, OH 44017	GPA: 3.6 SAT (ERW): 520-640 SAT (M): 520-620 ACT (C): 21-27 ED: No	Overall College Admit Rate: 70% Undergrad Enrollment: 2,860 Total Enrollment: 3,399	BM Music Theatre Degrees Awarded in the Program(s) (2020): N/A	Pre-screen optional Audition req.
Kent State University 1325 Theatre Drive, Kent, OH 44242	GPA: 3.61 SAT (ERW): 510-610 SAT (M): 510-600 ACT (C): 20-26 ED: No	Overall College Admit Rate: 84% Undergrad Enrollment: 21,621 Total Enrollment: 26,822	BFA Musical Theatre Degrees Awarded in the Program(s) (2020): 10	Pre-screen only req. for virtual auditions Audition req.
Ohio University Ohio University, Athens, OH 45701	GPA: 3.55 SAT (ERW): 530-630 SAT (M): 520-620 ACT (C): 21-26 ED: No	Overall College Admit Rate: 87% Undergrad Enrollment: 19,284 Total Enrollment: 25,714	BFA Performance, Musical Theatre Track Degrees Awarded in the Program(s) (2020): N/A	Pre-screen not req. Audition req.
Otterbein University 1 S Grove St, Westerville, OH 43081	GPA: N/A SAT (ERW): 490-625 SAT (M): 500-600 ACT (C): 20-27 ED: No	Overall College Admit Rate: 76% Undergrad Enrollment: 2,313 Total Enrollment: 2,652	BFA Musical Theatre BFA Musical Theatre, Concentration: Dance Degrees Awarded in the Program(s) (2020): 9	Pre-screen req. Audition req.

MUSICAL THEATRE PROGRAMS

School	Avg. GPA, SAT Evidence-Based Reading Writing (ERW), SAT Math (M), and ACT Composite (C) Early Decision (ED): Yes/No	Admission Statistics	Program(s)	Pre-Screen and/or Audition Required (Req.)
University of Cincinnati 2600 Clifton Ave, Cincinnati, OH 45221	GPA: 3.7 SAT (ERW): 560-650 SAT (M): 560-680 ACT (C): 23-29 ED: No	Overall College Admit Rate: 76% Undergrad Enrollment: 29,933 Total Enrollment: 40,826	BFA Musical Theatre Degrees Awarded in the Program(s) (2020): N/A	Pre-screen req. Audition req.
Wright State University 3640 Colonel Glenn Hwy, Dayton, OH 45435	GPA: 3.36 SAT (ERW): 478-620 SAT (M): 480-600 ACT (C): 18-25 ED: No	Overall College Admit Rate: 96% Undergrad Enrollment: 8,332 Total Enrollment: 10,936	BFA Musical Theatre Degrees Awarded in the Program(s) (2020): N/A	Pre-screen not req. Audition req.
Viterbo University 900 Viterbo Dr, La Crosse, WI 54601	GPA: 3.5 SAT (ERW): 520-600 SAT (M): 480-570 ACT (C): 20-25 ED: No	Overall College Admit Rate: 79% Undergrad Enrollment: 1,736 Total Enrollment: 2,516	BFA Music Theatre Degrees Awarded in the Program(s) (2020): 11	Pre-screen req. Audition req.

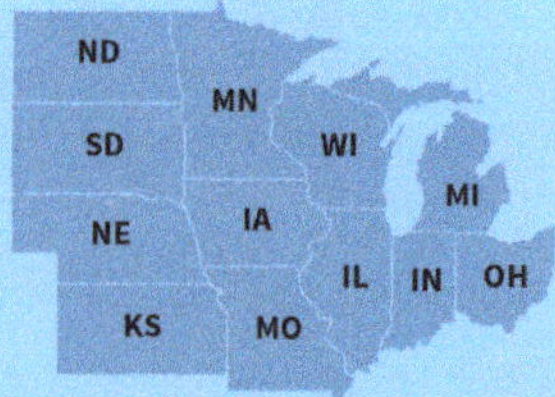

COLUMBIA COLLEGE CHICAGO

Address: 600 S Michigan Ave, Chicago, IL 60605
Website: *https://www.colum.edu/academics/programs/musical-theatre*
Contact: *https://www.colum.edu/contact*
Phone: (312) 369-1000
Email: admissions@colum.edu

COST OF ATTENDANCE:

Tuition & Fees: $35,716 | **Additional Expenses:** $18,000
Total: $53,716

Financial Aid: https://www.colum.edu/columbia-central/where-to-start/index

ADDITIONAL INFORMATION:

Available Degree(s)

- BA Musical Theatre
- BFA Musical Theatre Performance

Freshman Audition Requirement
Columbia College Chicago requires a pre-screen.

- 2 contrasting songs
- 1 monologue
- Choose 1 of 2 combinations
- Additional combination (Optional)
- Wild Card (Optional)
- Theatrical resume & headshot
- Written statement

Applicants then participate in an in-person group or virtual group audition.

Scholarships Offered
Students are automatically considered for renewable scholarships upon admission. For need-based scholarship, submit a FAFSA. For talent-based scholarships, submit an audition that demonstrates your best creative work. First-year, international students may be considered for talent-based scholarships.

Special Opportunities
The college stages 40 productions each year. Students are encouraged to audition as soon as they begin for both musical and non-musical productions. Students also perform in student films, devised production, off-campus productions, and Mainstage productions directly by faculty. Columbia hosts two internship fairs per year from theatres like Steppenwolf, Victory Gardens, and the Goodman. The Getz Theatre Center has four professional-quality stages, a state-of-the-art scene shop, and labs for costume, makeup, prosthetics, and lighting. Minors include Stage Combat, ASL, Theatre Directing, and Live and Performing Arts Management.

Notable Alumni
Scott Adsit, Jeremy Beiler, Aidy Bryant, Harter Clingman, Shantel Cribbs, Behzad Dabu, Michael George, Calle Johnson, Michael Kuroski, Courtney Mack, Mallory Maedke, Ashley Mondisa, Michelle Monaghan, Tonya Pinkins, Anna D. Shapiro, and Nadine Velazquez

ILLINOIS WESLEYAN UNIVERSITY

Address: 1312 Park Street, Bloomington, IL 61701
Website: *https://www.iwu.edu/theatre/courses/bfa-music-theatre.html*
Contact: *https://www.iwu.edu/admissions/contact/*
Phone: (309) 556-1000
Email: See contact link

COST OF ATTENDANCE:

Tuition & Fees: $53,610 | **Additional Expenses:** $12,652
Total: $66,262

Financial Aid: https://www.iwu.edu/financial-aid/tuition.html

ADDITIONAL INFORMATION:

Available Degree(s)

- BFA Music Theatre

Freshman Audition Requirement

Illinois Wesleyan University participates in the Paper Mill Playhouse Common Pre-Screen. For more information, please refer to Chapter 8. Submit via Acceptd.

- Songs (Option A)
- Monologues (Option A)
- Dance or Ballet (Optional)
- Wild Card

Applicants with a successful pre-screen are invited for a call-back, where they must audition and complete an interview.

Scholarships Offered

Music Theatre students may be considered for the Alumni Fine Arts for Theatre Scholarships. Awards go up to $34,000 per year and are renewable for four years. Students are evaluated based on their auditions/portfolio and high school academic achievement.

Special Opportunities

Students work with composers in the Music Theatre Workshop to shape their character. Students also participate in the Music Theatre Scene Study to work on scenes throughout the semester and participate in a showcase performance.

Notable Alumni

Bill Damaschke, Torri Newman, and Alex Pagels

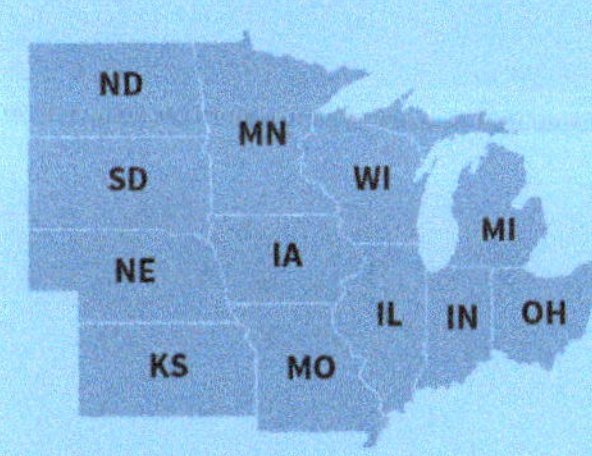

MILLIKIN UNIVERSITY

Address: 1184 W Main St, Decatur, IL 62522
Website: *https://millikin.edu/academics/cas/theatre-dance/areas-study/musical-theatre-bfa*
Contact: *https://millikin.edu/webform/contact-us*
Phone: (800) 373-7733
Email: admis@millikin.edu

COST OF ATTENDANCE:

Tuition & Fees: $38,800 | **Additional Expenses:** $13,582
Total: $52,382

Financial Aid: https://millikin.edu/cost-aid

ADDITIONAL INFORMATION:

Available Degree(s)

- BFA Musical Theatre

Freshman Audition Requirement

Millikin University participates in the Paper Mill Playhouse Common Pre-Screen. For more information, please refer to Chapter 8. Submit via Acceptd.

- Songs (Option A)
- Monologues (Option A)
- Dance Option (Required)
- Ballet Option (Optional)
- Wild Card (Optional)

Applicants with a successful pre-screen are invited for a call-back, where they must undergo an in-person or digital audition (under certain circumstances).

- Songs
- Monologues
- Dance combination

Scholarships Offered

The College of Fine Arts offers a scholarship for theatre students who show significant promise. This reward ranges from $4,000-$20,000 over four years.

Special Opportunities

At Millikin, students may gain onstage experience by auditioning for any of the university-held productions each season. Millikin holds 2 musicals, 2 plays, and 1 dance concert per season. Every other season, they hold an opera, co-produced with the School of Music. Furthermore, students enjoy the benefits of small class sizes and gain more individualized attention as well as faculty/student mentorships.

Notable Alumni

Jodi Benson, Polly Baker, Sierra Boggess, Joel Kim Booster, Hedy Burress, Brian Collier, Annamary Dickey, Katelyn Epperly, Tad Hilgenbrink, Ian Liberto, Michael Maize, Clinton Sherwood, Annie Wersching, and Jessica Wright

NORTHWESTERN UNIVERSITY

Address: 633 Clark St, Evanston, IL 60208
Website: *https://communication.northwestern.edu/academic-programs/music-theatre-certificate/*
Contact: *https://www.communication.northwestern.edu/contact*
Phone: (847) 491-3741
Email: dear-soc@northwestern.edu

COST OF ATTENDANCE:

Tuition & Fees: $60,768 | **Additional Expenses:** $23,070
Total: $83,838

Financial Aid: https://undergradaid.northwestern.edu/index.html

ADDITIONAL INFORMATION:

Available Degree(s)

- BA Theatre, Musical Theatre Certificate

Freshman Audition Requirement

Northwestern University does not require a pre-screen or audition for their Theatre major. However, applicants interested in the Musical Theatre Certificate may submit an optional Musical Theatre Supplement.

- Personal statement video
- 2 contrasting songs
- Monologue, dance, instruments (optional)

Students who are admitted to the Theatre program at Northwestern must undergo an in-person audition for full admittance to the Musical Theatre Certificate Program after beginning their first quarter of study.

Scholarships Offered

The Northwestern University Scholarship ($250 to over $40,000 per year) is based on financial need after other forms of aid have been applied. The Karr Achievement Scholarship ($2,500 annually) is a merit-based scholarship.

Special Opportunities

In the Musical Theatre Certificate Program, students take specialized courses in musicianship, dance, acting, and voice. Alumni of this program have been seen on Broadway and national tours.

Notable Alumni

Warren Beatty, Ann-Margret, Richard Benjamin, Greg Berlanti, Craig Bierko, Clancy Brown, Charles Busch, Stephen Colbert, Stephanie Shemin D'Abruzzo, Gregg Edelman, Frank Galati, Ana Gasteyer, Kathryn Hahn, Heather Headley, Marg Helgenberger, Brian d'Arcy James, Laura Innes, Charlton Heston, Jennifer Jones, Adam Kantor, Patricia Neal, Mary Beth Peil, and Michael Weston

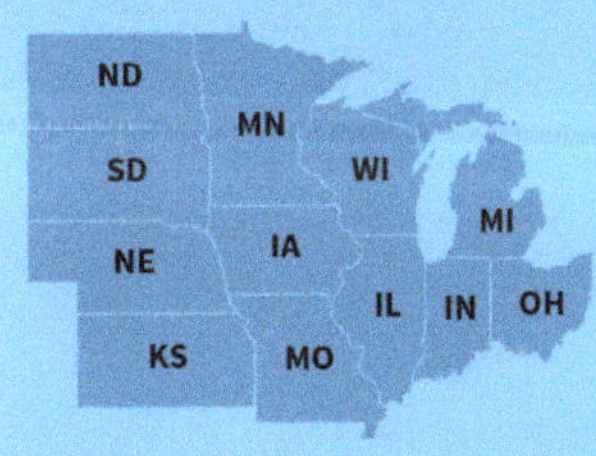

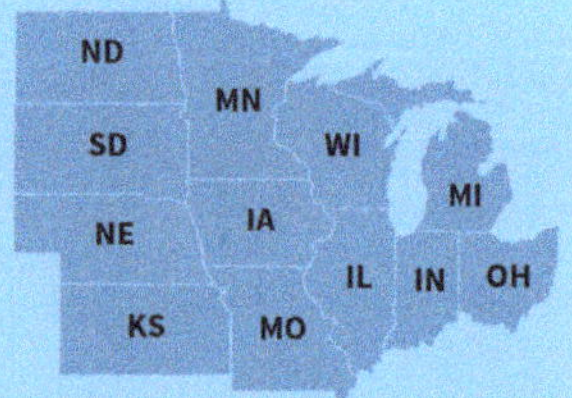

ROOSEVELT UNIVERSITY

Address: 430 S Michigan Ave, Chicago, IL 60605
Website: *https://www.roosevelt.edu/academics/programs/bachelors-in-musical-theatre-voice-bfa*
Contact: *https://www.roosevelt.edu/contact*
Phone: (312) 341-3500
Email: admission@roosevelt.edu

COST OF ATTENDANCE:

Tuition & Fees: $39,552 | **Additional Expenses:** $15,985
Total: $55,537

Financial Aid: https://www.roosevelt.edu/tuition-aid/learn-about-financial-aid-undergraduate

ADDITIONAL INFORMATION:

Available Degree(s)

- BFA Musical Theatre
- BFA Musical Theatre, concentration: Dance

Freshman Audition Requirement

Roosevelt University participates in the Paper Mill Playhouse Common Pre-Screen. For more information, please refer to Chapter 8. Submit via Acceptd.

- Songs (Option A or B)
- Monologues (Option A)
- Dance Option (Required)
- Ballet Option (Optional)
- Wild Card (Optional)

Applicants with a successful pre-screen are invited for a call-back, where they must undergo an in-person or live virtual audition.

- 1 monologue
- 2 songs

Scholarships Offered

Students are automatically considered for merit-based and need-based scholarships upon applying to Roosevelt University. Endowed scholarships are also available on a competitive basis, yearly.

Special Opportunities

Musical Theatre students study at Roosevelt University's Chicago College of Performing Arts (CCPA) Theatre Conservatory in the heart of downtown Chicago. This prime location offers students opportunities to perform at the Goodman Theatre, Steppenwolf Theatre Company, Lookingglass Theatre, and Chicago Shakespeare Theatre. Furthermore, all students are guaranteed onstage performance credit.

Notable Alumni

Major Attaway, Parvesh Cheena, Matt Crowle, Merle Dandridge, Andrea DeVriendt, J. Michael Finley, Damon Gillespie, Angela Grovey, Renee Keen, Courtney Reed, Mia Serafino, David Schmitz, and Travis Taylor

BALL STATE UNIVERSITY

Address: 2000 W University Ave, Muncie, IN 47306
Website: *https://www.bsu.edu/academics/collegesanddepartments/theatredance/what-we-offer/bachelors-degrees/musical-theatre*
Contact: *https://www.bsu.edu/admissions/undergraduate-admissions/contact-us*
Phone: (800) 482-4278
Email: askus@bsu.edu

COST OF ATTENDANCE:

In-State Tuition & Fees: $9,520 | **Additional Expenses:** $12,802
Total: $24,484

Out-of-State Tuition & Fees: $18,594 | **Additional Expenses:** $12,802
Total: $31,396

Financial Aid: https://www.bsu.edu/admissions/financial-aid-and-scholarships

ADDITIONAL INFORMATION:

Available Degree(s)

- BFA in Theatre, option: Musical Theatre

Freshman Audition Requirement

Ball State does not require a pre-screen. However, they require either a digital or in-person audition.

- Dance combinations
- 2 contrasting songs
- 2 contrasting monologues

Scholarships Offered

The Department of Theatre and Dance offers merit-based scholarships such as the University CFA Awards ($4,000 a year for in-state students and $2,000 a year for out-of-state students).

Special Opportunities

Ball State is an award-winning participant in the Kennedy Center American College Theatre Festival. Furthermore, musical theatre students are required to complete a senior capstone project, where they are part of a live group cabaret performance.

Notable Alumni

Meghan "Collins" Conley, Jessica Ervin, Talley Beth Gale, Matt Glassner, Joe Lino, David Merten, Erin Neufer, Grace Rex, Adam B. Shapiro, Mary Taylor, and Meg Warner

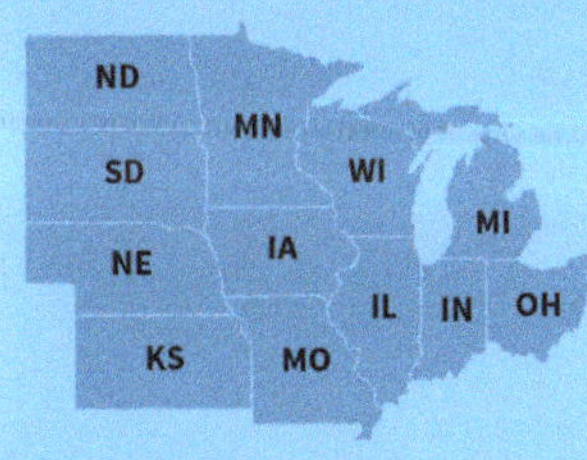

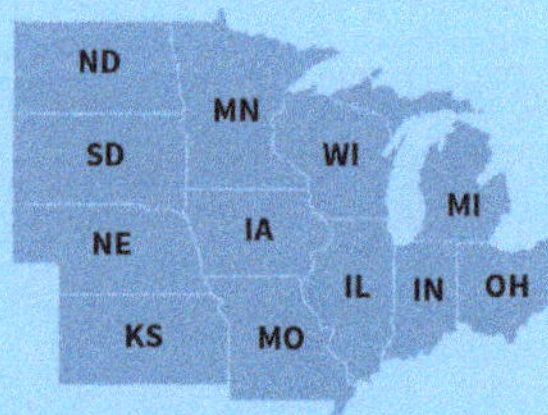

INDIANA UNIVERSITY BLOOMINGTON

Address: 107 S Indiana Ave, Bloomington, IN 47405
Website: *https://theatre.indiana.edu/undergraduate/musical-theatre-bfa/index.html*
Contact: *https://admissions.indiana.edu/contact/index.html*
Phone: (812) 855-4848
Email: admissions@indiana.edu

COST OF ATTENDANCE:

In-State Tuition & Fees: $11,332 | **Additional Expenses:** $15,966
Total: $27,298

Out-of-State Tuition & Fees: $38,352 | **Additional Expenses:** $15,966
Total: $54,318

Financial Aid: https://admissions.indiana.edu/cost-financial-aid/financial-aid.html

ADDITIONAL INFORMATION:

Available Degree(s)

- BFA Musical Theatre

Freshman Audition Requirement

Indiana University Bloomingtonparticipates in the Paper Mill Playhouse Common Pre-Screen. For more information, please refer to Chapter 8. Submit via Acceptd.

- Songs (Option A)
- Monologues (Option A)
- Dance (Required)
- Ballet (Optional)
- Wild Card (Required)

Applicants with a successful pre-screen are invited for an audition, where they must undergo an in-person or live virtual audition.

- Dance class
- Acting class
- 2 contrasting songs

Scholarships Offered

Indiana University Bloomington offers a variety of scholarships for in-state, out-of-state, and international students. Students applying before the early action deadline will receive consideration for IU Academic Scholarships ($1,000–$11,000) and for the invitation-only Selective Scholarship.

Special Opportunities

The musical theatre program at IUB encourages students to study choreography, instrumental studies, staging, backstage crew work, on top of musical theatre-focused coursework so that students gain a well-rounded understanding of the production process.

Notable Alumni

Jonathan Banks, Sarah Clarke, Laverne Cox, David C. Giuntoli, Tan Kheng Hua, Andraes Katsulas, Kevin Kline, J. Lee, Lee Majors, Arian Moayed, Nicole Parker, Julian Ramos, Ranveer Singh, Hana Slevin, Brian Stack, Jeri Taylor, Herb Vigran, Aaron Waltke, and Jaysen Wright

UNIVERSITY OF MICHIGAN

Address: 500 S. State St., Ann Arbor, MI 48109
Website: *https://smtd.umich.edu/programs-degrees/degree-programs/undergraduate/musical-theatre/bachelor-of-fine-arts-in-musical-theatre/*
Contact: *https://smtd.umich.edu/about/contact-us/*
Phone: (734) 764-0593
Email: smtd.admissions@umich.edu

COST OF ATTENDANCE:

In-State Tuition & Fees: $18,208 | **Additional Expenses:** $16,094
Total: $34,302

Out-of-State Tuition & Fees: $56,962 | **Additional Expenses:** $16,094
Total: $73,056

Financial Aid: https://finaid.umich.edu/

ADDITIONAL INFORMATION:

Available Degree(s)
- BFA Musical Theatre

Freshman Audition Requirement
Applicants must submit a resume, photograph, and personal statement to the Artistic Profile. All pre-screening materials must be submitted to the SMTD Artistic Profile.

- 2 contrasting monologues
- 2 songs
- 1 dance video
- 1 ballet video (Optional)
- Video Response
- Wild card (Optional)

Applicants with a successful pre-screen are invited for a live audition, either via Zoom or in person.

- 2 contrasting monologues
- 2 songs
- Ballet and jazz combinations

Scholarships Offered
The School of Music, Theatre, & Dance offers merit-based scholarships to musical theatre students. Additionally, University of Michigan offers several scholarships for incoming students. One of them is the Stamps Scholars Program, a prestigious merit-based program that offers the full cost of attendance. The HAIL Scholarship is an invitational award that covers four years of tuition and fees for low-income, high achieving Michigan students. Many scholarships are need-based, although some are merit-based as well.

Special Opportunities
Since only the best earn spots on and off-Broadway, the University of Michigan's highly competitive and renowned program accepts only top candidates, trains them intensely, and expects disciplined effort in acting, dance, and voice. Numerous opportunities are offered in mainstage productions, student-run theatre, and community organizations. Students study music theory, music theatre history, and the liberal arts. Private voice lessons are offered.

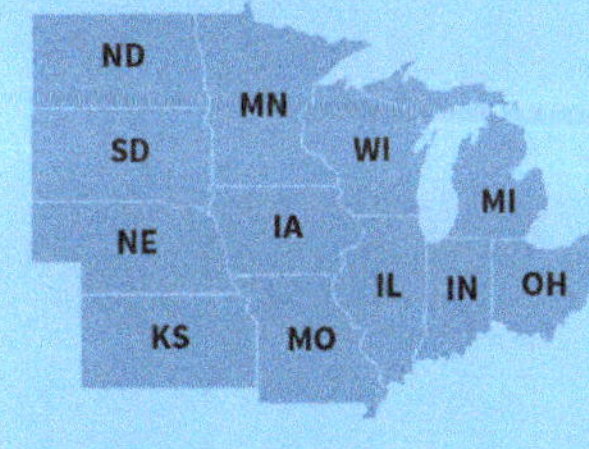

Notable Alumni
Gavin Creel, Erin Dilly, Hunter Foster, Andrew Keenan-Bolger, Celia Keenan-Bolger, Benj Pasek, Justin Paul, Andrew Lippa, Benj Pasek, Justin Paul, Jeffrey Seller, James D. Stern, and Jacqueline Toboni

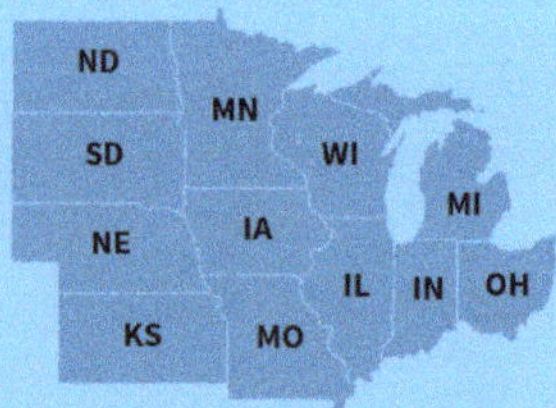

WESTERN MICHIGAN UNIVERSITY

Address: 1903 W Michigan Ave, Kalamazoo, MI 49008
Website: *https://wmich.edu/theatre/academics/performance*
Contact: *https://wmich.edu/contact*
Phone: (269) 387-1000
Email: Contact via phone.

COST OF ATTENDANCE:

Tuition & Fees: $16,646 | **Additional Expenses:** $14,945
Total: $31,591

Financial Aid: https://wmich.edu/finaid

ADDITIONAL INFORMATION:

Available Degree(s)

- BFA Theatre: Music Theatre Performance

Freshman Audition Requirement

Applicants must submit a pre-screen to Acceptd.

- Headshot & resume
- 2 references
- 30-second vocal audition

Applicants with a successful pre-screen are invited for a digital or in-person audition.

- 2 contrasting songs
- 1 monologue
- Dance call

Scholarships Offered

All students are considered for merit-based and need-based scholarships if they submit their university application by December. Awards range from $1,500 to $16,000 per year. Additionally, students in the College of Fine Arts may be eligible for talent-based scholarships.

Special Opportunities

Musical Theatre students are expected to participate in productions held by the university yearly. All theatre students must also pass a juried audition at the end of their sophomore year.

Notable Alumni

Victoria Blade, Cory Blevins, Amanda Cowper, Dayna Jarae Dantzler, Hannah Elless, Tiffany Frances, Larry Herron, Scott Jacobs, Darren Edward Johnson, Brian Martin, Crystal Lucas-Perry, Aaron C. Rutherford, Marcus Shane, Jonathan Scotcher Warner, Mikey Winslow, and Lauren Zakrin

SOUTHEAST MISSOURI STATE UNIVERSITY

Address: 1 University Plaza, Cape Girardeau, MO 63701
Website: *https://semo.edu/academics/programs/arts-media/conservatory/musical-theatre-bfa.html*
Contact: *https://semo.edu/contact.html*
Phone: (573) 651-2000
Email: admissions@semo.edu

COST OF ATTENDANCE:

In-State Tuition & Fees: $6,750 | **Additional Expenses:** $11,994
Total: $18,744

Out-of-State Tuition & Fees: $11,985 | **Additional Expenses:** $12,456
Total: $24,441

Financial Aid: https://semo.edu/sfs/financialaid/

ADDITIONAL INFORMATION:

Available Degree(s)

- BFA Theatre: Musical Theatre

Freshman Audition Requirement

Submit an online application audition form through the Southeast Missouri State University website.

- Headshot & resume
- Career goals
- 60-90 second video

Applicants must also select an in-person audition date or submit video links to audition videos.

- 2 contrasting songs
- 1 monologue
- Dance call

Scholarships Offered

The Copper Dome Scholarship is available to all incoming freshmen, and is based on a SAT/ACT and GPA. Awards range from $1,000 to $5,000. In addition, the President's Scholarship is awarded to five students and is based on academic achievement. This award is valued at approximately $10,000 per year.

Special Opportunities

According to SMSU, students may, "participate in one of two showcases: New York City with The CRY HAVOC Company or Los Angeles with Actors Connection." Furthermore, students may study abroad at NSKI University College in Oslo where they learn method acting and musical theatre.

Notable Alumni

Anna Hebrank, Cedric Kyles, Andrew Tebo, and Sarah Tochtrop

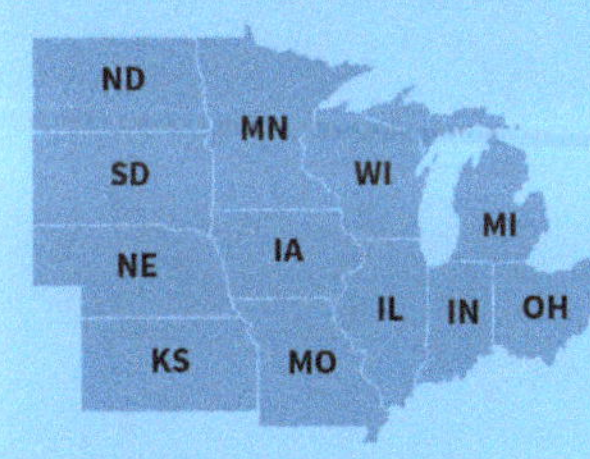

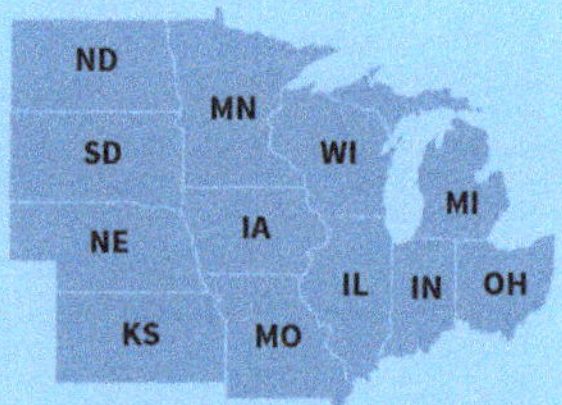

STEPHENS COLLEGE

Address: 1200 E Broadway, Columbia, MO 65215
Website: *https://www.stephens.edu/academics/conservatory-for-the-performing-arts/musical-theatre/*
Contact: *https://www.stephens.edu/campus-offices/*
Phone: (573) 442-2211
Email: info@stephens.edu

COST OF ATTENDANCE:

Tuition & Fees: $23,385 | **Additional Expenses:** $12,864
Total: $36,249

Financial Aid: https://www.stephens.edu/admission-aid/undergraduate/financial-aid/

ADDITIONAL INFORMATION:

Available Degree(s)

- BFA Musical Theatre

Freshman Audition Requirement

Stephens College participates in the Paper Mill Playhouse Common Pre-Screen, however they use the pre-screen in lieu of an audition. For more information, please refer to Chapter 8. Submit via Acceptd.

- Songs (Option A or B)
- Monologues (Option A or B)
- Dance Option (Required)
- Ballet Option (Optional)
- Wild Card (Required)

Scholarships Offered

Stephens College offers various institutional merit-based scholarships for incoming freshmen. The Academic Merit Scholarship awards $7,000 up to full tuition and is renewable for four years.

Special Opportunities

Focus is on individualized student technique and progress at Stephens College. This program is accelerated, and takes 3 years/2 summers to complete. Furthermore, students participate in the summer stock theatre internship to build a body of work.

Notable Alumni

Becca Ayers, Heather Ayers, Stephanie Beatriz, Carlos Carrasco, Judith Chapman, Chris Cooper, Joan Crawford, Missy Doty, Susan Flannery, Colleen Grate, Jennie Greenberry, Tammy Grimes, Mariah Lee, Susie McMonagle, Marjie Millar, Elizabeth Mitchell, Carrie Nye, Annie Potts, Jennifer Tilly, and Dawn Wells

UNIVERSITY OF CENTRAL MISSOURI

Address: 116 W South St, Warrensburg, MO 64093
Website: *https://www.ucmo.edu/academics/programs/majors/musical-theatre-bfa-47-586/index.php*
Contact: *https://www.ucmo.edu/public-safety/contact-our-staff/*
Phone: (877) 729-8266
Email: admit@ucmo.edu

COST OF ATTENDANCE:

In-State Tuition & Fees: $7,748 | **Additional Expenses:** $11,930
Total: $19,678

Out-of-State Tuition & Fees: $15,495 | **Additional Expenses:** $11,930
Total: $27,425

Financial Aid: https://www.ucmo.edu/future-students/financing-your-education/

ADDITIONAL INFORMATION:

Available Degree(s)

- BFA Musical Theatre

Freshman Audition Requirement

University of Central Missouri does not require a pre-screen. Auditions take place in person.

- Headshot & resume
- 2 contrasting monologues
- 1 ballad
- 1 song
- Dance
- Interview

Scholarships Offered

University of Central Missouri (UCM) offers merit-based and need-based scholarships of varying award amounts. They also have a scholarship finder link that allows students to apply to specific scholarships throughout their time as students at UCM.

Special Opportunities

Theatre students may opt in for designated theatre housing, known as the Theatre Special Housing Interest Program (SHIP). This location is in close proximity to the Black Box Theatre and contains a lounge for rehearsals, and a fully-equipped dance studio.

Notable Alumni

Gracie Heath, Charlotte Sipple, and Alyce Wilson

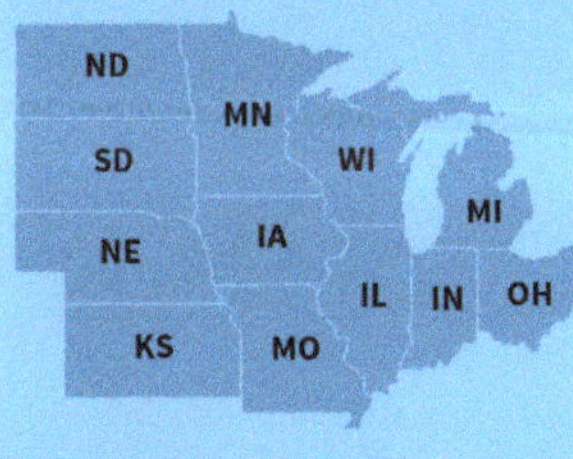

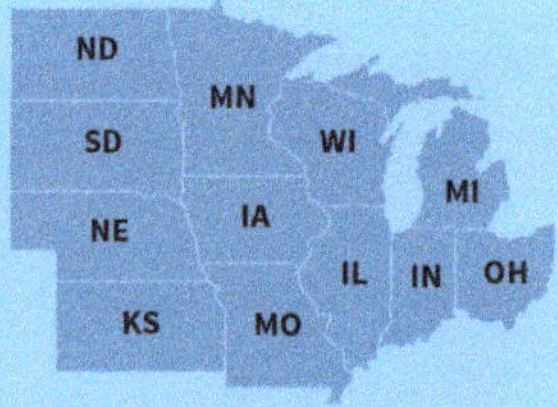

WEBSTER UNIVERSITY

Address: 470 E Lockwood Ave, Webster Groves, MO 63119
Website: *https://www.webster.edu/conservatory/programs/musicaltheatre.php*
Contact: *Via Email or phone*
Phone: (800) 981-9801
Email: admit@webster.edu

COST OF ATTENDANCE:

Tuition & Fees: $33,100 | **Additional Expenses:** $19,474
Total: $52,574

Financial Aid: https://www.webster.edu/financialaid/index.php

ADDITIONAL INFORMATION:

Available Degree(s)

- BFA Musical Theatre

Freshman Audition Requirement

Webster University does not require a pre-screen. However, all applicants must audition in-person, either on campus or at an off-campus location through Unified Auditions.

- 2 monologues
- 2 contrasting songs
- Dance (if requested)

Scholarships Offered

Webster University offers merit-based and need-based scholarships to all students. Most scholarships do not require a separate application. Awards go up to $19,000. Furthermore, students in the bordering states of Illinois, Iowa, Kentucky, Tennessee, Arkansas, or Oklahoma may receive a tuition grant.

Special Opportunities

Musical theater students learn cold reading skills, acting for the camera, cabaret performance, and more. By the first year, students join a showcase in New York and Los Angeles.

Notable Alumni

Hunter Bell, Nikki Boyer, Norbert Leo Butz, Adam Jamal Craig, Kevin Earley, Julie Ann Emery, Jodi Kingsley, Jenifer Lewis, Masha Mason, Danny McCarthy, Jerry Mitchel, Rob Riggle, and Dana Snyder

CREIGHTON UNIVERSITY

Address: 2500 California Plaza, Omaha, NE 68178
Website: *https://www.creighton.edu/academics/programs/musical-theatre*
Contact: *https://www.creighton.edu/ask*
Phone: (402) 280-2700
Email: admissions@creighton.edu

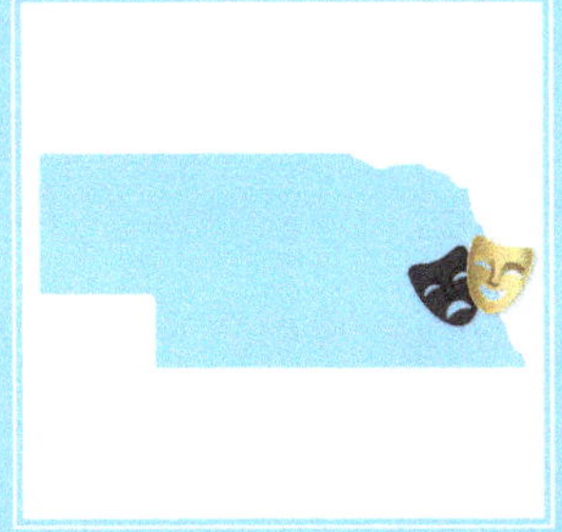

COST OF ATTENDANCE:

Tuition & Fees: $44,310 | **Additional Expenses:** $15,950
Total: $60,260

Financial Aid: https://www.creighton.edu/admission-aid

ADDITIONAL INFORMATION:

Available Degree(s)

- BFA Musical Theatre

Freshman Audition Requirement

There is no audition requirement for incoming freshmen, however there is later in the program to earn the BFA degree.

Scholarships Offered

All students who are accepted to Creighton automatically receive a $10,000 annual scholarship. Furthermore, Creighton offers additional merit scholarships. Applicants must submit a separate application.

Special Opportunities

Musical theatre students in all years are eligible to be cast in productions. Students perform on the Mainstage and in the Lied Education Center for the Arts.

Notable Alumni

Addie Barnhart, Bruce Hough, Lora Kaup, Mark Krejci, Amy Lane, Alexia Lorch, Michael J. McCandless, and Bill Van Deest

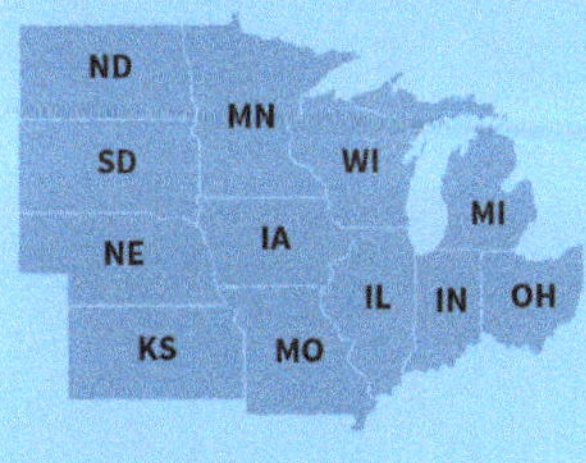

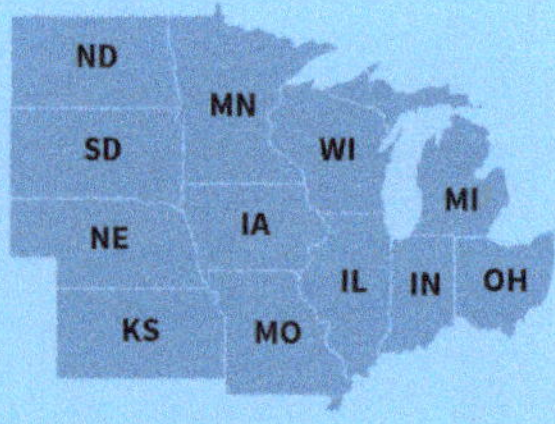

NEBRASKA WESLEYAN UNIVERSITY

Address: 51st and Huntington Ave., Lincoln, NE 68504
Website: *https://www.nebrwesleyan.edu/academics/majors-and-minors/theatre/theatre-degrees/musical-theatre-bfa*
Contact: *https://www.nebrwesleyan.edu/visit/contact-us*
Phone: (800) 541-3818
Email: admissions@nebrwesleyan.edu

COST OF ATTENDANCE:

Tuition & Fees: $35,964 | **Additional Expenses:** $11,148
Total: $47,112

Financial Aid: https://www.nebrwesleyan.edu/admissions/financial-aid-office/financial-aid-office

ADDITIONAL INFORMATION:

Available Degree(s)

- BFA Musical Theatre

Freshman Audition Requirement

Nebraska Wesleyan University does not require a pre-screen. Applicants may submit audition materials and participate in auditions in person on campus or through Chicago Unified Auditions, via Zoom, or on Acceptd.

- Headshot & resume
- Photograph
- 1 monologue
- 2 contrasting songs
- Dance (optional)

Scholarships Offered

All students receive a renewable, $1,000 grant when they attend a campus tour or virtual visit. Academic scholarships are based on GPA only or ACT/SAT and GPA combined. These awards range from $15,000-$20,000. Theatre Scholarships range from $500-$3000 and are based on the admission audition.

Special Opportunities

Each year, NWU produces 3-5 musicals, 1+ Shakespeare or Greek productions, and several dramas, comedies, and tragedies. Students have the opportunity to participate in these productions.

Notable Alumni

Kayli Jamison and Emily Kinney

BALDWIN WALLACE UNIVERSITY

Address: 275 Eastland Rd, Berea, OH 44017
Website: *https://www.bw.edu/academics/undergraduate/music-theatre/*
Contact: *https://www.bw.edu/admission/counselors/*
Phone: (440) 826-2222
Email: admission@bw.edu

COST OF ATTENDANCE:

Tuition & Fees: $35,366 | **Additional Expenses:** $13,024
Total: $48,390

Financial Aid: https://www.bw.edu/undergraduate-admission/first-year/tuition/

ADDITIONAL INFORMATION:

Available Degree(s)

- BM Music Theatre

Freshman Audition Requirement

Baldwin Wallace University has an optional pre-screen for applicants. This optional pre-screen is a video of 2, 16-bar cuts. All applicants must submit a few video materials prior to their audition.

- 1 monologue
- 1 wild card video
- 1 dance combination

The audition takes place live.

- 3 songs

Scholarships Offered

First-year applicants are automatically considered for merit scholarships ($12,000 to $21,000 a year) based on their cumulative weighted high school GPA. Baldwin Wallace University also offers numerous special awards up to $8,000.

Special Opportunities

Classical acting techniques in whole-body movement, vocal quality, tone, diction, and dialects for camera and theatre using the Stanislavsky systematic training, Meisner technique, and Alexander tension release and posture method. Students learn movement through ballet, jazz, tap, modern, and hip-hop and vocally with classical, musical theatre, and pop/rock. Three musicals per year along with plays and operas. Students graduate with their AEA card or EMC membership.

Notable Alumni

Zach Adkins, Ryan Garrett, Caitlin Houlahan, Kyle Jean-Baptiste, Corey Mach, Lauren Marshall, Chris McCarrell, Trista Moldovan, Sainty Nelsen, Shannon O'Boyle, Jill Paice, Kyle Post, Ciara Renee, and Kate Rockwell

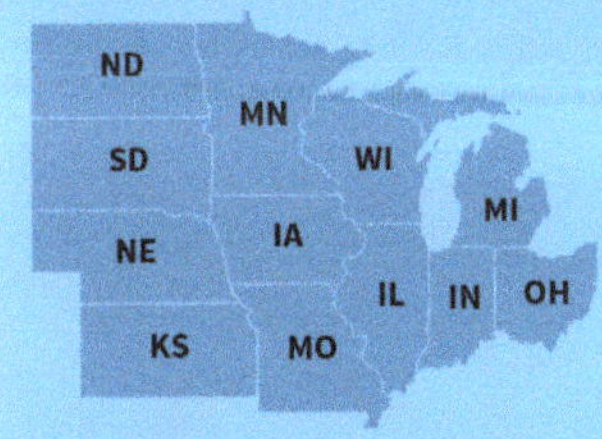

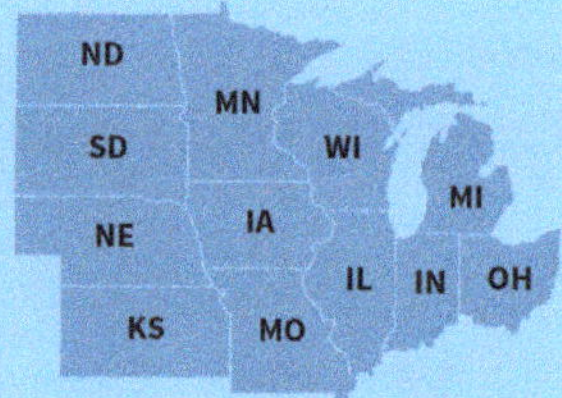

KENT STATE UNIVERSITY

Address: 1325 Theatre Drive, Kent, OH 44242
Website: *https://www.kent.edu/theatredance/bachelor-fine-arts-musical-theatre*
Contact: *https://www.kent.edu/theatredance/contact-us*
Phone: (330) 672-2082
Email: theatre@kent.edu

COST OF ATTENDANCE:

In-State Tuition & Fees: $11,923 | **Additional Expenses:** $17,745
Total: $29,668

Out-of-State Tuition & Fees: $20,799 | **Additional Expenses:** $17,745
Total: $38,544

Financial Aid: https://www.kent.edu/financialaid

ADDITIONAL INFORMATION:

Available Degree(s)

- BFA Musical Theatre

Freshman Audition Requirement

Kent State does not require a pre-screen for applicants who audition in-person. However, they require a pre-screen for applicants who choose to audition live, virtually.

- 1 monologue
- 2 contrasting songs
- Dance reel

Virtual applicants who pass the prescreen move onto a live virtual round.

- 1 monologue
- 2 songs

Students who audition in-person are only required to audition.

- 1 monologue
- 2 songs
- Dance call

Scholarships Offered

Out-of-state students may be eligible for merit-based awards, including the President's Achievement Award ($4,000-$12,500), the Honors Distinction Award ($1,000-$3,000), the Founders Scholarship ($1,000-$2,000) among others. In-state students may be eligible for the same scholarships.

Special Opportunities

The campus houses 3 theatres, rehearsal spaces, laboratories for costumes and scenery, and it oversees the outdoor venue Porthouse Theatre. In their senior year, students may participate in the New York City Musical Theatre Showcase.

Notable Alumni

Kaitlyn Black, Tee Boyich, Antoinette Comer, John de Lancie Jeff Richmond, Alice Ripley, and Ray Wise

OHIO UNIVERSITY

Address: Ohio University, Athens, OH 45701
Website: *https://www.ohio.edu/fine-arts/theater/bfa-performance*
Contact: *Same as above.*
Phone: (740) 593-4818
Email: theater@ohio.edu

COST OF ATTENDANCE:

In-State Tuition & Fees: $12,840 | **Additional Expenses:** $11,862
Total: $24,702

Out-of-State Tuition & Fees: $22,810 | **Additional Expenses:** $11,862
Total: $34,672

Financial Aid: https://www.ohio.edu/admissions/tuition/scholarships-financial-aid

ADDITIONAL INFORMATION:

Available Degree(s)

- BFA Performance, Musical Theatre Track

Freshman Audition Requirement

Applicants may enter the BFA program directly from high school or enter as a BA student and apply for the BFA at the end of their freshman year. BFA applicants must audition, either live virtually, in-person on campus, or in-person at the National Unified Auditions.

- 2 contrasting songs
- 1 monologue
- Dance call
- Wild Card (Optional)

Students may submit an optional video audition prior to their live audition.

- Dance video

Scholarships Offered

Students who submit their application by the Early Action deadline are automatically considered for the OHIO Excellence Awards. Award amounts vary. There is no separate application required.

Special Opportunities

Students may participate in readings, workshops, and full productions including at the Playwright's Festival of New Plays. Additionally, Broadway at OHIO is a yearly festival with master classes, performances, mock auditions, and the NextGen Voice Competition Auditions.

Notable Alumni

Richard Dean Anderson, Chuck Cooper, Thomas F. Duffy, Jonathan Freeman, Matthew Glave, David Hansen, Keith McDermott, Ed O'Neill, Paul Newman, and Betty Thomas

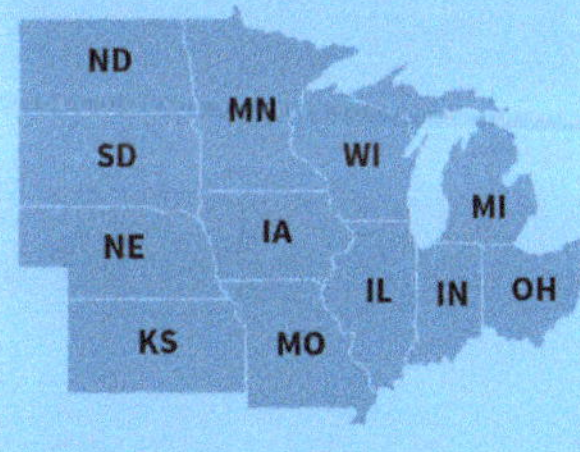

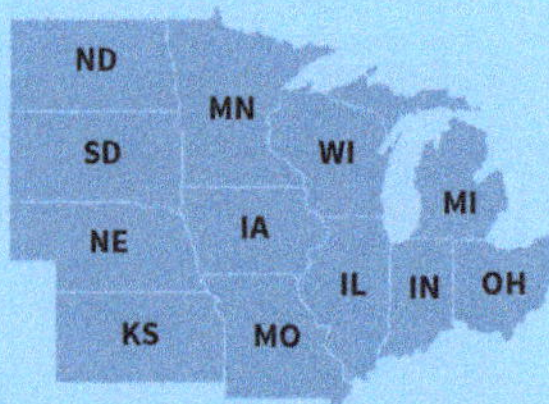

OTTERBEIN UNIVERSITY

Address: 1 S Grove St, Westerville, OH 43081
Website: *https://www.otterbein.edu/programs/bachelor-of-fine-arts-musical-theatre/*
Contact: *https://www.otterbein.edu/about/campus-addresses/*
Phone: (614) 890-3000
Email: uotterb@otterbein.edu

COST OF ATTENDANCE:

Tuition & Fees: $32,624 | **Additional Expenses:** $12,224
Total: $44,848

Financial Aid: https://www.otterbein.edu/financial-aid/

ADDITIONAL INFORMATION:

Available Degree(s)

- BFA Musical Theatre
- BFA Musical Theatre, Concentration: Dance

Freshman Audition Requirement

Otterbein University participates in the Paper Mill Playhouse Common Pre-Screen. For more information, please refer to Chapter 8. Submit via Acceptd.

- Songs (Option A)
- Monologues (Option B)
- Dance Option (Required)
- Ballet (Optional)
- Wild Card (Optional)

Applicants with a successful pre-screen are invited for a virtual audition or an in-person audition on campus or at the National Unified Auditions.

- Dance audition
- 2 vocal selections
- 1 monologue

Scholarships Offered

Applicants are automatically considered for merit-based and need-based scholarships when they apply to Otterbein. Awards go up to $18,000 per year. Talent awards are available to theatre students and range from $500 to $26,000.

Special Opportunities

The BFA in Musical Theatre is interdisciplinary. Students take courses in music theory, private voice study, jazz, ballet, tap, voice for stage, movement, and many other courses. Performance opportunities exist on mainstage productions, musicals, vocal ensembles, and workshops. Otterbein hosts a Senior Showcase as well, produced in New York City for casting directors which also allows students the chance to join a ten-week internship at a professional theatre.

Notable Alumni

Jonathan Bennett, Jeremy Bobb, Mandy Bruno, David Graf, Rachael Harris, Dee Hoty, Sam Jaeger, Gordon Jump, Karen Radcliffe, and Cory Michael Smith

UNIVERSITY OF CINCINNATI

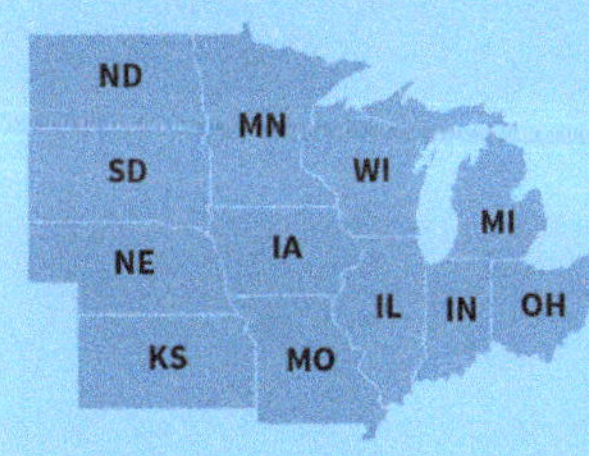

Address: 2600 Clifton Ave, Cincinnati, OH 45221
Website: *https://ccm.uc.edu/areas-of-study/academic-units/musical-theatre/bachelor-of-fine-arts.html*
Contact: *https://admissions.uc.edu/contact.html*
Phone: (513) 556-1100
Email: admissions@uc.edu

COST OF ATTENDANCE:

In-State Tuition & Fees: $12,598 | **Additional Expenses:** $16,510
Total: $29,108

Out-of-State Tuition & Fees: $27,932 | **Additional Expenses:** $11,874
Total: $44,442

Financial Aid: https://financialaid.uc.edu/

ADDITIONAL INFORMATION:

Available Degree(s)

- BFA Musical Theatre

Freshman Audition Requirement
University of Cincinnati participates in the Paper Mill Playhouse Common Pre-Screen. For more information, please refer to Chapter 8. Submit via Acceptd.

- Songs (Option A)
- Monologues (Option A)
- Dance Option (Required)
- Wild Card (Optional)

Applicants with a successful pre-screen are invited for an audition either live virtually, or in-person on-campus or at the National Unified Auditions.

- Jazz dance combination
- 2 contrasting songs
- 1 monologue

Scholarships Offered
The Cincinnatus Scholarship Program offers renewable scholarships to incoming first-year students based on merit. Applicants must submit their application and all accompanying materials by December 1 of their senior year to be considered.

Special Opportunities
With the oldest musical theatre program in the country, the University of Cincinnati is one of the top training grounds for musical theatre. Vocal training is emphasized with private voice coaching, musical theatre coaching, and group training. Classical actor training includes Chekov and Meisner techniques while dance training includes ballet, jazz, tap, and modern. Four musicals are presented per season along with workshops and concerts. Cast members may from any year. Seniors showcase their talents to agents and casting directors in New York.

Notable Alumni
Christy Altomare, Shoshana Bean, Ashley Brown, Josh Breckenridge, Ryan Breslin, Kristy Cates, Andrew Chappelle, Max Chernin, Max Clayton, Nikki Renée Daniels, Julian Decker, Alysha Deslorieux, Mickey Fisher, Mia Gentile, Jessica Hendy, Blaine Krauss, Marcia Lewis, Kevin McCollum, Pamela Myers, Karen Olivo, Faith Prince, Lee Roy Reams, Noah Ricketts, John Riddle, Raven Thomas, Tom Viola, Betsy Wolfe, and Kirsten Wyatt

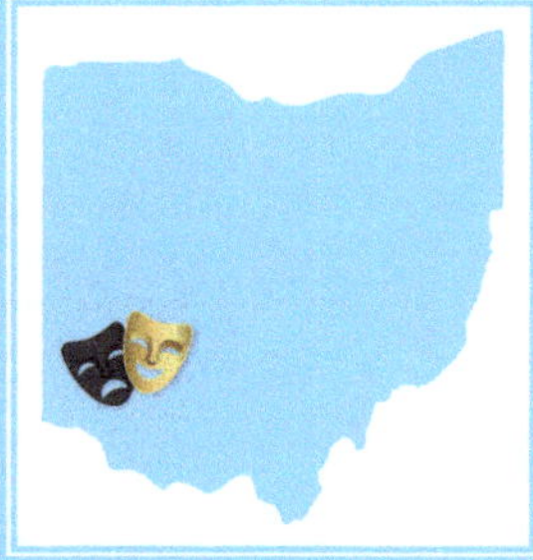

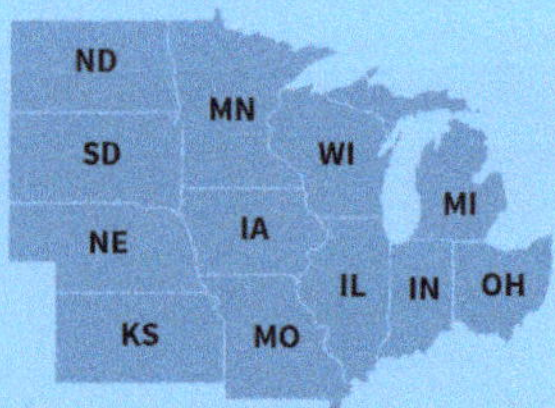

WRIGHT STATE UNIVERSITY

Address: 3640 Colonel Glenn Hwy, Dayton, OH 45435
Website: *https://liberal-arts.wright.edu/theatre-dance-and-motion-pictures/bachelor-of-fine-arts-in-acting-musical-theatre-concentration*
Contact: *https://www.wright.edu/admissions/undergraduate*
Phone: (937) 775-5700
Email: admissions@wright.edu

COST OF ATTENDANCE:

In-State Tuition & Fees: $9,962 | **Additional Expenses:** $11,948
Total: $21,910

Out-of-State Tuition & Fees: $19,380 | **Additional Expenses:** $11,948
Total: $31,328

Financial Aid: https://www.wright.edu/raiderconnect/financial-aid

ADDITIONAL INFORMATION:

Available Degree(s)

- BFA Musical Theatre

Freshman Audition Requirement

Wright State does not require a pre-screen. Auditions are required.

- 2 contrasting monologues
- 2 contrasting songs
- Dance audition required for placement

Scholarships Offered

The Department of Theatre, Dance, and Motion Pictures offers need-based and merit-based scholarships. The audition determines qualification. In addition, Wright State offers numerous merit and need-based scholarships for first-year students with awards as high as full tuition, room, and board.

Special Opportunities

Students may join the Honors program for acting and musical theatre. In this program, students create a capstone project. Students must apply to join this program. Musical theatre students may also participate in workshops to help prepare for the auditions for the Senior Showcase in New York City.

Notable Alumni

Hannah Beachler, Eddie McClintock, Joey Monda, Alicia Rodis, Nicole Scherzinger, Brad Sherwood, and Tricia Small

VITERBO UNIVERSITY

Address: 900 Viterbo Dr, La Crosse, WI 54601
Website: *https://www.viterbo.edu/theatre-and-music-theatre-department*
Contact: *https://www.viterbo.edu/about/contact-us*
Phone: (608) 796-3010
Email: admission@viterbo.edu

COST OF ATTENDANCE:

Tuition & Fees: $30,400 | **Additional Expenses:** $9,386
Total: $39,786

Financial Aid: https://www.viterbo.edu/first-year-admissions/first-year-cost-and-aid

ADDITIONAL INFORMATION:

Available Degree(s)

- BFA Music Theatre

Freshman Audition Requirement

Viterbo University participates in the Paper Mill Playhouse Common Pre-Screen. For more information, please refer to Chapter 8. Submit via Acceptd.

- Songs (Option A)
- Monologues (Option A)
- Dance Option (Required)
- Wild Card (Optional)

Applicants with a successful pre-screen are invited for an in-person or virtual audition.

- 1 monologue
- 2 contrasting songs
- Dance call
- Interview

Scholarships Offered

Renewable merit-based scholarships up to $16,000 are available to all students. Theatre students are also eligible for talent scholarships.

Special Opportunities

Students may audition to perform in any of the five, fully-mounted productions per year. Additionally, musical theatre students benefit from individualized attention due to the low, 9:1 student to faculty ratio. In their senior year, students participate in a Senior Showcase.

Notable Alumni

David Adamick, Linda Balgord, Matt Boehler, Abby DeSanto, Raisa Ellington, Kerby Joe Grubb, Rebecca Kaasa, Jhardon DiShon Milton, Troy Iverson, Ashley Pankow, Samantha Pauly, Maya Richardson, Arbender J. Robinson, and Nadia Wahhab

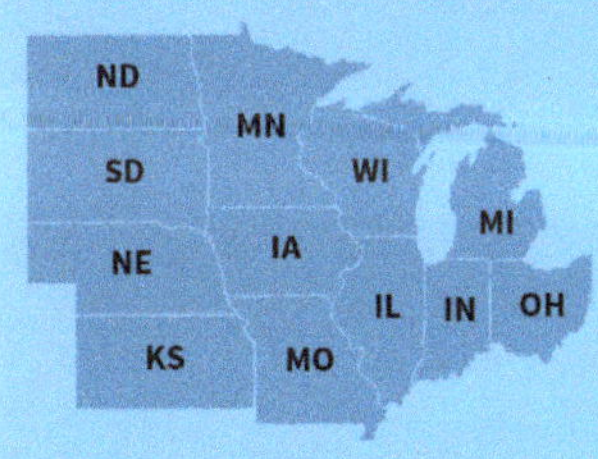

CHAPTER 15
REGION THREE
SOUTH

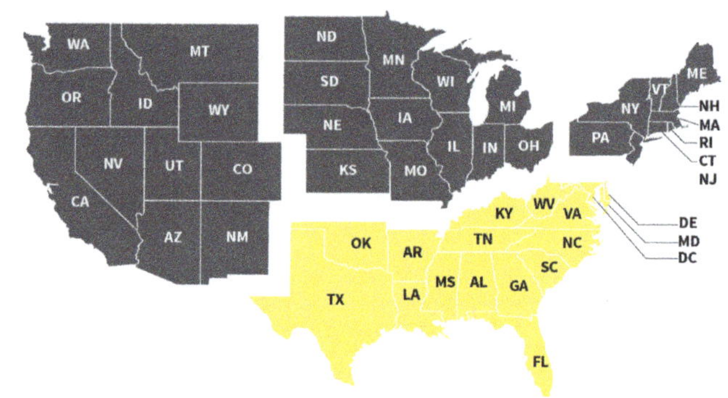

ALABAMA

ARKANSAS

DELAWARE

DISTRICT OF COLUMBIA

FLORIDA

GEORGIA

KENTUCKY

LOUISIANA

MARYLAND

MISSISSIPPI

NORTH CAROLINA

OKLAHOMA

SOUTH CAROLINA

TENNESSEE

TEXAS

VIRGINIA

WEST VIRGINIA

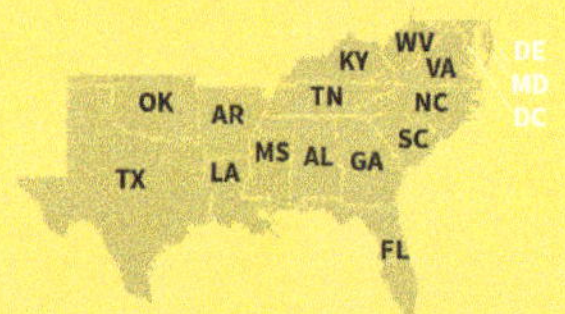

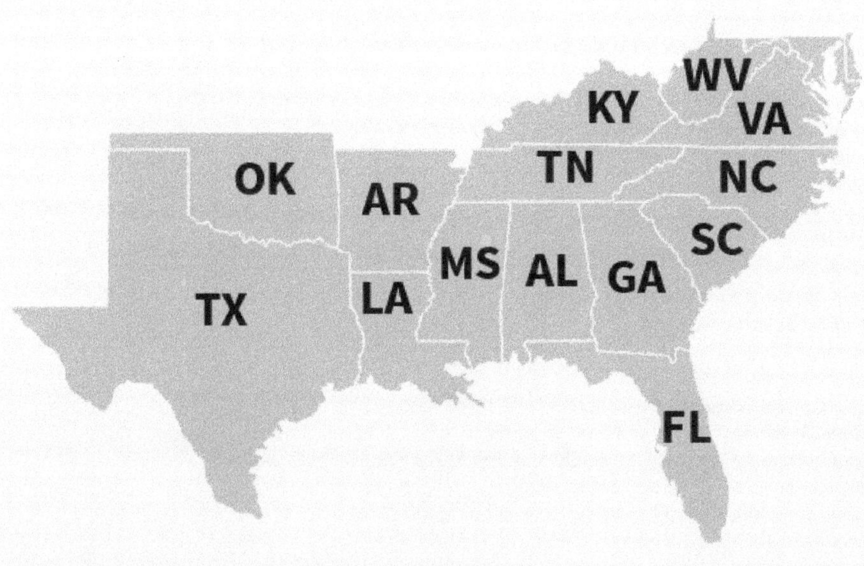

18 *Programs* | 16 *States*

1. *AL - Samford University*
2. *AL - University of Alabama*
3. *DC - American University*
4. *FL - Florida State University*
5. *FL – University of Miami*
6. *FL - University of Tampa*
7. *LA - Loyola University New Orleans*
8. *LA - Tulane University*
9. *NC - Elon University*
10. *OK - Oklahoma City University*
11. *OK - University of Oklahoma*
12. *SC - Coastal Carolina University*
13. *TN - Belmont University*
14. *TX - Sam Houston State*
15. *TX - Texas Christian University (TCU)*
16. *TX - Texas State University*
17. *VA - James Madison University*
18. *VA - Shenandoah University*

MUSICAL THEATRE PROGRAMS

School	Avg. GPA, SAT Evidence-Based Reading Writing (ERW), SAT Math (M), and ACT Composite (C) Early Decision (ED): Yes/No	Admission Statistics	Program(s)	Pre-Screen and/or Audition Required (Req.)
Samford University 800 Lakeshore Dr, Homewood, AL 35229	GPA: 3.8 SAT (ERW): 540-640 SAT (M): 520-600 ACT (C): 22-30 ED: No	Overall College Admit Rate: 84% Undergrad Enrollment: 3,576 Total Enrollment: 5,829	BFA Musical Theatre Degrees Awarded in the Program(s) (2020): 10	Pre-screen not req. Audition req.
University of Alabama at Birmingham 1720 University Blvd, Birmingham, AL 35294	GPA: 3.83 SAT (ERW): 560-668 SAT (M): 530-660 ACT (C): 22-30 ED: No	Overall College Admit Rate: 81% Undergrad Enrollment: 13,878 Total Enrollment: 22,563	BFA Musical Theatre Degrees Awarded in the Program(s) (2020): 9	Pre-screen req. Audition req.
American University 4400 Massachusetts Ave NW, Washington, DC 20016	GPA: 3.79 SAT (ERW): 630-710 SAT (M): 590-680 ACT (C): 27-32 ED: Yes	Overall College Admit Rate: 39% Undergrad Enrollment: 7,953 Total Enrollment: 14,001	BA Musical Theatre Degrees Awarded in the Program(s) (2020): 11	Pre-screen not req. Audition req.
Florida State University 600 W College Ave, Tallahassee, FL 32306	GPA: 3.59 SAT (ERW): 620-680 SAT (M): 600-670 ACT (C): 27-31 ED: No	Overall College Admit Rate: 81% Undergrad Enrollment: 13,878 Total Enrollment: 22,563	BFA Music Theatre Degrees Awarded in the Program(s) (2020): N/A	Pre-screen req. Audition req.

MUSICAL THEATRE PROGRAMS

School	Avg. GPA, SAT Evidence-Based Reading Writing (ERW), SAT Math (M), and ACT Composite (C) Early Decision (ED): Yes/No	Admission Statistics	Program(s)	Pre-Screen and/or Audition Required (Req.)
University of Miami University of Miami, Coral Gables, FL 33124	GPA: 3.6 SAT (ERW): 620-700 SAT (M): 630-720 ACT (C): 28-32 ED: Yes	Overall College Admit Rate: 33% Undergrad Enrollment: 11,334 Total Enrollment: 17,809	BFA Musical Theatre Degrees Awarded in the Program(s) (2020): N/A	Pre-screen optional Audition req.
University of Tampa 401 W Kennedy Blvd, Tampa, FL 33606	GPA: N/A SAT (ERW): 550-620 SAT (M): 540-610 ACT (C): 22-27 ED: No	Overall College Admit Rate: 56% Undergrad Enrollment: 8,657 Total Enrollment: 9,605	BFA Musical Theatre Degrees Awarded in the Program(s) (2020): 14	Pre-screen not req. Audition req.
Loyola University New Orleans 6363 St Charles Ave, New Orleans, LA 70118	GPA: 3.48 SAT (ERW): 540-640 SAT (M): 510-600 ACT (C): 21-26 ED: No	Overall College Admit Rate: 72% Undergrad Enrollment: 3,219 Total Enrollment: 4,497	BA Theatre Arts and Musical Theatre Degrees Awarded in the Program(s) (2020): 5	Pre-screen not req. Audition req.
Tulane University 6823 St Charles Ave, New Orleans, LA 70118	GPA: 3.64 SAT (ERW): 680-740 SAT (M): 680-770 ACT (C): 30-33 ED: No	Overall College Admit Rate: 10% Undergrad Enrollment: 7,780 Total Enrollment: 13,127	BFA Musical Theatre Degrees Awarded in the Program(s) (2020): N/A	Pre-screen not req. Audition req.

MUSICAL THEATRE PROGRAMS

School	Avg. GPA, SAT Evidence-Based Reading Writing (ERW), SAT Math (M), and ACT Composite (C) Early Decision (ED): Yes/No	Admission Statistics	Program(s)	Pre-Screen and/or Audition Required (Req.)
Elon University 100 Campus Dr., Elon, NC 27244	GPA: 4.07 SAT (ERW): 580-660 SAT (M): 560-660 ACT (C): 25-30 ED: Yes	Overall College Admit Rate: 72% Undergrad Enrollment: 6,291 Total Enrollment: 7,117	BFA Music Theatre Degrees Awarded in the Program(s) (2020): 17	Pre-screen req. Audition req.
Oklahoma City University 2501 N. Blackwelder, Oklahoma City, OK 73106	GPA: N/A SAT (ERW): 550-650 SAT (M): 530-610 ACT (C): 22-29 ED: No	Overall College Admit Rate: 73% Undergrad Enrollment: 1,527 Total Enrollment: 2,617	BM Music Theatre Degrees Awarded in the Program(s) (2020): N/A	Pre-screen req. Audition req.
University of Oklahoma 840 Asp Ave., Carpenter Hall Rm 104, Norman, OK 73019	GPA: 3.63 SAT (ERW): 560-650 SAT (M): 540-650 ACT (C): 23-29 ED: No	Overall College Admit Rate: 83% Undergrad Enrollment: 21,383 Total Enrollment: 27,772	BFA Musical Theatre Performance Degrees Awarded in the Program(s) (2020): 12	Pre-screen req. Audition req.
Coastal Carolina University Coastal Carolina University, Conway, SC 29528	GPA: 3.72 SAT (ERW): 510-600 SAT (M): 510-580 ACT (C): 19-25 ED: No	Overall College Admit Rate: 70% Undergrad Enrollment: 9,500 Total Enrollment: 10,118	BFA Theatre, concentration: Musical Theatre Degrees Awarded in the Program(s) (2020): N/A	Pre-screen req. Audition req.

MUSICAL THEATRE PROGRAMS

School	Avg. GPA, SAT Evidence-Based Reading Writing (ERW), SAT Math (M), and ACT Composite (C) Early Decision (ED): Yes/No	Admission Statistics	Program(s)	Pre-Screen and/or Audition Required (Req.)
Belmont University 1900 Belmont Blvd, Nashville, TN 37212	GPA: 3.79 SAT (ERW): 580-660 SAT (M): 540-640 ACT (C): 23-30 ED: No	Overall College Admit Rate: 83% Undergrad Enrollment: 6,631 Total Enrollment: 8,204	BFA Musical Theatre BM Musical Theatre BA Voice, emphasis: Musical Theatre Degrees Awarded in the Program(s) (2020): N/A	Pre-screen not req. Audition req.
Sam Houston State University 1905 University Ave, Huntsville, TX 77340	GPA: N/A SAT (ERW): 490-570 SAT (M): 480-550 ACT (C): 18-23 ED: No	Overall College Admit Rate: 92% Undergrad Enrollment: 18,811 Total Enrollment: 21,912	BFA Musical Theatre Degrees Awarded in the Program(s) (2020): 19	Pre-screen not req. Audition req.
Texas Christian University (TCU) 2800 South University Dr., Fort Worth, TX 76109	GPA: N/A SAT (ERW): 560-660 SAT (M): 550-660 ACT (C): 25-31 ED: No	Overall College Admit Rate: 48% Undergrad Enrollment: 9,704 Total Enrollment: 11,379	BFA Theatre, emphasis: Musical Theatre Degrees Awarded in the Program(s) (2020): 13	Pre-screen req. Audition req.

MUSICAL THEATRE PROGRAMS

School	Avg. GPA, SAT Evidence-Based Reading Writing (ERW), SAT Math (M), and ACT Composite (C) Early Decision (ED): Yes/No	Admission Statistics	Program(s)	Pre-Screen and/or Audition Required (Req.)
Texas State University 601 University Dr, San Marcos, TX 78666	GPA: N/A SAT (ERW): 510-600 SAT (M): 500-580 ACT (C): 20-25 ED: No	Overall College Admit Rate: 85% Undergrad Enrollment: 33,193 Total Enrollment: 37,812	BFA Musical Theatre Degrees Awarded in the Program(s) (2020): 11	Pre-screen req. Audition req.
James Madison University 800 S Main St, Harrisonburg, VA 22807	GPA: N/A SAT (ERW): 570-650 SAT (M): 550-630 ACT (C): 23-28 ED: No	Overall College Admit Rate: 80% Undergrad Enrollment: 19,727 Total Enrollment: 21,594	BA Musical Theatre Degrees Awarded in the Program(s) (2020): N/A	Pre-screen not req. Audition req.
Shenandoah University 1460 University Dr, Winchester, VA 22601	GPA: 3.55 SAT (ERW): 510-630 SAT (M): 500-600 ACT (C): 19-26 ED: No	Overall College Admit Rate: 74% Undergrad Enrollment: 2,267 Total Enrollment: 4,174	BFA Musical Theatre Degrees Awarded in the Program(s) (2020): 21	Pre-screen req. Audition req.

SAMFORD UNIVERSITY

Address: 800 Lakeshore Dr, Homewood, AL 35229
Website: *https://www.samford.edu/arts/theatre-and-dance/musical-theatre-major*
Contact: *https://www.samford.edu/admission/contact*
Phone: (205) 726-2011
Email: https://www.samford.edu/admission/contact

COST OF ATTENDANCE:

Tuition & Fees: $34,198 | **Additional Expenses:** $11,260
Total: $45,458

Financial Aid: https://www.samford.edu/admission/financial-aid?arts

ADDITIONAL INFORMATION:

Available Degree(s)

- BFA Musical Theatre

Freshman Audition Requirement

Samford University does not require a pre-screen. Auditions and interviews are held live, in-person or virtually.

- 3 songs
- 2 monologues
- 2 dance videos, one ballet
- Dance call

Scholarships Offered

Merit-based and need-based scholarships are available to all Samford University students.

Special Opportunities

School of the Arts students follow Catalyst, a multi-disciplinary and collaborative curriculum. Professional-level experience is required for graduating seniors.

Notable Alumni

Mary Anderson, Tony Hale, Gail Patrick, Susan Patterson, Jeanne Ellison Shaffer, Kristian Stanfill, and Perry Stephens

UNIVERSITY OF ALABAMA AT BIRMINGHAM

Address: 1720 University Blvd, Birmingham, AL 35294
Website: *https://www.uab.edu/cas/theatre/academics/bfa-musical-theatre*
Contact: *https://www.uab.edu/home/contact*
Phone: (205) 934-4011
Email: chooseuab@uab.edu

COST OF ATTENDANCE:

In-State Tuition & Fees: $8,568 | **Additional Expenses:** $19,062
Total: $27,630

Out-of-State Tuition & Fees: $20,400 | **Additional Expenses:** $19,751
Total: $40,151

Financial Aid: https://www.uab.edu/cost-aid/

ADDITIONAL INFORMATION:

Available Degree(s)

- BFA Musical Theatre

Freshman Audition Requirement

University of Alabama at Birmingham (UAB) participates in the Paper Mill Playhouse Common Pre-Screen. For more information, please refer to Chapter 8. Submit via Acceptd.

- Songs (Option A or B)
- Monologues (Option A)
- Dance Option (Required)
- Ballet Option (Optional)
- Wild Card (Required)

Applicants with a successful pre-screen are invited for an in-person or virtual audition.

Scholarships Offered

UAB offers merit-based scholarships, however applicants must submit a separate application to be considered. Awards range from $2,000-$10,000 for in-state students and $6,000-$20,000 for out-of-state students.

Special Opportunities

UAB produces four mainstage productions, four touring productions, and other performance opportunities each year. Musical theatre students have ample opportunities to gain experience on stage. Furthermore, musical theatre students are required to complete a capstone project focused on the business side of musical theatre.

Notable Alumni

The BFA in Musical Theatre program is 6 years old as of 2022. As such, many of their graduates are just in the middle of their first few contracts.

AMERICAN UNIVERSITY

Address: 4400 Massachusetts Ave NW, Washington, DC 20016
Website: *https://www.american.edu/cas/performing-arts/theatre/ba-must.cfm*
Contact: *https://www.american.edu/about/contact-us.cfm*
Phone: (202) 885-3420
Email: dpa@american.edu

COST OF ATTENDANCE:

Tuition & Fees: $51,062 | **Additional Expenses:** $17,530
Total: $68,592

Financial Aid: https://www.american.edu/financialaid/

ADDITIONAL INFORMATION:

Available Degree(s)

- BA Musical Theatre

Freshman Audition Requirement

American University does not require a pre-screen. Freshman applicants may only audition in Spring, preferably prior to starting their university studies. However, students may be admitted into AU and then transfer into the major after completing the Fall audition. Submit via SlideRoom.

- 1 monologue
- 2 contrasting songs
- Optional dance piece
- Theatre resume and headshot

Scholarships Offered

AU automatically considers all students for merit scholarships upon their university application. Scholarship awards range from $8,000-$22,000. Furthermore, all theatre and musical theatre students are eligible for specialized scholarships, based on their audition.

Special Opportunities

Musical Theatre majors are intensively trained in acting, voice, and dance. Students learn from internationally-recognized performers in seminars, workshops, and productions. Furthermore, AU students are eligible to apply for the combined Bachelor's/Master's Program.

Notable Alumni

Caroline Aaron, Aamir Ali, Bryan Callen, Elizabeth Chomko, America Ferrera, Gale Harold, Goldie Hawn, Benjamin Salisbury, Margo Seibert, Michele Snyder, and Vishal Vaidya

FLORIDA STATE UNIVERSITY

Address: 600 W College Ave, Tallahassee, FL 32306
Website: *https://theatre.fsu.edu/programs/undergraduate/music-theatre/*
Contact: *https://admissions.fsu.edu/contact/*
Phone: (850) 644-6200
Email: admissions@fsu.edu

COST OF ATTENDANCE:

In-State Tuition & Fees: $6,516 | **Additional Expenses:** $16,512
Total: $23,028

Out-of-State Tuition & Fees: $21,683 | **Additional Expenses:** $16,512
Total: $38,195

Financial Aid: https://financialaid.fsu.edu/

ADDITIONAL INFORMATION:

Available Degree(s)

- BFA Music Theatre

Freshman Audition Requirement
Florida State University participates in the Paper Mill Playhouse Common Pre-Screen. For more information, please refer to Chapter 8. Submit via Acceptd.

- Songs (Option A or B)
- Monologues (Option A)
- Dance Option (Required)
- Ballet (Required)
- Wild Card (Optional)

Applicants with a successful pre-screen are invited for a callback via Zoom.

- 2 dance combinations
- 2 contrasting songs
- 1 monologue

Applicants who pass the callback will be invited on campus for a live audition and dance workshop.

Scholarships Offered
The School of Theatre awards scholarships to selected incoming and continuing students. BFA students can qualify based on academic ability and potential.

Special Opportunities
The comprehensive program focused on professional acting on Broadway, regional theatre, entertainment, and graduate school. Seniors present a Showcase in NYC for producers, directors, agents, and casting directors.

Notable Alumni
Frankie Alvarez, Senait Ashenafi, King Bach, Vanessa Baden, Dan Bakkedahl, Trenesha Biggers, Ricou Browning, Cody Burger, Matt Cohen, Gregor Collins, Mekia Cox, Valerie Cruz, Dimitri Diatchenko, Faye Dunaway, Tiffany Fallon, Luis Fonsi, Suzanne Friedline, Joanna Garcia, Paul Gleason, Montego Glover, Andre Gordon, Jennifer Hammon, Joey Haro, Cheryl Hines, Andre Holland, Polly Holliday, Traylor Howard, Nancy Kulp, Billy Lane, Jon Locke, DeLane Matthews, Michelle McCool, Gerald McCullouch, Vic Morrow, Henry Polic II, John Preston, Burt Reynolds, Chay Santini, Amy Seimetz, Sonny Shroyer, Richard Simmons, Pat Skipper, J Smith-Cameron, Tonea Stewart, Erik Stolhanske, Gabriel Traversari, Robert Urich, Casper Van Dien, and Joseph Will

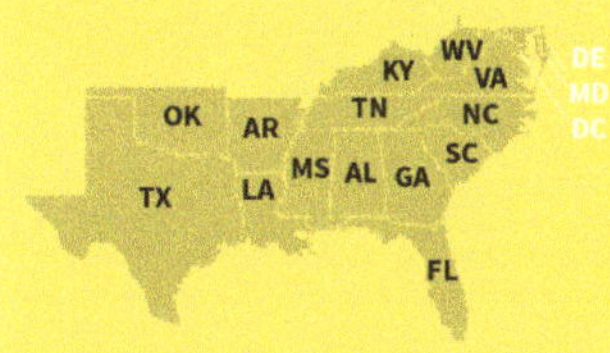

UNIVERSITY OF MIAMI

Address: University of Miami, Coral Gables, FL 33124
Website: *https://theatrearts.as.miami.edu/undergraduate-programs/bfa-musical-theatre-program/index.html*
Contact: *https://admissions.miami.edu/undergraduate/about/contact-us/index.html*
Phone: (305) 284-6000
Email: admission@miami.edu

COST OF ATTENDANCE:

Tuition & Fees: $53,682 | **Additional Expenses:** $20,030
Total: $73,712

Financial Aid: https://finaid.miami.edu/index.html

ADDITIONAL INFORMATION:

Available Degree(s)

- BFA Musical Theatre

Freshman Audition Requirement

University of Miami offers an optional pre-screening for applicants. It is not required, however it is highly recommended as it allows applicants to secure an audition date in the city of their choice.

The live audition is either on-campus or at the Pittsburgh Unified Auditions, CAP Auditions, Moonified Auditions, or the National Unified Auditions.

- 2 contrasting monologues
- 2 contrasting songs
- Dance call

Scholarships Offered

According to UM, "approximately 50% of incoming first-year students receive merit scholarships". The most prestigious merit award at UM is the Stamps Scholarship. This scholarship covers the student's full cost of attendance for four years of study, including a laptop allowance and access to a $12,000 enrichment fund that may be used towards educational purposes. Other UM scholarships also cover the full cost of tuition or cost of attendance for all four years. These are all based off merit and/or financial need. For more information on first-year merit scholarships, visit: https://admissions.miami.edu/undergraduate/financial-aid/scholarships/freshman/index.html

Special Opportunities

Students in the Comprehensive Musical Theatre program can enjoy a small student to faculty ratio. There are an average of 10 students to every teacher. Students also do not compete against graduate students for stage roles, as there is no MFA program. For more information, visit: https://theatrearts.as.miami.edu/undergraduate-programs/bfa-musical-theatre-program/index.html

Notable Alumni

Lewis Cleale, Joshua Henry, Ray Liotta, Jo Ann Pflug, Ernie Sabella, and Sylvester Stallone

UNIVERSITY OF TAMPA

Address: 401 W Kennedy Blvd, Tampa, FL 33606
Website: *https://www.ut.edu/academics/college-of-arts-and-letters/department-of-theatre-and-dance-degrees/bachelor-of-fine-arts-in-musical-theatre*
Contact: *https://www.ut.edu/admissions/admissions-contact-information*
Phone: (813) 253-6211
Email: admissions@ut.edu

COST OF ATTENDANCE:

Tuition & Fees: $31,274 | **Additional Expenses:** $11,750
Total: $43,024

Financial Aid: https://www.ut.edu/admissions/financial-aid

ADDITIONAL INFORMATION:

Available Degree(s)

- BFA Musical Theatre

Freshman Audition Requirement

University of Tampa (UT) does not require a pre-screen. However, applicants must audition either digitally or in person. Submit via the SpartanStart Portal.

- 2 contrasting songs
- 1 monologue

Scholarships Offered

All applicants are automatically considered for merit-based and need-based scholarships when they submit their university application. Awards range from $8,000-$18,000 per year. Departmental scholarships are available for musical theatre students.

Special Opportunities

Students will participate in musical theatre and dramatic productions, and cabarets. In-residentce workshops are offered with established musical theatre artists. Internship opportunities with local theme park and theatre companies. Other opportunities include Dance Happening, Spring Dance Concert, six theatre productions per year, and vocal ensembles.

Notable Alumni

Erin Leigh Knowles, Scott Leonard, Bobby Lord, John Matuszak, Marissa Volpe, and Charles White

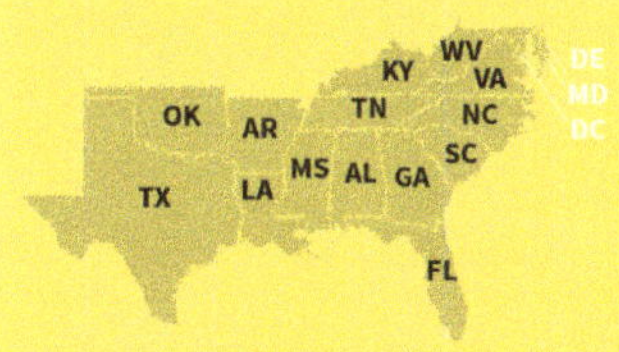

LOYOLA UNIVERSITY NEW ORLEANS

Address: 6363 St Charles Ave, New Orleans, LA 70118
Website: *http://cmm.loyno.edu/theatre/musical-theatre*
Contact: *https://www.loyno.edu/admissions/meet-your-counselor*
Phone: (504) 865-3240
Email: admit@loyno.edu

COST OF ATTENDANCE:

Tuition & Fees: $42,208 | **Additional Expenses:** $18,514
Total: $60,722

Financial Aid: https://www.loyno.edu/admissions/tuition-financial-aid/financial-aid

ADDITIONAL INFORMATION:

Available Degree(s)

- BA Theatre Arts and Musical Theatre

Freshman Audition Requirement

Loyola University New Orleans does not require a pre-screen. Students may audition on-campus or via video submission.

- Headshot & resume
- 1 monologue
- 2 contrasting songs

Scholarships Offered

Applicanst are automatically considered for merit-based scholarships. Awards range from $14,000-$23,000 per year. Students may apply separately for the Social Justice Scholarship and Ensemble Award in their application portal. Students who are admitted to the University Honors Program may also receive an award of $5,000 per year.

Special Opportunities

Loyola University New Orleans is a Jesuit school that contains an arts-focused community and ample performance opportunities for students. BA Theatre Arts and Musical Theatre students will improve their performance skills and study musical theatre, theatre management, theatrical technology, and design.

Notable Alumni

James Will McBride

TULANE UNIVERSITY

Address: 6823 St Charles Ave, New Orleans, LA 70118
Website: *https://liberalarts.tulane.edu/departments/music/academics/undergrad/bfa-musical-theatre*
Contact: *https://liberalarts.tulane.edu/departments/theatre-dance/contact-us*
Phone: (504) 865-5389
Email: undergrad.admission@tulane.edu

COST OF ATTENDANCE:

Tuition & Fees: $60,814 | **Additional Expenses:** $18,828
Total: $80,232

Financial Aid: https://admission.tulane.edu/tuition-aid

ADDITIONAL INFORMATION:

Available Degree(s)

- BFA Musical Theatre

Freshman Audition Requirement

Tulane University does not require a pre-screen. Auditions are required and must be submitted online to the Green Wave Portal.

- 3 contrasting songs
- 1 monologue (Optional)

Scholarships Offered

Tulane University offers two full-tuition merit scholarships: the Deans' Honor Scholarship and the Paul Tulane Award. They also offer one total-cost merit scholarship: the Stamps Scholarship. Musical Theatre students may be eligible for the $5,000/year Musicianship Scholarship.

Special Opportunities

Musical theatre majors take coursework in the Suzuki Method, tap dance, jazz, ballet, acting, and more.

Notable Alumni

Bryan Batt, Evan Farmer, Paul Michael Glaser, Rick Hurst, Anthony Laciura, Christian LeBlanc, Enrique Murciano, Ed Nelson, Al Shea, and Harold Sylvester

ALABAMA
ARKANSAS
DELAWARE
DISTRICT OF COLUMBIA
FLORIDA
GEORGIA
KENTUCKY
LOUISIANA
MARYLAND
MISSISSIPPI
NORTH CAROLINA
OKLAHOMA
SOUTH CAROLINA
TENNESSEE
TEXAS
VIRGINIA
WEST VIRGINIA

ELON UNIVERSITY

Address: 100 Campus Drive, Elon, NC 27244
Website: *https://www.elon.edu/u/academics/arts-and-sciences/performing-arts/majors-minors/*
Contact: *https://www.elon.edu/u/about/contact-elon/*
Phone: (336) 278-2000
Email: admissions@elon.edu

COST OF ATTENDANCE:

Tuition & Fees: $38,725 | **Additional Expenses:** $16,922
Total: $55,647

Financial Aid: https://www.elon.edu/u/admissions/undergraduate/financial-aid/

ADDITIONAL INFORMATION:

Available Degree(s)

- BFA Music Theatre

Freshman Audition Requirement
Elon University participates in the Paper Mill Playhouse Common Pre-Screen. For more information, please refer to Chapter 8. Submit via Acceptd.

- Songs (Option A or B)
- Monologues (Option A)
- Dance Option (Required)

Applicants with a successful pre-screen are invited for a live callback on campus or a virtual callback over Zoom.

- Live dance call
- Interview
- Prepare to sing if requested
- Dance video (if virtual)

Scholarships Offered
Elon University offers numerous merit-based scholarships, talent-based scholarships including Performing Arts Scholarships, as well as Fellows and Scholars programs (scholarships ranging from $7,500 to $13,500 per year).

Special Opportunities
Students study contemporary vocal techniques, music theory, musical theatre literature, scene study, acting for the camera, ballet, jazz, modern, tap, commedia, and Fosse. They can also participate in master classes taught by visiting artists who conduct seminars, workshops, and performances on campus. Students can take private voice lessons every semester. Two mainstage musical theatre productions, one black box production, two annual musical revues, and three plays are produced each year. Students also get to audition for visiting performer workshops, musical reviews, dance performances, student-run productions, and an annual senior thesis production.

Notable Alumni
John Bucchino, Rich Blomquist, Dave Clemmons, Reno Collier, Lisa Goldstein, Grant Gustin, Katie Hillard, Kelli O'Hara, Geof Pilkington, Martin Ritt, Ben Seay, Brent Sexton, Mike Trainor, Taylor Trensch, Kenneth Utt, Barrett Wilbert Weed, and Chris Wood

OKLAHOMA CITY UNIVERSITY

Address: 2501 N. Blackwelder, Oklahoma City, OK 73106
Website: *https://www.okcu.edu/music/academics/degree-programs/undergraduate/music-theater*
Contact: *https://www.okcu.edu/main/contact/*
Phone: (405) 208-5000
Email: N/A

COST OF ATTENDANCE:

Tuition & Fees: $33,404 | **Additional Expenses:** $16,276
Total: $49,680

Financial Aid: https://www.okcu.edu/financialaid/home/

ADDITIONAL INFORMATION:

Available Degree(s)

- BM Music Theatre

Freshman Audition Requirement

Oklahoma City University participates in the Paper Mill Playhouse Common Pre-Screen. For more information, please refer to Chapter 8. Submit via Acceptd.

- Songs (Option A)
- Monologues (Option B)
- Dance Option (Required)
- Wild Card (Required)

Applicants with a successful pre-screen are invited for a live virtual or on-campus callback.

- 2 contrasting songs
- 2 contrasting monologues
- Dance call

Scholarships Offered

Students in the School of Theatre are eligible for academic scholarships based on high school GPA and standardized test scores (up to $7,800 a year).

Special Opportunities

Oklahoma City University's program is focused on music but includes thorough training in acting and dance. Students take acting, dance, voice, and ensemble each term with additional classes in piano, diction, stagecraft, musical writing, costume, and makeup. Approximately one-fifth of the coursework is in performance/music training. Students audition for six shows and are cast in both musicals and operas. Each production integrates music/text/character analysis as well as acting, movement, dance, and diction. The New York City showcase allows students to work with casting directors and agents.

Notable Alumni

Belinda Allyn, Colin Anderson, Heather Botts, Jane Bunting, Kristin Chenoweth, Jacob Gutierrez, Wes Hart, Jeremy Hays, Eryn LeCroy, Stacey Logan, Elliott Mattox, Tiffany Mann, Will Mann, Matt McMahan, Manna Nichols, Kelli O'Hara, Minami Okamura, Destan Owens, Ernie Pruneda, Ron Raines, Molly Rushing, Jennifer Sanchez, Abby C. Smith, and Darius Wright

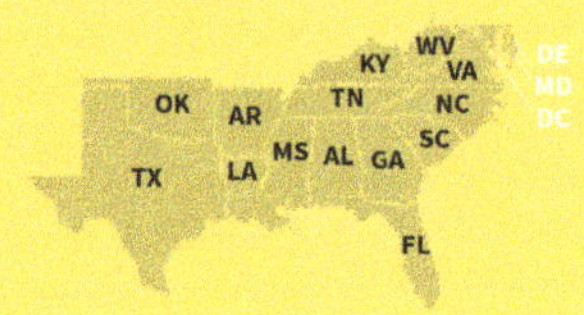

UNIVERSITY OF OKLAHOMA

Address: 840 Asp Ave., Carpenter Hall Rm 104, Norman, OK 73019
Website: *http://www.ou.edu/finearts/musicaltheatre*
Contact: *http://www.ou.edu/web/about_ou/contact*
Phone: (405) 325-2151
Email: admissions@ou.edu

COST OF ATTENDANCE:

In-State Tuition & Fees: $13,065 | **Additional Expenses:** $11,700
Total: $24,765

Out-of-State Tuition & Fees: $28,869 | Additional Expenses: $18,757
Total: $40,569

Financial Aid: http://www.ou.edu/admissions/affordability/financial-aid

ADDITIONAL INFORMATION:

Available Degree(s)

- BFA Musical Theatre Performance

Freshman Audition Requirement

University of Oklahoma participates in the Paper Mill Playhouse Common Pre-Screen. For more information, please refer to Chapter 8. Submit via Acceptd.

- Songs (Option A)
- Monologue (Option B)
- Dance Option (Required)
- Wild Card (Optional)

Applicants with a successful pre-screen are invited for a callback audition. Callbacks may occur on-campus, in person at various cities, or virtually.

Scholarships Offered

University of Oklahoma offers numerous test score and high school GPA-based scholarships (up to $16,000 over four years for in-state students and $60,000 over four years for out-of-state students and and international students) as well as National Merit Scholarships, Oklahoma State Regents' Academic Scholars Program scholarship and test-optional scholarships.

Special Opportunities

The University of Oklahoma's Weitzenhoffer School of Musical Theatre hosts the only full musical theatre program in the nation. There is a 50-student cap and a 5:1 student to teacher ratio.

Notable Alumni

Skyler Adams, Barry Busby, Stephen Dickson, Larry Drake, CK Edwards, Ronnie Claire Edwards, Annie Funke, James Garner, Alice Ghostley, Ed Harris, Van Heflin, Adrianna Hicks, Dan Horn, Rance Howard, Christian Kane, Roberta Knie, Eloise Kropp, Dorcas Leung, Cory Lingner, Luke Longacre, Kelly Mantle, Emily Mechler, Ez (Iris) Menas, Olivia Munn, Con O'Shea-Creal, Meg Randall, Jamard Richardson, Christopher Rice, Esther Stillwell, Sarah Quinn Taylor, Daryl Tofa, Matt Villines, MacKenzie Warren, Dennis Weaver, and Kristen Beth Williams

COASTAL CAROLINA UNIVERSITY

Address: Coastal Carolina University, Conway, SC 29528
Website: *https://www.coastal.edu/theatre/programs/bfa-musicaltheatreconcentration/*
Contact: *https://www.coastal.edu/aboutccu/contactus/*
Phone: (800) 277-7000
Email: admissions@coastal.edu

COST OF ATTENDANCE:

In-State Tuition & Fees: $11,640 | **Additional Expenses:** $14,084
Total: $25,724

Out-of-State Tuition & Fees: $27,394 | **Additional Expenses:** $14,084
Total: $41,478

Financial Aid: https://www.coastal.edu/financialaid/

ADDITIONAL INFORMATION:

Available Degree(s)

- BFA Theatre, concentration: Musical Theatre

Freshman Audition Requirement

Coastal Carolina University participates in the Paper Mill Playhouse Common Pre-Screen. For more information, please refer to Chapter 8. Submit via Acceptd.

- Songs (Option A)
- Monologue (Option A)
- Dance Option (Required)
- Wild Card (Optional)

Applicants with a successful pre-screen are invited for an on-campus audition/interview.

Scholarships Offered

CCU offers merit-based awards that consider cumulative high school GPA, SAT/ACT scores, high school coursework, class rank, recommendations, writing samples, and resumes. Awards range from 10% of tuition to 60% of tuition. The Visual and Performing Arts Award offers 25% of full-time tuition.

Special Opportunities

Students have the opportunity to earn roles in mainstage productions and the senior showcase in New York. Additionally, Coastal Carolina University hosts guest artists and workshops.

Notable Alumni

Madelyn Cline, Bailey Hanks, Michael Kelly, and Edwin McCain

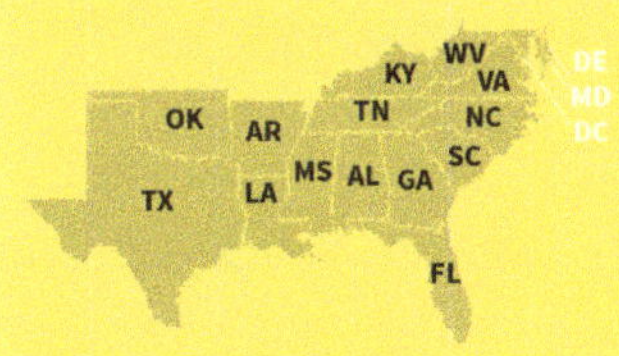

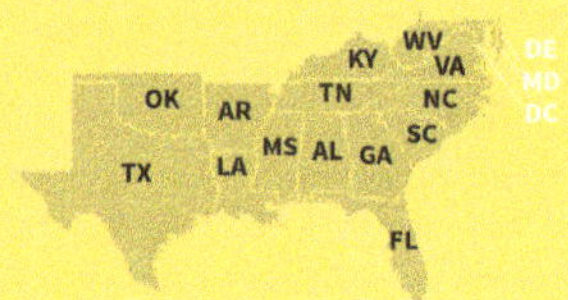

BELMONT UNIVERSITY

Address: 1900 Belmont Blvd, Nashville, TN 37212
Website: *https://www.belmont.edu/cmpa/music/undergrad/musical-theatre/index.html*
Contact: *https://www.belmont.edu/admissions/index.html*
Phone: (615) 460-6000
Email: N/A

COST OF ATTENDANCE:

Tuition & Fees: $38,430 | **Additional Expenses:** $19,875
Total: $58,305

Financial Aid: https://www.belmont.edu/sfs/aid/undergrad.html

ADDITIONAL INFORMATION:

Available Degree(s)

- BFA Musical Theatre
- BM Musical Theatre
- BA Voice, emphasis: Musical Theatre

Freshman Audition Requirement

Belmont University does not require a pre-screen. Auditions are required for all three majors. Below are the audition requirements for the BFA and BM in Musical Theatre.

- 1 aria song
- 2 musical theatre songs
- 1 monologue
- Group dance class
- Headshot & resume

The BA Voice, emphasis in Musical Theatre requires an audition as well, with separate requirements from the BM and BFA in Musical Theatre.

- 2 classical pieces
- 1 musical theatre song
- Repertory list
- Resume

Scholarships Offered

All applicants are automatically considered for merit scholarships when they submit their Belmont University application. Students who apply as test-optional will be considered for merit scholarships based on their high school GPA and overall strength of their application. General Freshman Academic Merit Scholarships ($3,000 to $10,000 annually) are awarded on a rolling basis following the offer of admission. Belmont also offers named awards, which recognize approximately the top two percent of all freshman applicants.

Special Opportunities

Several of Belmont University's productions have won the American Prize in Musical Theatre Performance. Students in Belmont's Musical Theatre program are known for the "Belmont Belt" - their open and healthy vocal sound.

Notable Alumni

McKinley Belcher III, Sean Hetherington, DJ Qualls, and Tony Vincent

SAM HOUSTON STATE UNIVERSITY

Address: 1905 University Ave, Huntsville, TX 77340
Website: *https://www.shsu.edu/academics/theatre/programs/musical-theatre/*
Contact: *https://www.shsu.edu/admissions/*
Phone: (936) 294-1828
Email: admissions@shsu.edu

COST OF ATTENDANCE:

In-State Tuition & Fees: $11,034 | **Additional Expenses:** $15,652
Total: $26,686

Out-of-State Tuition & Fees: $23,274 | **Additional Expenses:** $15,652
Total: $38,926

Financial Aid: https://www.shsu.edu/dept/financial-aid/

ADDITIONAL INFORMATION:

Available Degree(s)

- BFA Musical Theatre

Freshman Audition Requirement

Sam Houston State University does not require a pre-screen. Auditions are required, and are either on-campus or recorded.

- 2 contrasting monologues
- 2 songs
- Dance reel
- Wild card video

Scholarships Offered

Applicants must apply separately for scholarships through the Scholarships4Kats Portal. Scholarships are based on merit and need, and range in value. The audition acts as the talent-based scholarship portion for musical theatre applicants interested in the department scholarship.

Special Opportunities

All musical theatre students participate in workshops each semester that dive into dance and music. Students also learn about the business aspects of being a professional performer. Students also receive vocal belt training.

Notable Alumni

Dana Andrews, Katie Rose Clarke, Joel McDonald, and Richard Linklater

TEXAS CHRISTIAN UNIVERSITY (TCU)

Address: 2800 South University Dr., Fort Worth, TX 76109
Website: *https://finearts.tcu.edu/theatre/academics/areas-of-study/bfa-emphasis-in-musical-theatre/*
Contact: *https://admissions.tcu.edu/connect.php*
Phone: (817) 257-7000
Email: frogmail@tcu.edu

COST OF ATTENDANCE:

Tuition & Fees: $51,660 | **Additional Expenses:** $20,168
Total: $71,828

Financial Aid: https://financialaid.tcu.edu/

ADDITIONAL INFORMATION:

Available Degree(s)

- BFA Theatre, emphasis: Musical Theatre

Freshman Audition Requirement

Texas Christian University (TCU) participates in the Paper Mill Playhouse Common Pre-Screen. For more information, please refer to Chapter 8. Submit via Acceptd.

- Songs (Option B)
- Monologue (Option A)
- Dance Option (Required)
- Ballet Option (Optional)
- Wild Card (Optional)

Applicants with a successful pre-screen are invited for an in-person or virtual audition.

- 2 contrasting songs
- 1 monologue
- Dance call

Scholarships Offered

The Nordan Fine Arts Awards are competitive scholarships for students in the College of Fine Arts. The Nordan Young Artist Award is $10,000+ for incoming freshmen, based on application audition. Students may then renew this scholarship for their remaining years.

Special Opportunities

The student to faculty ratio for BFA performance classes is 12:1. All theatre students train together in fundamental performance coursework. BFA musical theatre students also get specific training on musical theatre performance, musical theatre dance, theory, history, and private voice lessons. Students are encouraged to audition for local theatres while they are enrolled at TCU.

Notable Alumni

Norman Alden, Betty Buckley, Frederic Forrest, Kristin Holt, Benton Jennings, Kames Kerwin, Chris Klein, William Lewis, Wendy Powell, Tudi Rouche, Travis Schuldt, Shantel VanSanten, Van Williams, and Travis Willingham

TEXAS STATE UNIVERSITY

Address: 601 University Dr, San Marcos, TX 78666
Website: *https://www.theatreanddance.txstate.edu/Undergraduate-Degrees/BFA-Musical-Theatre.html*
Phone: (512) 245-2111
Email: https://www.admissions.txstate.edu/contact.html

COST OF ATTENDANCE:

In-State Tuition & Fees: $11,540 | **Additional Expenses:** $15,080
Total: $26,620

Out-of-State Tuition & Fees: $23,820 | **Additional Expenses:** $15,080
Total: $38,900

Financial Aid: https://www.finaid.txstate.edu/

ADDITIONAL INFORMATION:

Available Degree(s)

- BFA Musical Theatre

Freshman Audition Requirement

Texas State University participates in the Paper Mill Playhouse Common Pre-Screen. For more information, please refer to Chapter 8. Submit via Acceptd.

- Songs (Option A or B)
- Monologues (Option A)
- Dance Option (Required)
- Ballet Option (Optional)
- Wild Card (Required)

Applicants with a successful pre-screen are invited for an in-person or virtual audition.

- 2 contrasting songs
- 2 contrasting monologues
- Dance class or video

Scholarships Offered

Out-of-state students may qualify for a nonresident tuition waiver if they, "qualify for at least $1,000 in Texas State competitive or merit scholarships…". In addition, all applicants are automatically awarded National Scholarships and Assured scholarships when they gain acceptance to TSU. A number of competitive scholarships are available as well. An application is required for the Department of Theatre and Dance scholarships.

Special Opportunities

Texas State University produces a dozen shows each year, including two musicals. Special opportunities include the Black and Latino Playwrights Conference, New Work Series, and Undergraduate Directing Festival. Individualized training in voice and acting are offered as well as on-camera acting, directing, speech/dialects, score/libretto analysis, musical theatre history, ballet, jazz, and tap. With close connections to summer theatre opportunities, many students gain additional preparation outside of the classroom. Texas State offers a "Business of the Business" lab series covering doing taxes while on tour, negotiating contracts (Equity, non-union, film, television), mock agent meetings, and how-tos for press interviews on shows. The annual senior showcase takes place in New York City.

Notable Alumni

Scott H. Biram, Powers Boothe, Johnny Brantley III, Stephen Brower, Thomas Carter, Roberta Colindrez, Nick Eibler, Julia Estrada, Jennifer Foster, Demond Green, Emma Hearn, Jesse Heiman, Jorrel Javier, Ben Mayne, Sean McGibbon, Chelcie Ross, George Strait, Anna Uzele, and Gianna Yanelli

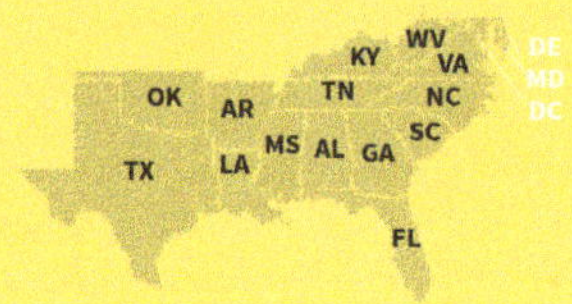

JAMES MADISON UNIVERSITY

Address: 800 S Main St, Harrisonburg, VA 22807
Website: https://www.jmu.edu/theatredance/majors/musical-theatre.shtml
Contact: https://www.jmu.edu/contact-us.shtml
Phone: (540) 568-6211
Email: admissions@jmu.edu

COST OF ATTENDANCE:

In-State Tuition & Fees: $12,914 | **Additional Expenses:** $16,174
Total: $29,088

Out-of-State Tuition & Fees: $29,868 | **Additional Expenses:** $16,174
Total: $46,042

Financial Aid: https://www.jmu.edu/financialaid/index.shtml

ADDITIONAL INFORMATION:

Available Degree(s)

- BA Musical Theatre

Freshman Audition Requirement

James Madison University does not require a pre-screen, however they do follow the Paper Mill Playhouse Common Pre-Screen. For more information, please refer to Chapter 8. Submit via SlideRoom.

- Songs (Option A or B)
- Monologues (Option A)
- Dance Option (Required)
- Ballet Option (Optional)
- Wild Card (Optional)

Live auditions are required.

- 2 contrasting songs
- 1 monologue
- Dance class

Scholarships Offered

James Madison University offers merit-based and need-based scholarships to all students. Students are encourage to apply for scholarships on their university portal.

Special Opportunities

James Madison University produces 3 plays and 2 musicals yearly as well as 5-8 student-produced plays/musicals. Students have every opportunity to gain on-stage experience through these performances. Furthermore, musical theatre students take coursework in dramaturgy, directing, choreography, playwriting, musical directing, and more.

Notable Alumni

Sarah Baker, Jackee Harry, Ashley Iaconetti, Wendy Maybury, and Reshma Shetty

SHENANDOAH UNIVERSITY

Address: 1460 University Dr, Winchester, VA 22601
Website: *https://www.su.edu/conservatory/areas-of-study/bachelor-of-fine-arts-in-musical-theatre/*
Contact: *https://www.su.edu/admissions/contact-us/*
Phone: (540) 665-4581
Email: Admit@su.edu

COST OF ATTENDANCE:

Tuition & Fees: $33,140 | **Additional Expenses:** $16,442
Total: $49,582

Financial Aid: https://www.su.edu/financial-aid/

ADDITIONAL INFORMATION:

Available Degree(s)

- BFA Musical Theatre

Freshman Audition Requirement

Shenandoah University participates in the Paper Mill Playhouse Common Pre-Screen. For more information, please refer to Chapter 8.

- Songs (Option A or B)
- Monologues (Option A)
- Dance Option (Optional)
- Wild Card (Optional)

Applicants with a successful pre-screen are invited for an in-person or live virtual audition.

Scholarships Offered

Musical theatre students may be eligible for the Shenandoah University Conservatory Scholarship, valued at $2,000-$19,500 per year. This renewable scholarship is based on the student's application and the audition. Students may also be eligible for other merit-based awards, ranging in value from $3,000-$20,000 per year.

Special Opportunities

All students at all levels are required to audition for the two main stage musicals and one black box musical occurring at Shenandoah University. There are also numerous student-produced performance opportunities to audition for.

Notable Alumni

Roman Banks, Carter Beauford, Kate Flannery, Aaron Galligan-Stierle, Harold Perrineau, J. Robert Spencer, Carl Tanner, Kathy Voytko, Anthony Wayne, Mac Wiseman, Laura Woyasz, and Richard Zarou

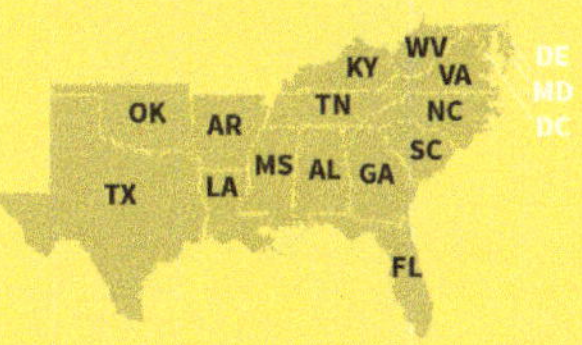

ALASKA

ARIZONA

CALIFORNIA

COLORADO

HAWAII

IDAHO

MONTANA

NEVADA

NEW MEXICO

OREGON

UTAH

WASHINGTON

WYOMING

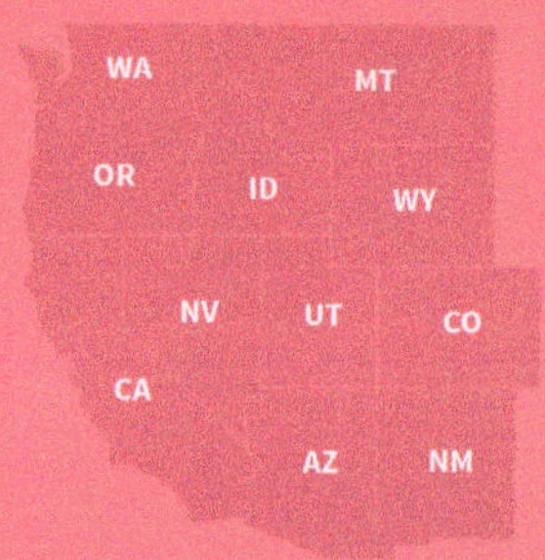

CHAPTER 16

REGION FOUR

WEST

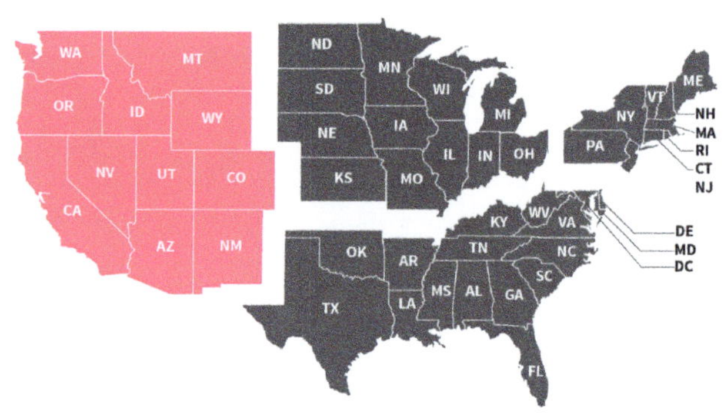

8 *Programs* | **13** *States*

1. *AZ - University of Arizona*
2. *CA - California State University, Chico*
3. *CA - California State University, Fullerton (CSUF)*
4. *CA - Chapman University*
5. *CA - Pepperdine University*
6. *CA - University of California, Irvine (UCI)*
7. *CA - University of Southern California (USC)*
8. *WA - Central Washington University*

MUSICAL THEATRE PROGRAMS

School	Avg. GPA, SAT Evidence-Based Reading Writing (ERW), SAT Math (M), and ACT Composite (C) Early Decision (ED): Yes/No	Admission Statistics	Program(s)	Pre-Screen and/or Audition Required (Req.)
University of Arizona The University of Arizona, Tucson, AZ 85721	GPA: 3.43 SAT (ERW): 550-660 SAT (M): 540-690 ACT (C): 21-29 ED: No	Overall College Admit Rate: 85% Undergrad Enrollment: 36,503 Total Enrollment: 46,932	BFA Musical Theatre Degrees Awarded in the Program(s) (2020): 7	Pre-screen req. Audition req.
California State University, Chico 400 W 1st St, Chico, CA 95929	GPA: 3.34 SAT (ERW): 490-590 SAT (M): 480-580 ACT (C): 18-24 ED: No	Overall College Admit Rate: 90% Undergrad Enrollment: 15,747 Total Enrollment: 16,746	BFA Musical Theatre Degrees Awarded in the Program(s) (2020): 7	Pre-screen not req. Audition not req.
California State University, Fullerton (CSUF) 800 N State College Blvd, Fullerton, CA 92831	GPA: N/A SAT (ERW): 500-590 SAT (M): 500-590 ACT (C): 18-23 ED: No	Overall College Admit Rate: 68% Undergrad Enrollment: 36,975 Total Enrollment: 42,051	BFA Theatre, Concentration: Musical Theatre Degrees Awarded in the Program(s) (2020): N/A	Pre-screen req. Audition req.
Chapman University 1 University Dr, Orange, CA 92866	GPA: N/A SAT (ERW): 590-670 SAT (M): 580-680 ACT (C): 25-30 ED: Yes	Overall College Admit Rate: 58% Undergrad Enrollment: 7,404 Total Enrollment: 9,761	BA Theatre Studies BFA Theatre Performance Musical Theatre Minor Degrees Awarded in the Program(s) (2020): N/A	BA Theatre Studies Pre-screen not req. Audition req. BFA Theatre Performance Pre-screen not req. Audition req.

School	Avg. GPA, SAT Evidence-Based Reading Writing (ERW), SAT Math (M), and ACT Composite (C) Early Decision (ED): Yes/No	Admission Statistics	Program(s)	Pre-Screen and/or Audition Required (Req.)
Pepperdine University 24255 Pacific Coast Hwy, Malibu, CA 90263	GPA: 3.69 SAT (ERW): 600-690 SAT (M): 600-720 ACT (C): 26-31 ED: No	Overall College Admit Rate: 42% Undergrad Enrollment: 3,459 Total Enrollment: 9,554	BA Theatre Arts, emphasis: Musical Theatre Degrees Awarded in the Program(s) (2020): N/A	Pre-screen not req. Audition req.
University of California, Irvine (UCI) 4000 Mesa Rd., Irvine, CA 92697	GPA: N/A SAT (ERW): 600-680 SAT (M): 630-750 ACT (C): 26-33 ED: No	Overall College Admit Rate: 30% Undergrad Enrollment: 29,638 Total Enrollment: 36,303	BFA Music Theatre Degrees Awarded in the Program(s) (2020): 9	Pre-screen not req. Audition not req.
University of Southern California (USC) University of Southern California, Los Angeles, CA 90007	GPA: 3.83 SAT (ERW): 660-740 SAT (M): 680-790 ACT (C): 30-34 ED: No	Overall College Admit Rate: 16% Undergrad Enrollment: 19,606 Total Enrollment: 46,107	BFA Musical Theatre Degrees Awarded in the Program(s) (2020): N/A	Pre-screen req. Audition req.
Central Washington University 400 E University Way, Ellensburg, WA 98926	GPA: 3.09 SAT (ERW): 470-580 SAT (M): 460-570 ACT (C): 17-24 ED: No	Overall College Admit Rate: 86% Undergrad Enrollment: 10,518 Total Enrollment: 11,174	BFA Theatre: Musical Theatre Degrees Awarded in the Program(s) (2020): 4	Pre-screen not req. Audition req.

UNIVERSITY OF ARIZONA

Address: The University of Arizona, Tucson, AZ 85721
Website: *https://tftv.arizona.edu/prospective-students/acting-musical-theatre/*
Contact: *https://www.arizona.edu/contact-us*
Phone: (520) 621-2211
Email: admissions@arizona.edu

COST OF ATTENDANCE:

In-State Tuition & Fees: $12,700 | **Additional Expenses:** $18,050
Total: $30,750

Out-of-State Tuition & Fees: $37,200 | **Additional Expenses:** $18,050
Total: $55,250

Financial Aid: https://financialaid.arizona.edu/

ADDITIONAL INFORMATION:

Available Degree(s)

- BFA Musical Theatre

Freshman Audition Requirement
University of Arizona participates in the Paper Mill Playhouse Common Pre-Screen. For more information, please refer to Chapter 8. Submit via Acceptd.

- Songs (Option A)
- Monologues (Option A)
- Dance Option (Required)
- Wild Card (Required)

Applicants with a successful pre-screen are invited for a callback either in person at the Chicago Unifieds or Anaheim Unifieds, or virtually.

- 2 contrasting songs
- 1 monologue
- Headshot & resume

Scholarships Offered
University of Arizona offers several merit-based and need-based awards. Arizona residents are eligible for the Resident Wildcat Awards, based on GPA and test scores. Awards range from $3,000-$15,000. The Non-Resident Arizona Awards range from $2,000-$35,000. The School of Theatre, Film & Television offers Theatre Student Awards such as the Baker Theatrical Lighting Scholarship and the G. Ann Blackmarr Endowment.

Special Opportunities
Upper division students have the opportunity to obtain professional internships with production companies and theaters across the country. Organizations students have interned at include Borderlands Theatre, Arizona Theatre Company, Immortal Cinema International, and more.

Notable Alumni
Samaire Armstrong, Michael Biehn, Lynn Borden, Jerry Bruckheimer, Fred Christenson, Rick Hoffman, Nicole Randall Johnson, Kourtney Kardashian, Greg Kinnear, Don Knotts, Tamika Lawrence, Marie MacKnight, Dipti Mehta, Labina Mitevska, Peter Murrieta, Craig T. Nelson, Caroline Rhea, Nicole Richie, Ron Shelton, Stephen Spinella, Barret Swatek, Jack Wagner, Kate Walsh, Kristen Wiig, and Christine Woods

CALIFORNIA STATE UNIVERSITY, CHICO

Address: 400 W 1st St, Chico, CA 95929
Website: *https://www.csuchico.edu/muta/programs/bfa-musical-theatre.shtml*
Contact: *https://www.csuchico.edu/contact/*
Phone: (530) 898-4636
Email: info@csuchico.edu

COST OF ATTENDANCE:

In-State Tuition & Fees: $7,972 | **Additional Expenses:** $18,756
Total: $26,728

Out-of-State Tuition & Fees: $17,476 | **Additional Expenses:** $18,756
Total: $36,232

Financial Aid: https://www.csuchico.edu/fa/

ADDITIONAL INFORMATION:

Available Degree(s)

- BFA Musical Theatre

Freshman Audition Requirement

California State University, Chico (Chico State) does not require a pre-screen or audition.

Scholarships Offered

Students may apply for merit-based or need-based scholarships via the Wildcat Scholarship Application. Award amounts vary.

Special Opportunities

Chico State is a member of the Musical Theatre Educators' Alliance. Musical theatre students may audition for any of the productions annually. Students often participate in master classes with Broadway professionals.

Notable Alumni

Amanda Detmer, Katie Morrill, and Paige Patterson

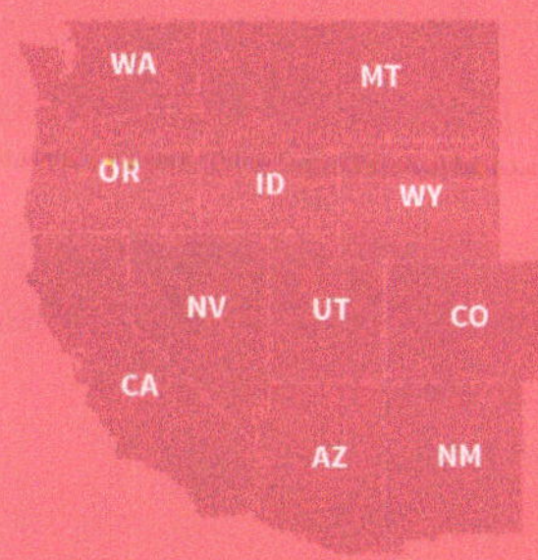

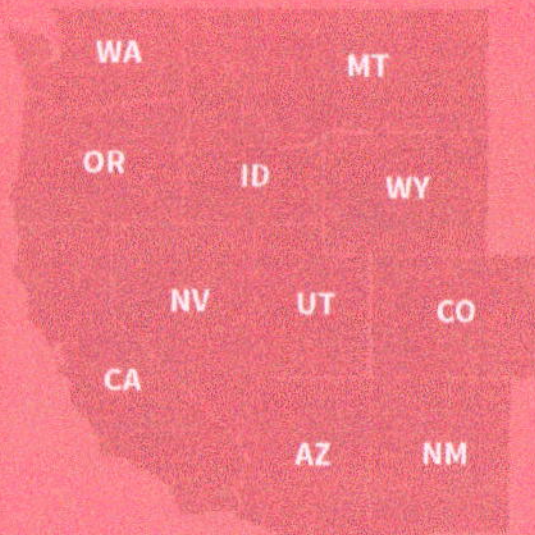

CALIFORNIA STATE UNIVERSITY, FULLERTON (CSUF)

Address: 800 N State College Blvd, Fullerton, CA 92831
Website: *https://www.fullerton.edu/arts/theatre/students/musical_theatre2.php*
Contact: *http://admissions.fullerton.edu/contact.php*
Phone: (657) 278-3100
Email: admissions@fullerton.edu

COST OF ATTENDANCE:

In-State Tuition & Fees: $6,870 | **Additional Expenses:** $20,912
Total: $27,782

Out-of-State Tuition & Fees: $16,358 | **Additional Expenses:** $20,492
Total: $36,850

Financial Aid: https://www.fullerton.edu/financialaid/

ADDITIONAL INFORMATION:

Available Degree(s)

- BFA Theatre, concentration: Musical Theatre

Freshman Audition Requirement

California State University, Fullerton (CSUF) participates in the Paper Mill Playhouse Common Pre-Screen. For more information, please refer to Chapter 8.

- Songs (Option A or B)
- Monologues (Option A)
- Dance Option (Required)
- Ballet Option (Optional)
- Wild Card (Optional)

Applicants with a successful pre-screen are invited for an in-person or virtual callback.

Scholarships Offered

Merit-based and need-based scholarships are available at CSUF. There are also numerous theatre-based scholarships available. Award amounts vary.

Special Opportunities

All theatre majors are guaranteed multiple performance opportunities during their time at CSUF. CSUF hosts 2 mainstage musicals and multiple studio plays.

Notable Alumni

Tanya Bracco and Linda Woolverton

CHAPMAN UNIVERSITY

Address: 1 University Dr, Orange, CA 92866
Website: *https://www.chapman.edu/copa/theatre/academic-programs/bfa-theatre-performance.aspx*
Contact: *https://www.chapman.edu/about/connect/index.aspx*
Phone: (714) 997-6815
Email: admit@chapman.edu

COST OF ATTENDANCE:

Tuition & Fees: $60,672 | **Additional Expenses:** $21,874
Total: $82,546

Financial Aid: https://www.chapman.edu/students/tuition-and-aid/financial-aid/undergraduate/index.aspx

ADDITIONAL INFORMATION:

Available Degree(s)

- BA Theatre Studies
- BFA Theatre Performance
- Musical Theatre Minor

Freshman Audition Requirement
Chapman University does not require a pre-screen for the programs listed here. Both the BA and BFA require a theatre resume, headshot, and goal statement. Submit via Common App.

BA Theatre Studies

- 5-8 pieces demonstrating skills
- Optional 60-sec monologue

BFA in Theatre Performance

- Intro video
- 2 monologue videos

Scholarships Offered
First-year scholarships range in amounts up to $36,000 per year. Select admitted students will also be offered institutional awards. These include awards for first-generation and underrepresented students, as well as awards from departments and schools/colleges.

The Department of Theatre has a limited number of Talent Awards for incoming first-year and transfer students. Students must be theatre majors. Consideration is made at the audition/interview and notified afterward.

Special Opportunities
The College of Performing Arts (CoPA) offers a unique collaboration with the Dodge College of Film and Media Arts. Theatre majors can take part in one of the film program's eight film productions each year. Students may work professionally but must attend all classes. CAST is a student group that organizes student-run productions, workshops, and guest artists. They produce events such as the 24-Hour Play Festival, From the Ground Up, Guerilla Shakespeare, and Beyond Stage (musical productions). USITT also organizes events and activities in technical theatre. Students can participate in Chapman On Broadway or the Player's Society. Film students at Dodge College hold open auditions for films.

Notable Alumni
Samantha Brown, Colin Hanks, Leslie Jones, Kellan Lutz, Linh Nga, Justin Simien, Roger Craig Smith, Joan Staley, Jodie Sweetin, Robin Thoren, and Esther Liang Veronin

ALASKA
ARIZONA
CALIFORNIA
COLORADO
HAWAII
IDAHO
MONTANA
NEVADA
NEW MEXICO
OREGON
UTAH
WASHINGTON
WYOMING

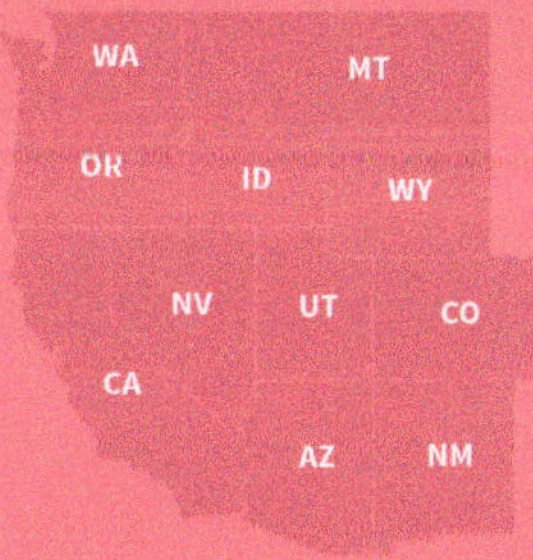

WEST

ALASKA
ARIZONA
CALIFORNIA
COLORADO
HAWAII
IDAHO
MONTANA
NEVADA
NEW MEXICO
OREGON
UTAH
WASHINGTON
WYOMING

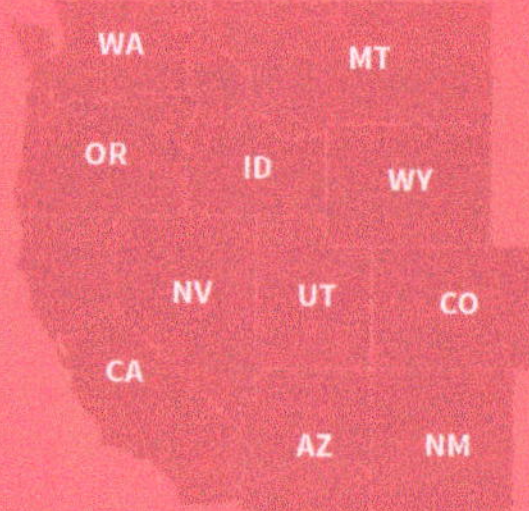

PEPPERDINE UNIVERSITY

Address: 24255 Pacific Coast Hwy, Malibu, CA 90263
Website: https://seaver.pepperdine.edu/fine-arts/undergraduate/theatre/
Contact: https://www.pepperdine.edu/contact/
Phone: (310) 506-4000
Email: admission-seaver@pepperdine.edu

COST OF ATTENDANCE:

Tuition & Fees: $59,450 | **Additional Expenses:** $20,770
Total: $80,220

Financial Aid: https://seaver.pepperdine.edu/admission/financial-aid/undergraduate/

ADDITIONAL INFORMATION:

Available Degree(s)

- BA Theatre Arts, emphasis: Musical Theatre

Freshman Audition Requirement

Pepperdine University does not require a pre-screen. Auditions are required and take place live virtually or on campus. Supplemental materials must be submitted via Slideroom.

- 2 contrasting songs
- 1 monologue
- Dance video

Scholarships Offered

Merit and need-based scholarships are available for Theatre/Musical Theatre students. Approximately 75% of theatre majors receive scholarships in varying amounts. Students must complete a FAFSA form.

Special Opportunities

In addition to rigorous training in acting, dance, and voice, and workshops with professional actors, Pepperdine's 8-week Theatre Program offers summer training through the Edinburgh Summer Program in Scotland. Pepperdine's Theatre department has participated in the International Edinburgh Fringe Festival since 1985. This popular, bi-annual, international program is exclusively for theatre majors. The Edinburgh program draws on the strengths of both Scottish and American theatre traditions, with a commitment to international collaboration through co-creation by artists from both Pepperdine and Scotland. Students employ the Linklater Voice technique.

Notable Alumni

Marshall Colt, Cami Edwards, Douglas Emerson, Kim Fields, Darby Hinton, Kelly Hu, Ashley Jones, Kate Mansi, Tahj Mowry, Tamera Mowry, Tia Mowry, Brandy Norwood, Eric Christian Olsen, Meredith Salenger, Francesca Marie Smith, and Clayton Snyder

UNIVERSITY OF CALIFORNIA, IRVINE

Address: 4000 Mesa Rd., Irvine, CA 92697
Website: *https://drama.arts.uci.edu/undergraduate-programs/music-theatre-bfa*
Contact: *https://www.arts.uci.edu/contact-us*
Phone: (949) 824-6614
Email: drama@uci.edu

COST OF ATTENDANCE:

In-State Tuition & Fees: $15,621 | **Additional Expenses:** $20,420
Total: $36,041

Out-of-State Tuition & Fees: $45,375 | **Additional Expenses:** $20,420
Total: $65,795

Financial Aid: https://www.ofas.uci.edu/content/

ADDITIONAL INFORMATION:

Available Degree(s)

- BFA Music Theatre

Freshman Audition Requirement

Students do not audition for the BFA Music Theatre program until they complete their first year at UCI.

Scholarships Offered

UCI offers numerous scholarships that are merit-based and/or need-based and are for residents, nonresidents, international students, or undocumented students. UCI's Distinguished Scholarships are merit-based and range from $3,000 per year to over $10,000. The Excellence in the Arts Scholarship is available for students in the Claire Trevor School of Arts with an award up to $3,000. International and undocumented students with financial need are eligible for $3,000 through the Anteater Uplift Scholarship. For more information on these and other available scholarships, visit: https://www.admissions.uci.edu/afford/scholarships/scholarship-central.php

Special Opportunities

Students may be eligible for Honors in Music Theatre if they maintain a certain GPA in their coursework. Additionally, UCI offers a four-week long intensive New York Satellite Program (NYSP) in Music Theatre. Auditions are held for this unique program. Students in this program meet in the Fall, start coursework for the program in the Winter, then go to New York City in the Spring. NYSP students participate in musicals written just for them. These works are presented Off-Broadway.

Notable Alumni

Grace Byers, Allison Case, Jenn Colella, Garrett Deagon, Ryan Farnsworth, Ben Jacoby, Madisen Johnson, Beth Malone, Alan Mingo Jr., Sepideh Moafi, Bree Murphy, Andrew Samonsky, and Teal Wicks.

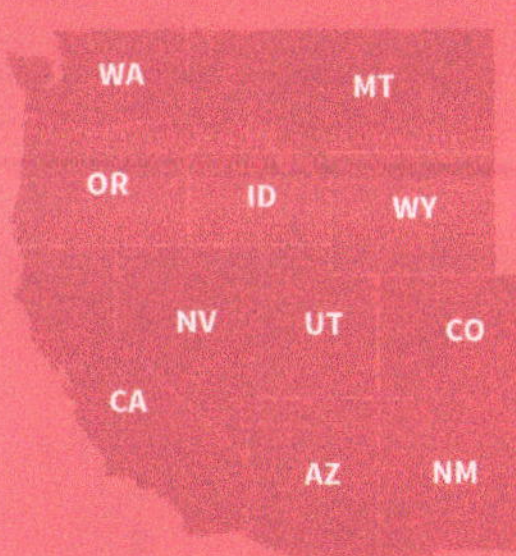

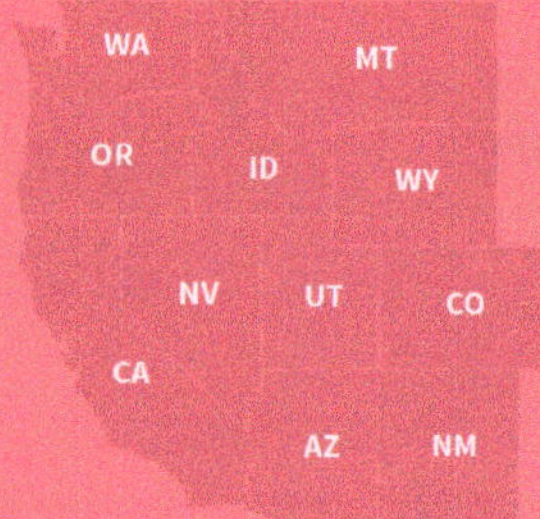

UNIVERSITY OF SOUTHERN CALIFORNIA (USC)

Address: University of Southern California, Los Angeles, CA 90007
Website: *https://dramaticarts.usc.edu/programs/undergraduate/musical-theatre/*
Contact: *https://dramaticarts.usc.edu/contact/*
Phone: (213) 821-2744
Email: sdainfo@usc.edu

COST OF ATTENDANCE:

Tuition & Fees: $57,256 | **Additional Expenses:** $19,264
Total: $76,520

Financial Aid: https://financialaid.usc.edu/undergraduates/students.html

ADDITIONAL INFORMATION:

Available Degree(s)

- BFA Musical Theatre

Freshman Audition Requirement

University of Southern California (USC) requires a pre-screen. Submit via SlideRoom.

- Headshot & resume
- 2 monologues
- 2 dance videos
- 2 contrasting songs
- Self-intro video

Applicants with a successful pre-screen are invited for a callback.

Scholarships Offered

The School of Dramatic Arts provides faculty-nominated merit-based awards to students who have completed at least one year as a Dramatic Arts major at USC.

Special Opportunities

Musical Theatre students at USC take coursework from the USC School of Dramatic Arts, USC Glorya Kaufman School of Dance, and USC Thornton School of Music. Students learn classical methodologies across cultures in drama, music, and dance.

Notable Alumni

Patrick J. Adams, Shiri Appleby, McKinley Belcher III, Troian Bellisario, Beck Bennett, Todd Black, Nichole Bloom, Charl Brown, LeVar Burton, Tate Donovan, Timothy Dowling, Anthony Edwards, Ryan Eggold, Greer Grammer, Daryl Hannah, Briga Heelan, Grant Heslov, Devin Kelley, Swoosie Kurtz, Eric Ladin, and James Lesure, Jaren Lewison, Chris Lowell, Alexander Ludwig, Joseph Mazzello, Bentley Mitchum, Fess Parker, Kelly Preston, Michael Pataki, Kyra Sedgwick, Tom Selleck, Cybill Shepherd, Chima Simone, Karan Soni, Robert Stack, Marlo Thomas, Robert Vaughn, John Wayne, Forest Whitaker, Mary Kate Wiles, and Anton Yelchin

CENTRAL WASHINGTON UNIVERSITY

Address: 400 E University Way, Ellensburg, WA 98926
Website: https://www.cwu.edu/theatre/musical-theatre
Contact: https://www.cwu.edu/theatre/contact-us-or-request-information
Phone: (509) 963-1750
Email: theatre@cwu.edu

COST OF ATTENDANCE:

In-State Tuition & Fees: $7,186 | **Additional Expenses:** $18,867
Total: $26,053

Out-of-State Tuition & Fees: $23,262 | **Additional Expenses:** $18,867
Total: $42,129

Financial Aid: https://www.cwu.edu/financial-aid/

ADDITIONAL INFORMATION:

Available Degree(s)

- BFA Theatre: Musical Theatre

Freshman Audition Requirement

Central Washington University does not require a pre-screen. Recorded auditions are required. Submit via Acceptd.

- Headshot & resume
- 2 songs
- 1 monologue
- Dance video
- Introductory video
- Letter of recommendation
- Second dance video (Optional)
- Third song (Optional)
- Applicant in a production (Optional)

Scholarships Offered

Students are encouraged to apply for scholarships via the Scholarship Central online application.

Special Opportunities

Musical theatre students at Central Washington University perform in the McConnell Auditorium, a 750-seat proscenium theatre. Students also use spaces such as the black box theatres at Milo Smith Tower Theatre and Studio 119.

Notable Alumni

Sara Coiley, Annie Demartino, Ryan Hormer, Delonda Johnson, and Aaron Siebol

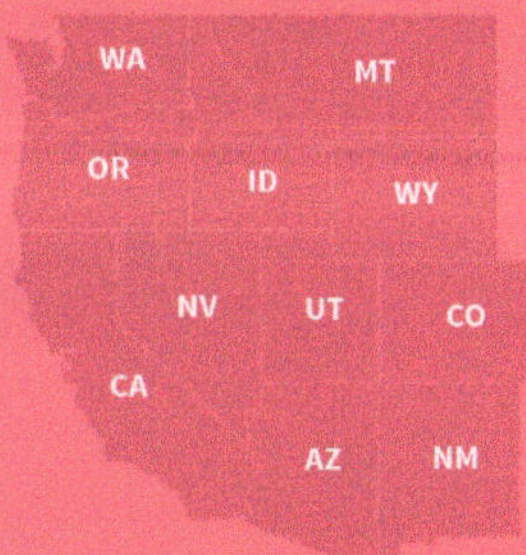

CHAPTER 17

MUSICAL THEATRE SCHOOLS BY CITY/STATE

School	City	State
University of Alabama at Birmingham	Birmingham	Alabama
Samford University	Homewood	Alabama
University of Arizona	Tucson	Arizona
California State University, Chico	Chico	California
California State University, Fullerton (CSUF)	Fullerton	California
UCI	Irvine	California
University of Southern California (USC)	Los Angeles	California
Pepperdine University	Malibu	California
Chapman University	Orange	California
University of Hartford - Hartt School	West Hartford	Connecticut
American University	Washington	District of Columbia (DC)
University of Miami	Coral Gables	Florida
Florida State University	Tallahassee	Florida
University of Tampa	Tampa	Florida
Illinois Wesleyan University	Bloomington	Illinois
Columbia College Chicago	Chicago	Illinois
Roosevelt University	Chicago	Illinois
Millikin University	Decatur	Illinois
Northwestern University	Evanston	Illinois
Indiana University Bloomington	Bloomington	Indiana
Ball State University	Muncie	Indiana
Loyola University New Orleans	New Orleans	Louisiana
Tulane University	New Orleans	Louisiana
Boston Conservatory at Berklee	Boston	Massachusetts
Emerson College	Boston	Massachusetts
University of Michigan	Ann Arbor	Michigan
Western Michigan University	Kalamazoo	Michigan
Southeast Missouri State University	Cape Girardeau	Missouri
Stephens College	Columbia	Missouri
University of Central Missouri	Warrensburg	Missouri
Webster University	Webster Groves	Missouri

School	City	State
Nebraska Wesleyan University	Lincoln	Nebraska
Creighton University	Omaha	Nebraska
Rider University	Lawrenceville	New Jersey
Montclair State University	Montclair	New Jersey
University at Buffalo	Buffalo	New York
SUNY Cortland	Cortland	New York
Long Island University Post	Greenvale	New York
Ithaca College	Ithaca	New York
American Musical & Dramatic Academy (AMDA)	New York	New York
The Juilliard School	New York	New York
Manhattan School of Music	New York	New York
Marymount Manhattan College	New York	New York
The New School	New York	New York
New York University	New York	New York
Pace University	New York	New York
Molloy College	Rockville Centre	New York
Syracuse University	Syracuse	New York
Elon University	Elon	North Carolina
Ohio University	Athens	Ohio
Baldwin Wallace University	Berea	Ohio
University of Cincinnati	Cincinnati	Ohio
Wright State University	Dayton	Ohio
Kent State University	Kent	Ohio
Otterbein University	Westerville	Ohio
University of Oklahoma	Norman	Oklahoma
Oklahoma City University	Oklahoma City	Oklahoma
Temple University	Philadelphia	Pennsylvania
University of the Arts	Philadelphia	Pennsylvania
Carnegie Mellon University	Pittsburgh	Pennsylvania
Point Park University	Pittsburgh	Pennsylvania
Pennsylvania State University	University Park	Pennsylvania
Coastal Carolina University	Conway	South Carolina
Belmont University	Nashville	Tennessee
Texas Christian University (TCU)	Fort Worth	Texas
Sam Houston State University	Huntsville	Texas

School	City	State
Texas State University	San Marcos	Texas
James Madison University	Harrisonburg	Virginia
Shenandoah University	Winchester	Virginia
Central Washington University	Ellensburg	Washington
Viterbo University	La Crosse	Wisconsin

CHAPTER 18

TOP 20 MUSICAL THEATRE PROGRAMS (ALPHABETIZED)

Ranking	School
1	American Musical & Dramatic Academy (AMDA)
2	Baldwin Wallace University
3	Boston Conservatory at Berklee
4	Carnegie Mellon University
5	Elon University
6	Emerson College
7	Ithaca College
8	The Juilliard School
9	Marymount Manhattan College
10	Montclair State University
11	New York University
12	Pace University
13	Pennsylvania State University
14	Point Park University
15	Oklahoma City University
16	Shenandoah University
17	Syracuse University
18	Texas State University
19	The University of Cincinnati
20	The University of Michigan

CHAPTER 19

MUSICAL THEATRE SCHOOLS BY AVERAGE TEST SCORE

MUSICAL THEATRE SCHOOLS BY AVERAGE SAT SCORE

School	Avg. SAT
Roosevelt University	450-580 (ERW) 450-550 (M)
Central Washington University	470-580 (ERW) 460-570 (M)
Millikin University	470-590 (ERW) 470-570 (M)
Wright State University	478-620 (ERW) 480-600 (M)
Stephens College	480-540 (ERW) 470-580 (M)
Point Park University	483-610 (ERW) 470-570 (M)
Sam Houston State University	490-570 (ERW) 480-550 (M)
California State University, Chico	490-590 (ERW) 480-580 (M)
Otterbein University	490-625 (ERW) 500-600 (M)
Nebraska Wesleyan University	490-640 (ERW) 500-610 (M)
Marymount Manhattan College	500-580 (ERW) 460-620 (M)
California State University, Fullerton (CSUF)	500-590 (ERW) 500-590 (M)
Southeast Missouri State University	500-600 (ERW) 500-590 (M)
Western Michigan University	500-610 (ERW) 510-610 (M)
Texas State University	510-600 (ERW) 500-580 (M)
Coastal Carolina University	510-600 (ERW) 510-580 (M)
Kent State University	510-610 (ERW) 510-600 (M)
University of Hartford - Hartt School	510-610 (ERW) 510-600 (M)

School	Avg. SAT
Rider University	510-620 (ERW) 510-600 (M)
Shenandoah University	510-630 (ERW) 500-600 (M)
Viterbo University	520-600 (ERW) 480-570 (M)
Baldwin Wallace University	520-640 (ERW) 520-620 (M)
Ohio University	530-630 (ERW) 520-620 (M)
Molloy College	540-620 (ERW) 540-630 (M)
Pace University	540-630 (ERW) 520-610 (M)
Loyola University New Orleans	540-640 (ERW) 510-600 (M)
Samford University	540-640 (ERW) 520-600 (M)
Long Island University Post	540-640 (ERW) 540-650 (M)
Webster University	548-650 (ERW) 530-610 (M)
SUNY Cortland	550-610 (ERW) 550-610 (M)
University of Tampa	550-620 (ERW) 540-610 (M)
Illinois Wesleyan University	550-640 (ERW) 550-660 (M)
Oklahoma City University	550-650 (ERW) 530-610 (M)
University of Arizona	550-660 (ERW) 540-690 (M)
University at Buffalo	560-640 (ERW) 580-670 (M)
University of Oklahoma	560-650 (ERW) 540-650 (M)

School	Avg. SAT
University of Cincinnati	560-650 (ERW) 560-680 (M)
Texas Christian University (TCU)	560-660 (ERW) 550-660 (M)
University of Alabama at Birmingham	560-668 (ERW) 530-660 (M)
James Madison University	570-650 (ERW) 550-630 (M)
Belmont University	580-660 (ERW) 540-640 (M)
Elon University	580-660 (ERW) 560-660 (M)
Pennsylvania State University	580-670 (ERW) 580-700 (M)
The New School	580-680 (ERW) 560-680 (M)
Indiana University Bloomington	580-700 (ERW) 560-680 (M)
Chapman University	590-670 (ERW) 580-680 (M)
Ithaca College	600-680 (ERW) 580-670 (M)
UCI	600-680 (ERW) 630-750 (M)
Pepperdine University	600-690 (ERW) 600-720 (M)
Emerson College	610-690 (ERW) 580-690 (M)
Florida State University	620-680 (ERW) 600-670 (M)
University of Miami	620-700 (ERW) 630-720 (M)
American University	630-710 (ERW) 590-680 (M)
University of Michigan	660-740 (ERW) 680-780 (M)

School	Avg. SAT
University of Southern California (USC)	660-740 (ERW) 680-790 (M)
New York University	670-740 (ERW) 700-800 (M)
Tulane University	680-740 (ERW) 680-770 (M)
Northwestern University	700-760 (ERW) 730-790 (M)
Carnegie Mellon University	700-760 (ERW) 760-800 (M)
Creighton University	N/A
Syracuse University	N/A
American Musical & Dramatic Academy (AMDA)	N/A *Test optional
Ball State University	N/A *Test optional
Boston Conservatory at Berklee	N/A *Test optional
Columbia College Chicago	N/A *Test optional
Manhattan School of Music	N/A *Test optional
Montclair State University	N/A *Test optional
Temple University	N/A *Test optional
The Juilliard School	N/A *Test optional
University of Central Missouri	N/A *Test optional
University of the Arts	N/A *Test optional

MUSICAL THEATRE SCHOOLS BY AVERAGE ACT SCORE

School	Avg. ACT
Central Washington University	17-24 (ACT C)
California State University, Fullerton (CSUF)	18-23 (ACT C)
Sam Houston State University	18-23 (ACT C)
California State University, Chico	18-24 (ACT C)
Wright State University	18-25 (ACT C)
Point Park University	18-26 (ACT C)
Roosevelt University	18-26 (ACT)
Coastal Carolina University	19-25 (ACT C)
Southeast Missouri State University	19-25 (ACT C)
University of Central Missouri	19-25 (ACT C)
Shenandoah University	19-26 (ACT C)
Stephens College	20-24 (ACT C)
Texas State University	20-25 (ACT C)
Viterbo University	20-25 (ACT C)
Kent State University	20-26 (ACT C)
Rider University	20-26 (ACT C)
Millikin University	20-27 (ACT C)
Otterbein University	20-27 (ACT C)
Webster University	20-27 (ACT C)
Western Michigan University	20-27 (ACT C)
Marymount Manhattan College	20-28 (ACT C)
Loyola University New Orleans	21-26 (ACT C)
Ohio University	21-26 (ACT C)
Baldwin Wallace University	21-27 (ACT C)
Molloy College	21-28 (ACT C)
University of Arizona	21-29 (ACT C)
SUNY Cortland	22-26 (ACT C)
University of Tampa	22-27 (ACT C)
Pace University	22-28 (ACT C) *Test optional
Long Island University Post	22-29 (ACT C)
Nebraska Wesleyan University	22-29 (ACT C)
Oklahoma City University	22-29 (ACT C)
University of Hartford - Hartt School	22-29 (ACT C)
University of Alabama at Birmingham	22-30 (ACT C)

School	Avg. ACT
James Madison University	23-28 (ACT C)
Samford University	23-29 (ACT C)
University at Buffalo	23-29 (ACT C)
University of Cincinnati	23-29 (ACT C)
University of Oklahoma	23-29 (ACT C)
Belmont University	23-30 (ACT C)
Illinois Wesleyan University	24-29 (ACT C)
Chapman University	25-30 (ACT C)
Elon University	25-30 (ACT C)
Pennsylvania State University	25-30 (ACT C)
Texas Christian University (TCU)	25-31 (ACT C)
The New School	26-30 (ACT C)
Pepperdine University	26-31 (ACT C)
Indiana University Bloomington	26-32 (ACT C)
UCI	26-33 (ACT C)
Emerson College	27-31 (ACT C)
Florida State University	27-31 (ACT C)
Ithaca College	27-31 (ACT C)
American University	27-32 (ACT C)
University of Miami	28-32 (ACT C)
Tulane University	30-33 (ACT C)
University of Southern California (USC)	30-34 (ACT C)
New York University	31-34 (ACT C)
University of Michigan	31-34 (ACT C)
Carnegie Mellon University	33-35 (ACT C)
Northwestern University	33-35 (ACT)
Creighton University	N/A
Syracuse University	N/A
American Musical & Dramatic Academy (AMDA)	N/A *Test optional
Ball State University	N/A *Test optional
Boston Conservatory at Berklee	N/A *Test optional
Columbia College Chicago	N/A *Test optional
Manhattan School of Music	N/A *Test optional
Montclair State University	N/A *Test optional
Temple University	N/A *Test optional
The Juilliard School	N/A *Test optional
University of the Arts	N/A *Test optional

MUSICAL THEATRE SCHOOLS BY AVERAGE GPA

School	Avg. GPA
Central Washington University	3.09
California State University, Chico	3.34
Wright State University	3.36
University of Arizona	3.43
University of Central Missouri	3.44
Point Park University	3.46
Western Michigan University	3.47
Loyola University New Orleans	3.48
Temple University	3.48
Emerson College	3.5
Viterbo University	3.5
Ball State University	3.52
Southeast Missouri State University	3.54
Ohio University	3.55
Shenandoah University	3.55
Florida State University	3.59
Baldwin Wallace University	3.6
University of Miami	3.6
Kent State University	3.61
University of Oklahoma	3.63
Tulane University	3.64
Syracuse University	3.67
Pepperdine University	3.69
University at Buffalo	3.7
University of Cincinnati	3.7
New York University	3.71
Coastal Carolina University	3.72
Indiana University Bloomington	3.74
American University	3.79
Belmont University	3.79
Illinois Wesleyan University	3.8
Samford University	3.8
University of Alabama at Birmingham	3.83
University of Southern California (USC)	3.83
Carnegie Mellon University	3.85
University of Michigan	3.87

School	Avg. SAT
Elon University	4.07
American Musical & Dramatic Academy (AMDA)	N/A
Boston Conservatory at Berklee	N/A
California State University, Fullerton (CSUF)	N/A
Chapman University	N/A
Columbia College Chicago	N/A
Creighton University	N/A
Ithaca College	N/A
James Madison University	N/A
Long Island University Post	N/A
Manhattan School of Music	N/A
Marymount Manhattan College	N/A
Millikin University	N/A
Molloy College	N/A
Montclair State University	N/A
Nebraska Wesleyan University	N/A
Northwestern University	N/A
Oklahoma City University	N/A
Otterbein University	N/A
Pace University	N/A
Pennsylvania State University	N/A
Rider University	N/A
Roosevelt University	N/A
Sam Houston State University	N/A
Stephens College	N/A
SUNY Cortland	N/A
Texas Christian University (TCU)	N/A
Texas State University	N/A
The Juilliard School	N/A
The New School	N/A
UCI	N/A
University of Hartford - Hartt School	N/A
University of Tampa	N/A
University of the Arts	N/A
Webster University	N/A

JOURNEY TO ART, DANCE, MUSIC, THEATRE, FILM, AND FASHION SERIES

JOURNEY TO

Fashion Design

COLLEGE ADMISSIONS & PROFILES

JOURNEY TO

Fashion Merchandising

COLLEGE ADMISSIONS & PROFILES

JOURNEY TO

COLLEGE ADMISSIONS & PROFILES

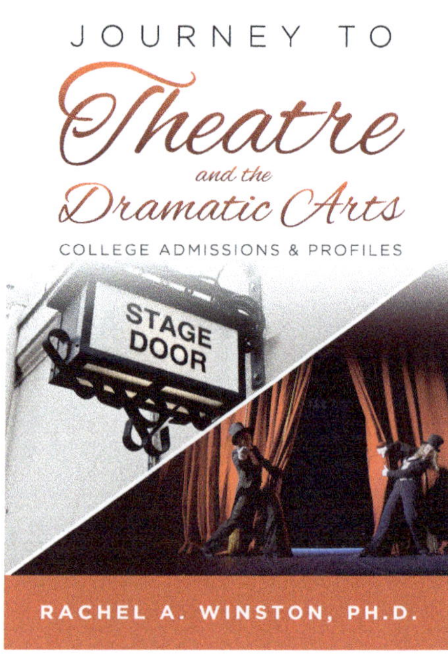

Live your dreams today remembering that discipline is the bridge between dreams and achievement!

"We believe in the American Dream that all people rich or poor can go as far in life as their talents and persistence will take them."
– Lizard Publishing Vision

At Lizard, we help you make your dreams come true.

CONTACT INFORMATION

Phone: 949-833-7706

E-mail: collegeguide@yahoo.com

Website: collegelizard.com and Lizard-publishing.com

COMPREHENSIVE HEALTH CARE SERIES

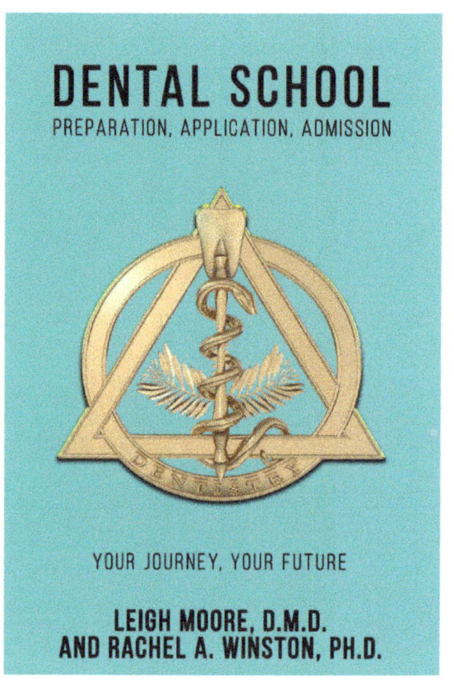

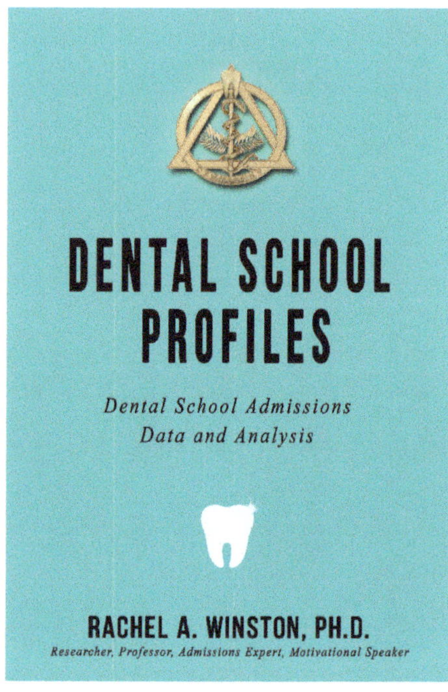

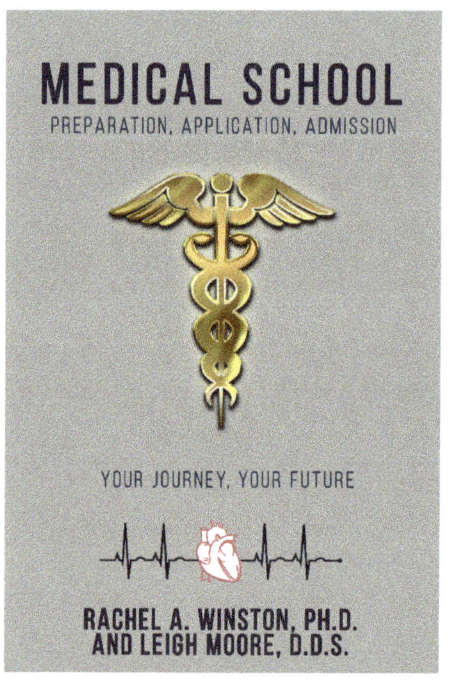

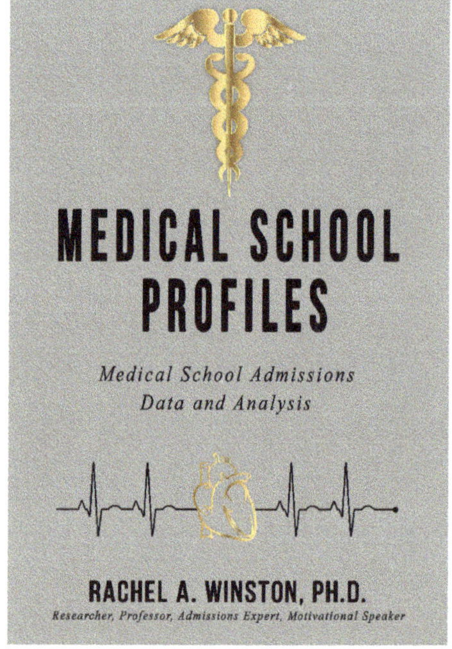

VET SCHOOL
PREPARATION, APPLICATION, ADMISSION
YOUR JOURNEY, YOUR FUTURE
RACHEL A. WINSTON, PH.D.
Researcher, Professor, Admissions Expert, Motivational Speaker

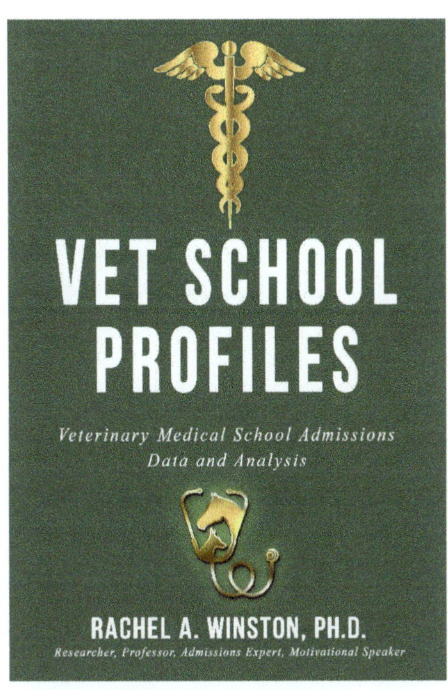
VET SCHOOL
PROFILES
Veterinary Medical School Admissions
Data and Analysis
RACHEL A. WINSTON, PH.D.
Researcher, Professor, Admissions Expert, Motivational Speaker

PHYSICIAN
ASST. (PA) SCHOOL
PREPARATION, APPLICATION, ADMISSION
YOUR JOURNEY, YOUR FUTURE
RACHEL A. WINSTON, PH.D.
Researcher, Professor, Admissions Expert, Motivational Speaker

PHYSICIAN ASST.
SCHOOL PROFILES
P.A. School Admissions
Data and Analysis
RACHEL A. WINSTON, PH.D.
Researcher, Professor, Admissions Expert, Motivational Speaker

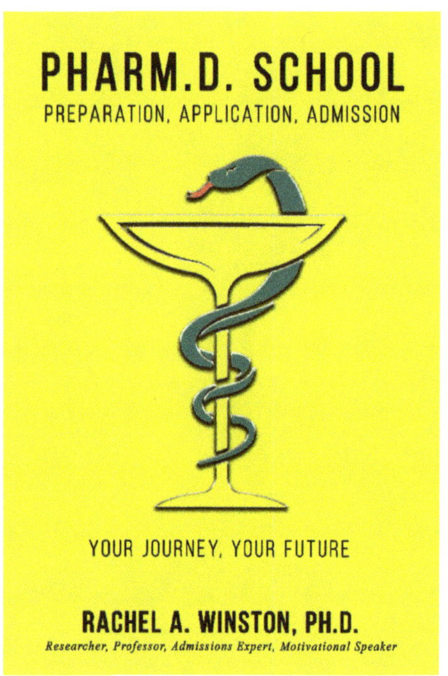
PHARM.D. SCHOOL
PREPARATION, APPLICATION, ADMISSION
YOUR JOURNEY, YOUR FUTURE
RACHEL A. WINSTON, PH.D.
Researcher, Professor, Admissions Expert, Motivational Speaker

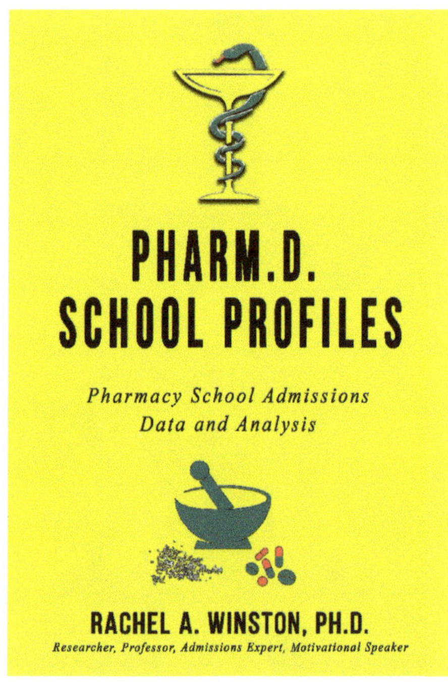
PHARM.D.
SCHOOL PROFILES
Pharmacy School Admissions
Data and Analysis
RACHEL A. WINSTON, PH.D.
Researcher, Professor, Admissions Expert, Motivational Speaker

OSTEOPATHIC
MEDICAL SCHOOL
PREPARATION, APPLICATION, ADMISSION
YOUR JOURNEY, YOUR FUTURE
RACHEL A. WINSTON, PH.D.
Researcher, Professor, Admissions Expert, Motivational Speaker

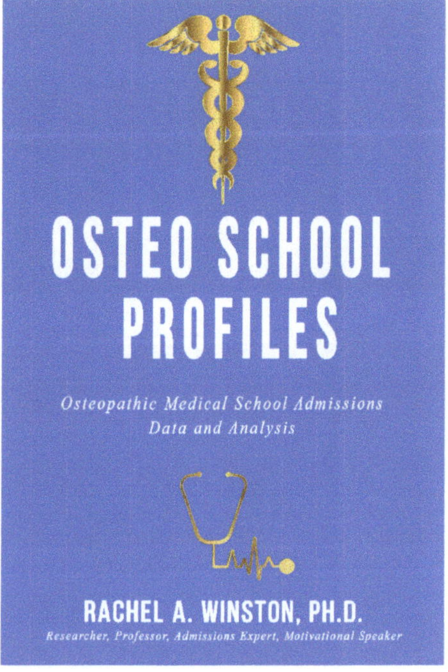
OSTEO SCHOOL
PROFILES
Osteopathic Medical School Admissions
Data and Analysis
RACHEL A. WINSTON, PH.D.
Researcher, Professor, Admissions Expert, Motivational Speaker

INDEX

Symbols

A

B

C

D

E

F

N

O

P

R

S

T

U

W

Z

www.ingramcontent.com/pod-product-compliance
Lightning Source LLC
Chambersburg PA
CBHW041936260326
41914CB00010B/1319
* 9 7 8 1 9 4 6 4 3 2 6 1 2 *